T0355536

FREEDOM
FIRST

MATTHEW KLAN

FREEDOM FIRST

ESCAPE THE INCOME TRAP, UNLOCK YOUR POTENTIAL
AND BE FINANCIALLY FREE, *NOW*

WILEY

First published in 2020 by John Wiley & Sons Australia, Ltd
42 McDougall St, Milton Qld 4064

Office also in Melbourne

Typeset in Liberation Serif Regular 11pt/13pt

© Matthew Klan 2020

The moral rights of the author have been asserted

ISBN: 978-0-730-38167-9

A catalogue record for this book is available from the National Library of Australia

A Cataloguing in Publication record for this book is available from the U.S. Library of Congress.

Freedom First® is a registered trademark of WEALTH CREATION TECHNOLOGIES PTY LTD

Dominant Value, Motivation Equation, Values Audit, Freedom Escape Velocity, Freedom First Wealth Creation Formula, Income Trap, Freedom Quadrant, Straight Line Thinking and all associated concepts, brands, names, and illustrations are TM of WEALTH CREATION TECHNOLOGIES PTY LTD.

The Freedom First concept and related concepts were developed by Matthew Klan in 2007 and shared and tested from 2007-2019.

Cover design by Wiley

Cover image © vvvita/Shutterstock

Quotes from *Fight Club* on pages 26 and 104: Copyright © 1997 Chuck Palahniuk. Reprinted by permission of ICM Partners.

10 9 8 7 6 5 4 3 2 1

Disclaimer

For my family.
You make freedom worth fighting for.

Contents

Introduction

Do you want to be financially free?

Plenty of people will answer yes; but what if I told you that we've been going about it backwards all along?

Decades ago in what feels like another life, I achieved what many people nowadays consider the ultimate: I'd studied hard, gotten into a good university and graduated with a professional degree that promised me a good career.

And then I made a decision I didn't really understand the importance of at the time, one that would shape my life from then on. Having achieved what society told me I should desire—the security of a good job, a secure pay cheque, with the promise of a secure retirement—I threw it all away and chose my freedom instead.

At the time, many people told me I was crazy. What was I thinking giving up not just a job but a career, and the guarantee of financial security? But I sensed back then what many people are starting to realise now: that the promise of security was only an illusion. I couldn't bear the thought of spending a lifetime working a job, hoping at best that at the end of many years I might be able to stop—perhaps in comfort, perhaps not.

When I first quit my job I wasn't rich.

I didn't have enough passive income to buy back all of my time—or enough capital saved to do the same—before I chose to do something different.

I could see that the path I was on wasn't going to buy back my time for another 40 years, and even then there was no guarantee. I'd known retirees who worked their whole life to buy back their time and still weren't financially free.

They had become dependent on the stock market, dependent on their pensions and, despite working hard their whole lives, they had only ever really learned one strategy, one skill for creating wealth: work and save. And if circumstances changed after retirement, derailing their carefully laid plans, then they had run out of time to repeat that strategy all over again.

I saw that it was more important to get onto a new path first, rather than just try to race to the end of the same path sooner: the path where you need to be rich, or at least moderately well off *first*, if you want to be financially free.

Because that's what both 'responsible financial planning' advice as well as 'get-rich-quick' advice tells us to do …

You probably think that there is no similarity between responsible financial planning and get-rich-quick thinking. Most people think they're polar opposites: working hard and saving is the responsible path, while trying to get rich quick is the irresponsible path.

But when it comes to financial freedom they are both the same path: rich, *then* free!

Those who have low time preference and an aversion to risk travel on the path more slowly, while those with high time preference and tolerance to risk try to race down the path more quickly!

But the speed you travel at is irrelevant if you are heading in the wrong direction.

What do you mean by 'Freedom First'?

If you want to become rich so you can be financially free, you need to *start* by getting free *first*.

Freedom First is not about replacing *all* of your income before you can quit your job; it's not about building up your passive income or building up enough equity — which pays you income — before you can be free.

It's not about getting financially free in three to five years, instead of 30 years. It's not about getting financially free *fast*.

Freedom First is about *getting free first*.

Freedom First is a principle.

People *say* they want to get rich so that they can finally be free …

I say you need to get free if you want to get rich in the first place.

The freer you get, the richer you'll become.

Although it might sound radical, the idea that freedom is necessary for the creation of wealth is not new: plenty of economists have pointed out the relationship between freedom and wealth when it comes to a nation's prosperity. American economist Brian S Wesbury has said, 'When freedom prevails, the ingenuity and inventiveness of people creates incredible wealth.'

But when it comes to an individual's ability to produce wealth, this incredible relationship has been ignored.

> ## One of the greatest pains to human nature is the pain of a new idea.
> *Walter Bagehot*

Perhaps it has always been more profitable to sell people security, rather than freedom?

Saying you want to get free, then doing everything in your power to do the opposite — going into debt, chasing security, locking away your money, tying yourself down and becoming dependent on a job and on the market for decades at a time — is insanity.

> ## Those who would give up essential liberty to purchase a little temporary security deserve neither liberty nor security.
> *Benjamin Franklin*

It's obvious in hindsight that if you want to get completely free *financially*, the way to do that is to start by getting a little freer *first*, and growing from there.

Plenty of people have gotten rich, only to discover they are not free.

Plenty of people get rich in booms, only to lose it all in a bust.

What I'm most proud of is not that I got rich.

It's that I got free, *then* rich.

And when the market changed in 2007–09 and we saw the biggest correction in most people's lifetimes, and fortunes that were made in the boom were lost, I stayed free.

And got freer. And richer.

If you know that for the rich the ultimate currency stops becoming money after a certain point, and starts becoming both the *time* and the *freedom* to act, then it makes sense that you should aim to build up those assets from the beginning.

Buy back your time.

Strive to have more choices: free people choose, unfree people comply.

These are the things that really matter in the end, and so if you want to be rich *and* financially free, they are precisely the things that should matter in the beginning.

The two sides of Freedom First

There are two sides to Freedom First: getting free first and valuing freedom first.

You've got to *get free first* if you want to be able to unlock the creative potential of your mind, and have the time and the resources to take advantage of opportunities that you create or that come your way. (I'll explain this in part III of the book.)

But you also have to *value being free* if you ever want to get free in the first place (as I'll explain in part I). Plenty of people say they value freedom; some even say they put it 'first', but do they? If your only conception of financial freedom is having a lot of money, passive income or flashy cars and houses, you might want to think about whether you really value freedom at all.

And while there are two parts to Freedom First, there's a third part to this book as well. If you've ever felt that you truly wanted to become financially free, and have done everything you can to get there, but with no success, in part II I'll look at the traps that come from not being free that might be holding you back.

When I first quit my job, I threw myself into the task of learning everything I could about money, investing the time I'd bought myself and my savings in wresting at first a living, then eventually wealth from the market. Once my endeavours had paid off and I managed to make myself rich, I tried to teach others what I'd learned. At first I shared the techniques and strategies I'd developed in a hostile market, hoping to help people make the most of the boom I saw coming, ahead of the correction I knew would be inevitable.

But having trained as a professional, without realising it I was sticking to the facts, the nitty gritty of what I was doing.

I came to realise that knowing *what* to do was not enough. While I had skin in the game, while I was living in the market, the people I taught were not.

And that made all the difference.

After more than 40 years of expanding credit and 90 years of inflating prices, and after watching bubbles rotate from one asset class to the next as newly created money from the government and banks sought out a home, for most people, constantly rising prices from shares to property had come to seem the norm.

Growing up with parents who had a job for life, when degrees were rare and valuable and pensions were secure, it was easy for many people to feel like we'd flattened out the world, rounded off the edges, and straightened out the curves and cycles: that we'd tamed the nature of the econo-system.

As a result of this, most people tended to think in straight lines and failed to see both incredible risks such as the global financial crisis (GFC), or the incredible opportunities that were on the horizon.

Freedom First is unique

I had the example of my own life, but it took me a long time to understand what lesson to take from it. It wasn't until I had been free for a long time, that I realised there was something fundamentally important about the decision I had made.

The idea truly is revolutionary: that if you want to be financially free, you've got to get free first — that freedom creates wealth.

> **The idea truly is revolutionary: that if you want to be financially free, you've got to get free first — that freedom creates wealth.**

The safe route, the secure route, hell, the responsible route is to tell people, 'get a good education and then get a good job. While you're in that good job you can think about learning to invest, maybe one day starting a business'.

Except in the real world that very rarely happens.

By the time people have worked hard enough to get a good job locked down, they have often run out of the energy or the time to explore anything else. Our youthful years are gone and we are just happy to pay the bills and have some time off. But what if a good education doesn't lead to a good job in the first place, or when it does, that job is not even that secure?

What if our safe, secure path was just a historical aberration?

For most of our history we were more like small-business people than modern employees: small farmers who settled the lands; artisans and guild members who travelled from town to town plying their trades. Tribespeople who herded, or hunted, worked skins and bones and traded with other tribes thousands of miles apart, long before we had written language.

It's not trading, exchanging, bartering and creating that are abnormal. It's not learning skills on the job and growing and changing as the world around you changes that are without historical precedent.

No, the thing that is absolutely unnatural is for a whole nation of people for several generations to be raised to expect that it's normal to get up in the morning and head out to work in somebody else's factory, or more recently somebody else's office; to start work when they say, and continue until they say you can stop—what you can do, and what you can't do, is decided for you—all in exchange for a little time off each week, a short break each year and, provided you take on debt, a roof over your head and a 'comfortable' life.

The only historical precedent I can think of that comes close to matching our culture of mass employment is a culture of mass slavery.

Freedom: something everyone can value

Most financial advice seems to fall into two broad groups that appeal to what people already value. It's either low-end nuts and bolts: 20 good tips to not be poor; or big picture: how some famous entrepreneur started out sleeping on a couch and went on to build a fortune, often losing a fortune and building another along the way (which doesn't sound that secure or free to me—who wants to get rich in a way that means you could lose it all?).

Each is only covering half of the story: either good financial defence with no offence, or good offence with no defence.

Each of these largely appeals to people who already have the personality to do these things. Some people love to share tips on how to cut coupons, others to 'fire up' and 'get excited'. Even if you could nudge your personality in one direction, you can't be both of these people.

I was neither of them. What I was, was someone who valued being free, and what I realised was that I was driven by a motivation that anyone can tap into, regardless of personality: a motivation that could take care of your financial offence, as well as defence, and drive you to do the things that make you financially free.

Some of those things may seem counterintuitive. In this book, I'll share why you shouldn't save for retirement, or for emergencies; why rent money is not dead money; and why you need to buy back *your* time if you want to buy back *more* time.

I'll introduce concepts such as Freedom Escape Velocity and the Freedom First Wealth Creation Formula. I'll teach you the *real* tax secrets of the rich, and explain tax in a way so simple you'll wonder why nobody has described it that way before.

I'll show you counterintuitive ways to save and pay off debt and build active income and active growth, as well as teach you why things like earning a steady pay cheque could be costing you your freedom and your chance to build wealth.

I'll show you how debt, dependence and income trap us into straight-line thinking and blind us to growth, as well as how to quit your job sooner than you ever thought possible.

Reading the stories of other successful people, I quickly realised that most people don't really understand what it was that drove them to success. Some have plenty of theories — but for the majority, their own motivations can be hard to divine. Which is why it took a while for me to understand what was different about what I valued, and why so many people *say* they want to be financially free first, while heading in the opposite direction.

But you don't have to take my word for it.

Instead of just my story, in this book I'm going to share with you the story of a young woman I met who, like a lot of people, wanted to be free, but having grown up in a society that encourages the opposite didn't know that she could be, or how to go about it.

It's one thing to think that I had discovered something powerful based on my own life, but it wasn't until I saw that it could be applied to others that I could be sure that Freedom First was truly a unique and universal principle.

Prologue

16 August 2007

My phone rang just as Melissa stood up to order us a second round of coffees. I had met Melissa a few weeks earlier at kung fu. With plenty of time on your hands, you find yourself taking up some interesting hobbies.

While kung fu was a bit of fun for me, on one of the few occasions we'd had to speak, Melissa had told me that she had taken it up after beginning a new job in real estate that required her to go out by herself and show houses to strangers.

It was in one of those breaks between sets that she had asked me the question I always find difficult to answer when I first meet someone — 'So what do you do for a living?'

I'd said something to her about how I used to be a physiotherapist. I'd found in the past that, if I tried to explain to people that I'd retired in my twenties and now I just managed my investments, I would be met with blank stares or disbelief. People are much more comfortable if you can just quickly give them a job title so they can size up where you belong in society.

Rather than stare blankly, Melissa had been curious, which is how I'd come to be having coffee with her in the middle of a weekday.

As she left the table, I checked my phone. It was my broker.

I had put on a trade the day before: selling 50 puts for $1635 each, while buying further puts to insure my position.[1]

You've probably heard that it is wise not to try to time the market, and that's true. And it's also true that if you find yourself in the middle of a gold rush it's better to be the guy who is selling the shovels, rather than one of the many who are buying the shovels in the hope of striking it rich.

This is pretty much what I was doing—selling something the market wanted. Basically it was a trade where I was taking advantage of the volatility that was present, rather than betting which way the market would go. I was selling things that were overpriced and buying things that were relatively underpriced to insure my position. The market could go up and I'd make money. Or it could go sideways. It could even go down a certain amount and, provided the volatility decreased, I could still make money as I was taking advantage of a market mispricing—arbitraging if you like.

My view was that after a healthy stock correction, the odds were higher that the market would rise, but I wasn't relying on that either.

It was a trade I'd been looking out for for a couple of months and once the correction started I'd waited a couple of weeks for it to fully develop.

'Christ, have you been watching this?' Marty said.

'No I've been out all morning, and anyway hello to you too, mate …'

Brokers always seemed to get more emotionally caught up in the market—perhaps it's a function of having anxious clients ringing their phone off the hook all morning.

'What's up?' I enquired.

'We're down over 200 points and still falling. Nobody's on the bid. You can feel the panic in the air this morning.'

The correction had started 16 days ago. While it's foolish to rely on guessing where the market will go, it is prudent to understand that there are cycles to the econo-system; and within those cycles there are predictable seasons. Each year that the market is booming—what we call a bull market—there are usually one or two reliable corrections where the market heads down for a couple of weeks.

---

[1] The technical name for this trade is 'bull put spread'. I'd gone short XJO 5700 PUTS for 163.5 each and insured my position with 5500 puts at 110 each. Don't worry if you don't understand a word of this! You don't need to know anything about trading to be financially free, as Melissa was about to learn.

Reliable in the sense that they will happen sometime within the year—but that can be narrowed down too. There are several times a year, historically, that corrections tend to happen based on predictable and repeatable human patterns—such as tax loss selling at the end of the financial year, or mutual fund redemptions and so on. In a bull market a correction is when the market pulls back a little.

It's actually quite a healthy thing. The market pulls back on average 5 per cent, sometimes 7 per cent, but usually no more than 10 per cent over a couple of weeks. The role of a correction is to 'let off steam'—when people have bid the price of stocks up more than they're worth, a correction can return things to saner values. And then the market will be free to continue to grow from there.

So I had been waiting for the market to pause and finally, two weeks ago, the correction had started. I waited until it had pulled back just over 9 per cent. There had been quite a big sell-off the day before and the market had been smacked down 176 points (or –2.96 per cent) and closed on its lows for the day. With such heavy selling there had been talk of a lot of people getting margin called throughout the day. (A margin call is when you borrow money from the bank and the bank asks you to pay off some of your loan because the value of the shares you own is at risk of falling below the amount of money you owe.)

'What are your clients doing?'

I've found it useful to have a broker with a lot of clients as a barometer of what people in the market were thinking.

'I'm getting clients who aren't being forced to sell, ringing me up to get them out.'

It's not until the end of a bull market, when everybody is getting into investing, that the sell-offs tend to get larger and larger. When a boom starts, it doesn't take much at all to scare people back out of the market. But by the time your cab driver is giving you stock tips, everybody is so confident after seeing several years of double-digit growth that it takes quite a lot to shake anyone's confidence.

And that's usually when the boom years are about to end. Instead of nice yearly pullbacks, we end up with a bear market, when the market continues to fall month after month until the average investor has lost all hope and has fled the market altogether.

'So what's behind it?'

'I don't know, the US was only down –1.3 per cent last night on fears of liquidity for Countrywide, but all the local papers this morning led with yesterday's 3 per cent fall here,' Marty explained.

'There were some people who didn't get called yesterday hanging out for a bounce this morning that didn't happen. They're panicking. I talked to my mate in margin lending and he said they are looking at more margin calls today than he's seen since September 11.'

As a market continues to boom, the average investor not only gets more and more confident to buy shares, but gets more and more confident to borrow money to do so. You see the same with property when people's equity rises: they get confident and draw that equity out and perhaps buy another property.

If the boom goes long enough, people can end up really highly leveraged.

But to my way of thinking that's completely the wrong way to go about it.

Being highly leveraged at the end of the boom right when the situation is about to change is really dangerous. As this boom had been progressing, I'd been lessening my leverage—my LTV ratio. The longer a boom goes on for me the closer we probably are getting to the next stage of the cycle.

But most people don't think cyclically; they think in a straight line. People with jobs are busy working day after day with a steady, predictable income, and don't really have any awareness of the *nature* of investing.

The value of being free

A lot of people thought that Warren Buffett had lost his edge and gone crazy in the late 1990s when he sat out of the tech boom while everyone around him was making a fortune. For Warren, the tech boom just didn't make sense. There was nothing he could use to gauge what these companies should really be worth. There was no income or earnings to justify the prices that people were paying for them.

Therefore there was nothing predictable; there were no fundamentals that he could rely on. Prices were going up, but it was due to a combination of easy money and just plain euphoria. Everyone was relying on someone else to come along and pay a little bit more, and in investing that's known as 'the greater fool theory'.

So just when everyone else was getting in, Warren sat out. And had he timed it perfectly he may have made a killing in the tech boom too, like others had, but had he got it wrong he could have lost a fortune, like so many more did.

By sitting out of the tech boom, Warren gave up short-term profits to survive the long-term seasons—which allowed him to continue to get richer. And that's what being free really is: once you have bought your time back you don't want to have to rely on the market, or property, doubling in value for you to stay free. And although I hadn't been sitting out of the recent boom in our market, I was taking the opportunity as the market rose to decrease my leverage, which is what allowed me the freedom to take advantage of this pullback that I'd been waiting for.

So after an almost 3 per cent sell-off the day before, many people had been margin called, forcing them to sell shares first thing in the morning. However, as the market had pulled back almost 10 per cent already so far this correction, and had come down to my technical support levels, I felt that any further sell-off this morning would be short lived as the last of the margin sellers were shaken out, and institutional investors would come back in to buy the market up in the afternoon.

As I sat at the table waiting for Melissa to return with our coffees, I tried to visualise where the market was, based on my charts. This was crazy. We were clearly oversold yesterday for a bull market correction. Had we started something else?

Even so, the news from overseas didn't justify today's falls, and even if we had started to head into bear-market territory, nothing falls in a straight line.

Most things don't break the first time they are tested. The market can always fall further than you think, but never indefinitely.

If I'd learned anything it was that on average people are terrible at forecasting trends, and the market rejoices in changing direction the minute everyone agrees that they know which direction it is heading. It seemed like this morning everyone agreed that the market was going straight to hell.

'Good thing I bought insurance yesterday, huh? I wonder what those puts I wrote are selling for? I bet I could make a killing selling some more today,' I said with a smile on my face.

'Or get killed. You're not thinking of doing something today are you?' Marty said, a hint of panic in his voice.

'This has to be the textbook definition of irrational pricing, right?'

'Well … the volatility is off the charts …' he agreed, reluctantly.

It sounded like the market was pricing in Armageddon. I could sell an 'insurance contract' today, the market could open down tomorrow and, provided it didn't drop through the floor, I could still make money as the spreads came back in and the risk premiums contracted.

'… and those puts you wrote yesterday, you could have gotten twice as much today or more I reckon, but I wouldn't go near them,' Marty advised.

'Alright. Well, keep me posted.'

I put the phone down just as Melissa was coming back to the table with our coffees.

'Thanks for the coffee,' I said, picking up our conversation where we'd left off. 'I hope I didn't give you the wrong idea when I said I invested for a living. I'm not a stockbroker or anything.'

'That's okay; I wasn't looking for any stock tips. I don't own shares and I don't really have any money to invest anyway,' she replied.

'Oh, that's good,' I said, surprised, relaxing. I quickly added, 'Sorry, I don't mean it's good that you have no money.'

She smiled.

'I just mean that when most people find out that I retired in my twenties they want a quick tip on the stock market or want to know where I think property's going next or whatever.'

'I'm not really looking for tips or to get rich,' Melissa said. 'I guess I was just curious that you'd had a good career and decided to walk away from it.

'I've always thought in the back of my mind that if I had a profession I might find it easier to tough it out in a job. As it is I can't last long in one job without it driving me crazy. I don't want to spend the rest of my life doing mindless work waiting for the weekend or retirement.

'I just want to feel I'm following a plan — going somewhere.'

'You're a millennial, right?' I enquired. 'So I bet you've been told: why can't you just get serious, get a good career and do your time like everyone else?'

'Absolutely. My parents never really gave me any financial advice, but when they did manage to have an opinion it was always "get a good job, buy property", and then what? Save for retirement? Rely on the pension? But how's that supposed to work nowadays? We get told, "don't make the same mistakes we did—you should put off getting married and enjoy yourself, develop your career, travel". And then in the next breath we're told "why haven't you knuckled down and bought a house yet?" Seriously?'

'I know, right? Irony much?' My attempt to sound millennial went unnoticed.

Melissa continued, 'It used to take two people to buy a house in their early twenties, and now we are expected to do it on our own with prices that are through the roof? I'm working in real estate at the moment and all you hear is "you've got to get on the property ladder because property always goes up".'

'Look, there are plenty of people who will take cheap shots at your generation. You've lived your whole life without a recession. We've had 20 years of uninterrupted growth here. You're coming in at the tail end of a historically unprecedented period of easy money; interest rates have been low for decades driving the price of assets up. But while your parents' generation may give you a hard time for not sticking to one career or job, that aspect of what you're doing isn't that crazy at all,' I reassured her. 'It's actually a pretty reasonable response to a world where the idea of a lifetime career is coming to an end.'

'Well, every time I get a new job I try to make sure it's better than the last one.'

'Right. You can't just work for one company your whole life and expect to get taken care of,' I replied. 'Instead the company will quite happily employ somebody over you who has gone out and gained more experience. So jumping around and getting a whole bunch of different work experience is a pretty reasonable adaptation to make.

'The thing is, each generation has something that they do right, and something they feel a little guilty about that their parents' generation did, that they didn't.

'Take the boomers: they may give their kids a hard time about not sticking to one job or buying property, but they in turn had parents who gave them a hard time about not saving much and taking on debt for things that their generation didn't. The fact is, in each generation the average person manages to do the things that will ensure that they end up ... about average.

'Those who lived through or were born in the Great Depression, they placed a lot of importance on the need to save money. And at the time that wasn't a bad thing to do. The great depression was a deflationary time, and during deflation the price of nearly everything goes down, which means that the value of savings actually goes up—basically the opposite of inflation. When stuff is getting cheaper, you can buy more tomorrow with the same amount of money. So saving money was quite a 'smart' thing for their generation to do.

'However, take the 1980s, when inflation was running pretty high: back then, not saving and instead borrowing money to buy a house turned out to be the smart thing to do—if you wanted to be average. Each generation gets a part of the picture right—and usually just enough to ensure that they don't fall too far behind. So what your generation is doing right is it's staying flexible.'

'Well that wasn't intentional!' Melissa replied. 'So what are we doing wrong?'

'Where do I start?' I joked. 'I remember an article I read a while ago in USA Today about millennials where they were asked: "What are your goals in life?" Over 80 per cent said they wanted to be rich, and more than half said they wanted to be famous. As if that was a life goal: to be famous!'

'I don't relate to that at all. I can't imagine anything I'd hate more than being famous.'

'Introvert, huh?' I smiled. 'I can relate.'

'I mean, don't get me wrong,' Melissa replied quickly. 'I want money, but not because I want to live it up or be famous—I want it so I don't have to do this for the rest of my life.'

Our coffee had turned into a late lunch when my phone rang again. It was my broker, the excitement evident in his voice. I excused myself and stepped outside.

'Well, we're about to start trading again, but we've fallen another 100 points over lunch. We're down –304 points or 5 per cent for the day. It's insane.'

'You know what?' I said. 'I know this wasn't the trade we planned on, but how often do you get a day like today? I want you to try to put the same spread on that we did yesterday.'

'You sure mate?'

'Yep, just make sure it's a contingent order. I don't want to end up naked.' ('Going naked' means placing a trade without any insurance.)

'Alright — I'll get back to you in a tick.'

The lunchtime crowd was packing up and hurrying back to their jobs in the city, leaving the café reasonably deserted. Not for the first time I appreciated the advantages of being free to do things outside of the normal hours that most people keep.

For one thing, the lines were shorter.

'They're not coming near it. The market makers will buy your written puts, but they're refusing to sell you insurance.'

'Aren't they obligated to provide a market?'

'Yeah, but it seems like none of them are too keen to stick to their obligations today. Not at any price.'

What was happening was that there are institutions in the stock market, usually the trading desks of large banks, whose job it is to provide a market within a certain spread of something called the Black–Scholes formula, so that if you wanted to buy or sell something there was always someone there to do it with. In exchange for providing a market, the market makers picked up a premium on every trade they did.

But that's not what the market makers were doing today. They didn't want to provide a market like they were supposed to; they just wanted to cover their risk. The risk they were being paid danger money every day to compensate them for. Who would have thought: banks happy to make a mint in the good times, then running for the hills from their obligations when things got bad?

'Typical … banksters,' I replied. 'It's a shame, too, those puts are seriously overpriced. I can almost guarantee that this is about to

turn around. Down 5 per cent in one day, after what? –3 per cent yesterday? And closing seriously oversold at that? After we've already corrected 9 per cent over the last few weeks?'

'… What about the calls?' I asked after a pause.

'You'll have to pay up for them.'

'Do it.'

The smarter trade would have been to follow the plan I had and add to the trade I did the other day—sell the volatility and bet that at the very least the market wouldn't continue to go straight down. But the market makers were running a mile from their obligations, and I wasn't about to write them the contracts they wanted, when they wouldn't sell me the ones I needed to insure my position.

Even though I was sure I was right.

I could go naked, but that would open me up to unlimited downside risk. I didn't get financially free, and more importantly stay free, by risking losing everything for a quick win.

So instead of selling something that was overpriced, I would be buying it.

Instead of doing the safe thing and arbitraging, I would be taking a view: that the market would go up.

If it did anything other than go straight up, if it went sideways for a while first, the fact that I was paying a high premium for these contracts would see me lose money. But only the money I put out there and no more.

'You've just bought 20 of the 5800 calls for 120 or $1200 each.'

It was done; I'd committed now, so I relaxed and Melissa and I spent the next few hours talking. I told her more about how I had first made the decision to quit my career and head off on a path very different from the one most people tread. And also about how, as I was teaching investing, I had started to notice something very important about that decision that I had made all those years ago.

I shared with Melissa something I'd come to understand about what really motivated us: I told her how our parents and others influenced the way we saw money. And I shared with her (as I will with you in Part I of the book) the secrets of the three generations of wealth, and my concept of a hierarchy of values. We talked more about how her generation valued being rich *and* famous, and how it's so important to know what your dominant value was. Because, despite what you hear, the rich aren't all evil or all good; in fact, they're not one monolithic group at all, with identical ideas, or secrets, or beliefs.

'You know, it's always felt so wrong going to a job every day, but I've always felt that I'm just supposed to ignore that feeling,' Melissa confided. 'I wasn't even aware that other people felt this sense of unease. You get the message from every direction that you should do what everyone else is doing—focus on security, get a good education or you're toast.

'Get a good job or you'll never be able to get a good house and you better hurry up and get on the property ladder too or you'll miss out. Slave away to pay down that mortgage or you'll never be able to save up for your retirement. It never ends. You're the first person to tell me that's it's okay to ignore the whole "security" path, or at least not to sacrifice everything for it or cling to it so much.'

'Yeah, I think it was Benjamin Franklin who said if you are willing to sacrifice your freedom for a little security you deserve neither freedom nor security,' I replied.

'But our society certainly seems geared to push us in the opposite direction: "Hey, freedom's great, but you can put that off until you've spent your life chasing security first, okay? Gotta get that security first … even if you have to go into debt to get it".'

'And you're right to feel some unease,' I continued. 'The responsible life plan is on its last legs. If my view of what will happen at the end of the decade turns out to be correct, then not killing yourself to get into the housing market straightaway might turn out to be not such a bad thing after all.'

'So,' I concluded, 'you want to get financially free?'

'Absolutely.'

'Well, if you want to be financially free, you've got to start by getting free first.'

'Okay, but how do I do that?' Melissa asked.

'Well, that can be different for every person, but look, I'll make you a deal. I'll teach you as much as you're willing to do.'

'Deal! So what should I do first?'

'Well, here's your first assignment, and this is pretty advanced stuff … I want you to save.

'But here's the catch: I don't want you to save for anything. I want you to save for nothing.'

She looked at me quizzically.

*'Do you remember that show **Seinfeld**?' I asked.*

*'**Friends** was more my era.'*

I groaned.

'So, all I do is save up some money, for nothing in particular?' Melissa asked.

'Not quite. The secret is in the way you say it: I want you to save for No-Thing,' I said slowly for effect.

'What you are really going to be saving up is some freedom. Saving itself is not going to make you rich. Or even that secure. It's not supposed to.

'It's supposed to make you free.

'Freedom is more than just having more time—freedom is also about having more choices.

'I'm not asking you to save for the rest of your life. In fact, I'm definitely not asking you to do that. That's boring, and ineffective, and there are reasons a lot of people can't do it anyway.

'No, I'm asking you to save for the short term, but for a different reason than nearly everyone else does. Most people, when they think of short-term saving, think of saving for "stuff", or if they are financially aware they think of short-term savings as a type of emergency insurance.

'Not only do many people find it hard to be motivated by that—even if you are the sort to be motivated by a need for security you might find that no matter how hard you try to be financially secure, you'll find it difficult to ever become truly financially free.

'In fact what I'm really asking you to do is to place a value on freedom.

'You don't really value something until you are prepared to give up something for it. For most people freedom is a far-off goal—or a close-up fantasy—but it's never a reality, because they don't value it.

'I want you to save up money for your freedom — not in the future, not for your retirement — for now. You won't need much, but I'll let you work that out for yourself.

'You can only spend what you've saved on getting yourself freer, if you spend it at all. And you may not even know what that is at first because most people don't even notice how free they aren't on a day-to-day basis.'

My phone had been buzzing, but the trade was set and there was nothing left to do now until tomorrow.

When I finally spoke to my broker, he told me what I had hoped to hear all day — the market had finally rallied. And hard.

I had thought yesterday that the margin selling *may* continue first thing this morning, but I expected that the panic of yesterday would subside as the margin sellers were all shaken out early, and the bigger institutional money came back in and bought up the market.

And I was right … eventually. But I had no idea that the panic and margin selling of the morning would drive the market down a further –304 points or 5 per cent at its lowest during the day, after falling nearly 10 per cent already over the past 16 days since this global sell-off began. The carnage continued after lunch, and it wasn't until the final hours of trading that sanity would prevail and the market began to bounce back an incredible 224 points, or 3.7 per cent, in the final two hours of the day.

The fear that was present in the morning had evaporated, replaced with a high-spirited camaraderie around the trading desks: there was an air of having narrowly escaped a disaster and I could hear the relief in my broker's voice. Emails would be forwarded later that day as the various broking houses passed around jokes about brokers and windows and parachutes and so on to each other and their clients, in a bizarre type of 'survivor's humour'.

But over the next few days, and weeks, I noticed something strange. We'd had a brush with death: the bull market was close to ending its run that day, but what should have been a clear sign that we were late in the boom was soon quickly forgotten by most.

The market roared back up. The arbitrage trade that I had done — the one that I had planned for — made me $25 710, which was nice. The 'risky' trade I did on the day I met with Melissa when the market was melting down: those contracts more than doubled in value over the next couple of days.

The fact that the market would correct, that it would fall anywhere from 3 to 10 per cent—and after bottoming out would recover over the next month or two—was reasonably predictable. That's quite normal for a healthy bull market, and even to be expected at this particular time of year.

What wasn't expected was that a couple of years earlier than I'd first anticipated, we'd have the craziest day in the market since September 11.

It gave me a warning that the inevitable correction I'd been talking about for years was coming. You can't fight demographics—and plenty of people had been talking about a correction coming with the imminent retirement of the baby boomers—but the question was when, how big and how long? And what would be the effects afterwards?

By effects I wasn't thinking about just the stock market. An inevitable chain of events was coming: demographics guaranteed that the baby boomers in the West, being the largest generation of consumers to date, would hit retirement and naturally consume less. Less consumption would lead to deflation as asset prices fell and people looking to retire paid off debt. As credit contracts, deficit spending soars to stimulate the economy and to combat deflation. Eventually, though, entitlements as we know them get deferred, then cut, and the last remnants of the standard life plan are swept away. The years of ever-expanding credit, constantly rising house prices and guaranteed retirement pensions would pass—just as the era of jobs for life had disappeared before them—forcing a rethink about our relationships to money, employment and security on the most fundamental level.

Over the next couple of months I would go on to reach out to all my former students, warning them that the big correction was coming, possibly sooner than I had expected, and it was time to change techniques to survive and to even prosper in the turbulent times we were about to face. But not everyone will adapt, because real change happens deep down on the level of values, and while you value comfort and security it can be hard to change, even with the best techniques and the earliest warning.

Which is why I would continue to touch base with Melissa over the coming weeks and expand upon some of the ideas we'd talked about. Unlike my clients, Melissa wasn't an investor. How would the principle I'd discovered work with someone who was starting from scratch? With the world changing, and security becoming even more elusive, would valuing freedom instead be the answer we needed?

PART I

Putting freedom first

CHAPTER 1

The primacy of values

Values, beliefs and results.

Most people want to be thin. And most people want to be rich. It's not like there aren't new techniques, new recipes or formulas to do either of these things freely available and easily accessible on the internet today. So why don't we do them? It's not for lack of a secret technique that we haven't achieved our greatest desires. Though it is very tempting to think this, which is why each year millions of dollars are spent by people who want to hear that the only reason they haven't got what they wanted — why they haven't gotten thin, or haven't gotten rich — is because they didn't have the right techniques. There is a persistent and very modern belief that there must be something more complex — a more sophisticated set of actions we could take — that could get us the result that eludes us.

The truth is that creating wealth is really very simple. But it's really very simple in the way that losing weight is very simple: simple *in theory*. The steps you need to take are straightforward, but taking those steps is not. And like weight loss, we find it hard to believe that if the steps seem so easy, why haven't we taken them? Why aren't we rich?

We have lost the focus we once had on *values* and the power they can have over our actions, so we think that the reason we don't succeed must be that there is a secret we are unaware of.

The Okinawans' secret

The Okinawans of Japan have a culture that results in longevity. They have a set of values that turns on its head the way we think about food, eating and pleasure. As a culture, they put much prestige on living a long life; they value the 1000-year-old wisdom of Confucius and in doing so they end up valuing things we don't. They value eating communally and they value eating 'until you are eight parts out of ten full' — a practice known as Hara Hachi Bu. What this means practically, is that they consume on average 1785 calories a day, compared with more than 2000 for the average Westerner. Their BMI measures between 18 and 22 compared to the average 26 or 27 of Westerners.

You can understand their success in two ways: from the bottom up — their culture promotes values that determine their beliefs and drive their actions — or from the top down: the thing that creates their extraordinary longevity is caloric restriction. It wasn't until the 1930s that biochemists at Cornell University first observed that rats fed a restricted diet lived up to twice as long as those that were fed normally. Yet the Okinawans are the only human population to have a self-imposed habit of calorie restriction. So you can focus on techniques and count all your calories and weigh your food precisely; you can look up nutrient balancing charts, search out substitutes and so on. But the truth is, even with more sophisticated techniques than the ancient Okinawans ever had at their disposal, they still beat us hands down at actually 'getting it done'. And that's because we are hanging onto our values and trying to fight against them with more and more techniques. We are making a thousand hackings at the leaves when we could make one chop at the roots.

Sometimes we look inside ourselves for answers, asking, Maybe something inside me is holding me back, if I haven't achieved what I want?

Although it's a step in the right direction to look within for answers, our search is usually only cursory, as we tend to look to things that are readily accessible to our conscious minds. Things like, 'The rich must have different beliefs from the poor and middle classes.'

Beliefs

You can believe that carbs will make you fat, and that the secret to losing weight is to eat a more natural diet. You can believe that exercising will give you energy and make you feel better, and eating rich foods will make you bloated and feel worse. Your beliefs may all be correct, but you are still not getting the result you want. Why?

Alternatively, you can harbour incorrect beliefs and still manage to get the result you want anyway. The best example I've seen of this is people who've attended a course, looking to improve their financial skills in a particular area so that they can be more prosperous. When asked, many will admit to the belief that they feel that the rich are 'evil'. We certainly get that message loud and clear from our culture. Yet if you truly believe that, how can you want to become rich yourself? If it's your beliefs that were holding you back from creating wealth, shouldn't this particular belief hold you back from *desiring* to create wealth too?

Nobody wants to be evil. Not even Google.

So clearly there is something deeper that motivates us. A desire that is greater than your negative belief, which is pushing you forward *despite* what you believe. If you truly believe that someone is evil, yet you still greatly desire to be in their position, then *desires can override beliefs.* Nobody wants to be evil, but you clearly want to be rich — so much so that you are willing to make an exception to your beliefs if you achieve your goal: 'I still believe that the rich are evil, but I'll be different when I become rich.'

You probably should get rid of that belief. The rich are neither inherently good, nor evil. Having superpowers doesn't make you a superhero any more than a supervillain. And wealth is like a superpower, the power to do more with the precious little time we have. It can even give you the power to fly when, without it you'd have to walk or take the bus! In the world of comics how you use your power determines whether you are good or bad. In that world, powers come to people randomly, but in our world wealth can be earned, created, stolen or, like a mutation, just inherited. Which is why I think *how* the rich get wealthy is far more important in deciding whether they are good or evil than just the fact that they *are* wealthy, and it is even more important than what they do with their wealth.

So it could help to rid yourself of the belief that being rich is evil, just as having better knowledge and beliefs about food and exercise should surely help the person who desires to lose weight to more easily achieve their goal. But it's not enough on its own — even with all the information that's available we're still fatter than ever before.

Values come before beliefs

Obviously we need to dig a little deeper. We need to understand what actually motivates us. In fact, understanding what motivates us — how to get the most out of ourselves — could be the most important skill to have in our modern world, which places more and more cognitive demands on us each year.

Subconscious desires — or 'what we value' — are what motivate us.

Values are literally the level where we choose between the things we want — that is, we choose which things we value more. Economists call these 'revealed preferences'. Take service stations, for example. People say they wish they could go back to the days when you could pull into a service station and actually get service. Someone would come out and pump your petrol for you, clean your windscreen, the whole nine yards. But if you say to those people would they be willing to pay as little as one cent more per litre for that service, would they pay it? It turns out the answer is no. When faced with a competing value — the desire to save money — people would rather hang onto their money and fill their own tank.

What does it mean to say that you really value being thin, for example, provided of course that you can shed the kilos by clicking your fingers or doing one weird trick? In any given situation we face competing values.

We often say we value being healthy and eating right, but when it comes down to a choice between the salad and eating until we are only eight parts out of ten full, and filling up on the hot/sweet/salty alternative, you know what we choose. Our actions reveal our preferences; we value *comfort* from food more than we value health or quality of life. So it's not just that values are more important than beliefs, or techniques, but *which* value is dominant, that is important. It's not what we say we value, but what we *really value* — our subconscious desires — that determines our results.

> It's not what we say we value, but what we *really value* — our subconscious desires — that determines our results.

No matter how much you want to copy someone's success by copying their techniques or their beliefs, you won't succeed until you come to value what they value too.

What are values?

When I say 'values', that shouldn't be mistaken for morals. When most people hear 'values', they either think conservative ('old fashioned' values) or progressive (tolerance, diversity etc.).

The power of values

As an aside, isn't it funny that some of the most powerful people today want to tell us what to value? Sure, they tell us what to believe too, but beliefs can be disproven and change with the times. Values can stay constant. Which can suggest to us just how powerful it can be to change what we value.

Your values are what you *personally* value in any situation. You could call them 'what you desire', but that doesn't really cover it. People say they desire to be thin — but they value the comfort, taste, stress relief and so on that food brings more. So for me the word 'desire' tends to make people think about what they *consciously* desire. 'Motivations' — or 'money motivations' — could be another term, but I like to use motivation as an action word. Something either motivates you or it doesn't, based on how much you desire, or value it.

If you value feeling light, if you value the feeling that you are doing something virtuous (like following the 1000-year-old teachings of a venerated wise man) then finishing a meal when you are only 80 per cent full (as the Okinawans do) may *feel* like success. But if you value comfort, the exact same thing (restricting your calories) will *feel* like a hardship, like you've missed out. In both cases it comes down to what we value *feeling*.

So what I call our 'values' are our *subconscious desires* about how we want to *feel*.

> ## There are a thousand hacking at the branches of evil to one who is striking at the root.
>
> *Henry David Thoreau*

Our emotions evolved before our forebrain. Our forebrain is the more recent part of our mind that we traditionally associate with making conscious and rational decisions, but a lot of research that has been conducted suggests that a large part of what our amazing forebrains do is to provide a narrative explanation — almost an excuse after the fact — for decisions and desires that well up from within us almost automatically, layering a perception of control and choice onto reality.

Values → Beliefs → Actions

If you value the states or feelings that lead to health, then you automatically ask different questions when facing an opportunity to eat. Likewise, rather than having to force yourself to 'think' like the rich or learn the beliefs of the rich, you should instead copy the motivations of the people who became rich.

So who are those people?

A Quick Recap

What we personally value—our subconscious desires about how we want to feel—motivates us and determines our results more than our beliefs or our habits. However, because values are subconscious, most people don't know what it is they really value.

CHAPTER 2

Is it our family's fault we aren't rich?

Do you need a 'Rich Dad' to be rich?

The fact is that the majority of wealth created today is first generational wealth. Let that sink in. What that means is that if you're rich, there's a good chance your parents weren't. Of course, the wealthy do try to pass their wealth on to their children—as we'll see in a moment—but much new wealth besides that is created as well.

> **The whole idea that the rich teach their kids stuff about money that the poor and middle class don't may be true, but it isn't the reason you're poor.**
>
> *Matthew Klan*

It's important to note that while income mobility is greater than most people believe, it's also not as great as it could be, especially since the most recent economic 'recovery'. (Later I'll introduce you to the idea of economic seasons, and why it's so important to be in touch with them if you want to create wealth.) However, what we've been seeing around the world is a rejection of natural seasons—cycles are being flattened out, seasons are being tampered with.

The most natural thing after a big correction like the GFC is that the gap between the rich and the poor should *decrease*— after all, the rich have more to lose (the poor are already at the bottom).

What we saw instead was a massive stimulus that only served to re-inflate the assets of the rich, while the wages for the rest of the economy remained flat, due in part to other policies that were designed to kick-start the economy by indirectly keeping wages low. Trying to 'fix' the natural seasons of money has led to greater inequality.

Don't get me wrong, there's a good chance poor people do model poor financial skills for their kids and having wealthy parents does increase the chance that you would be exposed to better financial habits. But if the only way, or even the *major* way, that people became rich was by learning techniques or secrets from a rich parent, then the majority of wealth *wouldn't* be first generation at all.

This is good news if you want to become rich but don't have a rich parent. It's bad news, of course, if you only want an excuse for not becoming rich! Though chances are, if you had a poor parent it probably *was* a handicap. But luckily one you can overcome without changing parents!

In fact, copying the behaviours, habits, even beliefs of the successful is not enough. The behaviours that make you rich will change with each generation; it's only the fundamental principles that won't. For example, saving money as a primary strategy can be good in a deflationary period, but bad in an inflationary one.

If you are going to model someone, copy their goal, their destination. Two people can arrive at the same destination taking very different paths. If you only copy someone's *steps* you need to make sure you copy them *exactly* if you want to arrive at the same place. And this is providing the terrain hasn't changed in the meantime. But don't just copy their goal; copy their reason, their motivation for choosing that goal. In other words copy what they value, that is driving them towards their goal.

We are all following paths that have led *previous* generations to wealth, security and so on—but will following those paths get us the same results today?

By focusing on the goal and the thing you subconsciously desire, you've got a reference point. Will doing the same thing as the previous generation still get me where I want to be? Or can I come up with my own unique way of getting there? Perhaps then, the most important influence from your parents is what they taught you to subconsciously desire.

Three generations of wealth

In 1901 Thomas Mann wrote the novel *Buddenbrooks*, in which he narrated the decline of German merchant familial wealth over several generations, giving rise to the phrase 'the Buddenbrooks effect' to describe how family wealth declines over time. Often the first generation, seeking money, becomes rich; the second generation, born into money, seeks social and civil position; while the third generation, having been born into comfort and prestige, looks to a life of music and the arts, until eventually the family wealth declines.

> **Men fight for liberty and win it with hard knocks. Their children, brought up easy, let it slip away again, poor fools. And their grandchildren are once more slaves.**
>
> *DH Lawrence*

You find this story echoed throughout history and around the world. In the UK, somewhere around Lancashire circa 1700, the saying 'from clogs to clogs in three generations' arose, based on a similar observation regarding the three generations of wealth and the types of shoes that peasants wore. Later in the 20th century this evolved into 'from shirtsleeves to shirtsleeves in three generations'.

More recently, author Amy Chau noted a similar phenomenon in Chinese culture, explaining: 'There's an old Chinese saying that prosperity can never last more than three generations.'

In the United States, the bestselling book *The Richest Man in Babylon* related the fable of 'The Luckiest Man in Babylon': the tale of Arad Gula and his grandson Hadan Gula. In this story the socialite grandson of a wealthy merchant laments how neither he nor his father could divine his grandfather's secret for attracting the gold coins, and subsequently they were facing financial ruin. A wise old friend of his grandfather's tries to teach young Hadan how his grandfather had valued very different things than his socialite grandson.

What all these different stories tell us is that there seems to be a cyclical nature to building wealth. Wealth doesn't increase in a straight line. Having a rich parent doesn't guarantee you'll be rich and having a poor parent doesn't mean you're stuck being poor either. In fact, it seems that instead of blindly copying our family's values, beliefs and behaviours, we instead end up valuing the things we do in *reaction* to our family.

The arc

Families aren't the only institutions that seem to follow a generational arc: starting with wealth building, followed by consolidation and sometimes decline. Civilisations also seem to follow cycles.

The reason we talk of 'golden ages' is because there are periods that are more prosperous than the periods before, or after them. If there was no arc, history would be just one long golden age, but it isn't. At what stage of the arc is our civilisation today?

The upward trend

Fortunately, the overall arc does bend upwards, and over time humanity has become more prosperous. From 1990 to 2010 the world poverty rate halved: more than one billion people rose out of poverty.

It can be very trendy to prophesise civilisational decline—and it's not always unfounded! But fortunately, regardless of whether our civilisation is advancing or declining, there are many arcs within a bigger crest. Think of tides ebbing and flowing when thinking of civilisations and golden ages. And think of waves cresting and breaking when thinking of the fortunes of families rising and falling. At any one point in time what moves the ocean in or out the furthest are the waves. Over a longer time frame, it's the tides. That's why it doesn't matter to your individual situation so much where we are in the civilisational cycle—but where are you in your family's arc? Is your wave rising, cresting or falling?

Of course, understanding the bigger cycles can be vital to help you to position yourself to create wealth, especially over the longer term. But thinking you can change those cycles is like King Canute sitting in front of the rising tide and ordering the ocean to advance no further. (King Canute was king of England from 1016 to 1035. He didn't actually think he could command the ocean to retreat: that's a modern misconception. He was proving a point to his obsequious courtiers who were constantly flattering him, that despite what they said he wasn't in fact omnipotent.) I'll talk more about cycles in part II.

So why do we see that most of the wealth that's created is first-generation wealth? Why does wealth seem to only last a couple of generations in some families? Our families are a big source of where we get ideas about money, but perhaps not in the way you would think. We don't learn our money beliefs and habits based on observing the beliefs and habits of our parents alone; we also learn about money by how our families influence us to earn or receive it (I focus on how you earn or receive money and the effect that has on you in part II). What does that mean?

Rich parents practising good money habits to create their wealth may inadvertently teach their children bad money habits. Wealthy parents who want children to 'have their lifestyle' may actually rob their children of the ability to create that lifestyle for themselves. They may set their kids up in a home to help them get started, for example. The book *The Millionaire Next Door* addresses this well, as we'll see later.

Probably the best examples though, come from immigrant families. The parents move to a new country because they value something strongly that they feel they couldn't get at home. Perhaps they value freedom, or in many cases security. Those immigrants who go on to be successful often do so because they have a strong motivating value — what I call a Dominant Value — that drives them to success.

But as we will see later, while there are many paths that can lead to wealth, not all of them lead to financial *freedom*. The hardworking immigrant parents who scrimp and save their whole lives often want their kids to grow up without the same fears that drive them. And who can blame them?

> **...while there are many paths that can lead to wealth, not all of them lead to financial *freedom*.**

Wealth that comes at the cost of fear will not feel very freeing at all. And it would be a cruel parent who wants their kids to feel fearful just so they can be prosperous. This often leads them to *encourage* their kids to value different things. The kids of successful immigrants may grow up in an environment where there is material wealth, but their parents are often set on encouraging them to value different things than they did when they created that wealth in the first place.

And often they are not bad things to value either; they are encouraged to value education, for example, and of course the status that may come with that. So, the kids of rich immigrants are sent off to university to become professionals. In turn, their children, the third generation, grow up in families where money isn't a big concern, and neither is family status. They are the kids of well-off professionals, and their parents—having been driven to value status by their immigrant parents—want their kids in turn to value something different again.

And the cycle repeats.

On the other hand, our families may also indirectly influence what we value because of the environment they create for us growing up. In fact, some of the children of poor families may actually go on to become wealthy precisely *because* all the responsibility fell on them growing up. As journalist Katharine Whitehorn noted, 'The easiest way for your children to learn about money is for you not to have any.'

But if they are driven by fear to create their wealth—fear of being poor or of living in chaos—what chance do they have to ever feel free themselves? And like the successful immigrants referred to above, how do they pass on the secrets of their success to their children when their motivation was based on a fear they would never want their children to have?

A Quick Recap

You don't need a 'Rich Dad' to be rich. Family *wealth* tends to rise and fall in cycles. Perhaps the most important influence your parents have on your financial success is what they *caused* you to value.

CHAPTER 3

We can choose what we value

The hierarchy of values.

In 1943 a psychologist by the name of Abraham Maslow, in a paper titled 'A Theory of Human Motivation', proposed his famous hierarchy of needs pyramid, which is still quite well known today.

He asked the questions, What motivates people? What makes people value what they do? What drives humans to value things like security, comfort, belonging, status, esteem or freedom? Maslow believed that people were motivated by what they valued at any one time, and proposed that what they valued in turn depended on what *needs* they had already met.

Maslow split our needs into a series of levels that transition from what he called 'lower order' needs to 'higher order' needs. According to Maslow, a person has to satisfy basic physiological needs such as the need for food and water or sleep before they can value or be motivated to pursue other things.

Once fed and rested, he said, we tend to value safety, security, employment and health. Then, if those needs are met, we can start to care about our position in the group: valuing love and belonging, seeking out friendships and connections.

Only after meeting those needs do we start to value meeting higher level needs, such as self-esteem and confidence, and further self-actualisation, including creativity, spontaneity, problem solving and so on.

Maslow's Hierarchy of Needs

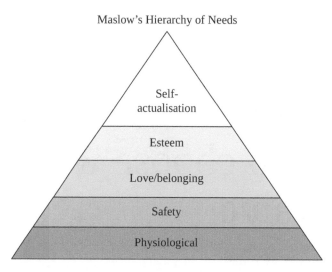

So is what we value determined for us by our environment? By needs we have or haven't met?

Do we need to ensure that physical needs such as satiation, safety and security are met before we can hope to reach for something more?

There was some precedent for what Maslow was proposing in works by earlier thinkers. The French philosopher Michel de Montaigne lived in the 16th century. While Montaigne's father was a soldier, his great-grandfather, Ramon Felipe Eyquem, had made the family fortune as a herring merchant and as a result Montaigne grew up with the finest education available in the classics.

But where the early Greek and Roman thinkers — who gave us the scientific method — praised the human ability to think rationally to overcome our circumstances, Montaigne disagreed. He placed an unusual focus on the human body and its effect on our supposed rational minds.

Montaigne reminded us that we are all animals, and that it is pretty hard to think lofty thoughts when your stomach is empty, or your bladder is full (giving Maslow a precedent for his ideas about the primacy of lower order needs).

The observation that family wealth often lasts only three generations seems to support Maslow's hierarchy too. In chapter 2 we saw that those wealthy immigrant parents who perhaps were very focused on safety and security — to the point where they never felt they could accumulate enough—often encouraged their kids to value different things from what they did. But could the *environment* they provide be responsible for the change in values from one generation to the next?

The wealthy parents raised children who never knew the hardships of their parents and had every material need taken care of. Perhaps being freed from the need to worry about survival or security would cause them to seek out status—a higher need in Maslow's pyramid—thereby preserving the family's wealth; but rather than growing it, they become more concerned with *legitimising* it. The children of a family that got rich in the plumbing business may go on to become doctors. In turn, their children—born with both security and status needs met—focus instead on pleasure or self-actualisation, and the wealth of the family and how it was created is forgotten.

So are we trapped, only being able to value higher needs in life after all our basic needs are met?

Fortunately not.

Testing the hierarchy

The rigidity of Maslow's hierarchy was broken in what is possibly the cutest and saddest psychology experiment to date. Psychologists Harry and Margaret Harlow set out to investigate attachment theory, which asks: What makes an infant attach to its mother? Is it the need for food, a basic biological need or something else? They used orphaned infant monkeys who had been separated from their mothers at birth to test this. These sad little monkeys were given a choice: would they rather go to a surrogate dummy 'mother' that was shaped out of chicken wire, but had a bottle of milk attached to her, or would they choose a second surrogate mother that, instead of being made of cold chicken wire, was made out of cloth and fur, but had no milk to offer?

The baby monkeys chose the 'mother' that was made out of fur—despite her lack of milk, and despite their hunger. Their hunger for comfort and love overrode their desire for basic sustenance. Subconscious needs higher up Maslow's pyramid were being valued despite lower level objective physiological needs not being met.

Turning the pyramid on its head

Although Maslow's pyramid has remained popular, he formed his hierarchy of needs long before we really started thinking evolutionarily about our psychology. Later researchers have pointed out that we don't stick to a strict progression from one level to another, although it can sometimes seem like we do.

Despite all our supposed progress, we as a society are still focused on security. All it takes is a little fearmongering and we seem to be easily convinced to give up our freedoms in the name of a little more security.

It's clear that we don't adhere to a strict hierarchical progression when meeting other needs as well. The middle of Maslow's pyramid concerns the need for connection, attention and belonging. Social networks like Facebook are making it easier than ever before to connect with other people, so in theory we should all be free from these particular needs, able to pursue needs at a higher level. Yet Facebook, YouTube and Twitter—which should be meeting our needs for connection, approval and attention—only seem to be inflaming them. We seem more desperate for attention than ever before!

But that's the good news. We don't have to wait until every lower need is met before we reach for higher levels, meaning we can unlock the creative energy that can produce the abundance that enriches us all.

We know that we can choose to value or pursue higher level needs before meeting every lower level need. And yet the advice we are still being given hasn't changed: if you want to get financially free, don't focus on the higher level need for freedom or self-actualisation. First you must get secure.

> **Spending your life pursuing security in the hope of winding up with freedom is insane.**
> *Matthew Klan*

People have speculated before that if we could just tip Maslow's pyramid upside down—if we could start by valuing the things on the higher levels of his pyramid—then we could meet lower level needs simultaneously ...

What should you choose to value more if you want to become rich?

Maslow may have been a little off in his understanding of what motivates us, but he got a lot of people thinking about the order or hierarchy of what we value.

And that's a good thing because while we may not have a hierarchy of needs, we do have what I call a hierarchy of values.

Hierarchy of values

What do I mean by 'hierarchy of values'? Simply that our values compete with each other. At any one time, one thing you value will take precedence over another. In the conscious mind, the difficulty we have in holding two competing ideas at once is called cognitive dissonance. Not many people can handle it. The subconscious mind is even more primitive. It's impossible to be elated and depressed at the same time. You can be one, then the other. But you can't be both simultaneously. It's the same with subconscious desires. One desire will take precedence. You can value freedom, then security; or security, then freedom, for example.

So your values compete with each other and form a hierarchy, but the order is not set because you can choose what you value most. And although what you value can be influenced by your parents or by your upbringing, there are many other things that can influence what you value too. Your environment, heredity, the personality you are born with, how you earn money and the stage of life you are at can all influence what you value most at any one time.

In fact, it's this last point that I find particularly sad about the post-GFC economy. A whole generation of kids who are finding it so hard to enter the job market are missing out on a critical time in their lives. Most people don't tend to value one particular thing their whole lives—at different stages we value different things—but the one time in most people's lives when they really do value freedom, however briefly, is when they reach their late teens and have the urge to be free, to get away from their parents and start a new life.

Instead, we have a generation now that quite rationally are staying in the family home, sometimes for years, and possibly missing the one time in their lives where it is easiest to strike out on their own, take risks and be free.

So, despite all these outside influences that shape what we value, and the fact that most people will change to an extent what they value most over time, some people do seem to develop one particular value that they hold dear throughout their lives. What can they teach us about becoming rich?

A Quick Recap

You can't value two things simultaneously. At any one time one value will take precedence over others, but your hierarchy of values can change. You can choose what to value.

CHAPTER 4
Dominant Values

**What you value – and how much – determines
your success. But will the path you are following
lead where you expect?**

When we think of those who become rich we tend to think of driven people who were single-minded in their pursuit of something, who successfully pursued some value. Individuals who were driven by a need that was stronger than the average person's, causing them to accumulate a larger-than-average fortune over their lifetimes.

This awareness is scratching at the surface of the reality that what we subconsciously desire — what we value — and how strongly we value it, determines our results or success in life.

For example, it's no coincidence that when we talk about the rich, we talk about the 'rich and powerful', the 'rich and famous' or the 'rich and successful'. We even talk about the 'rich and miserly', bringing to mind people who are driven perhaps by fear, or a greater-than-normal need for security. These people all have what I call a Dominant Value. This is a value that tends to assert itself ahead of other values in many situations.

While it is quite normal for us to change what we value the most over time, these people tend to continue to place the same value first in their hierarchy of values. They tend to keep valuing some subconscious need, even when it would seem to others that they have objectively ticked that box.

There is more than one path to riches

What should you choose to value if you want to be financially free?

I think many people are put off the idea of becoming wealthy because of a lack of awareness of there being more than one way to get rich. How often have you heard 'the rich' this or 'the rich' that? We think of the most visible types of rich people and then think to ourselves: 'Who wants to be a shameless attention hound, or be tight and fearful, if that's what it takes to be rich?'

Most people don't really know what motivates them, what they subconsciously value. And many of the people who share with us the secrets of their success are sharing just that—the secrets of *their* success, at least as far as they are aware. Even when they do get their own motivations right, that advice is useless to us unless we first adopt their Dominant Value.

So the 'rich and famous' advise us that the secret to getting wealthy is to increase your profile. Get yourself out there!

The 'rich and powerful' tell us (when they are not lying) that it is all about connections—the secret to success is networking!

The 'busy business person', motivated perhaps by status, tells us it's all about looking the part (buying status objects), or 'kicking goals', constantly striving for success. They have made millions, yet they are still running around. What's with that? Why do they keep working at such a high-stress job when they already have more than most of us could want? We can see now that it's because they are driven by something other than the money. And so the question becomes: If you want what they have, can you be driven by what they are driven by?

Most people I've taught just want to be financially free. They don't want to keep accumulating runs on the board until the game is over. They just want to be free to enjoy the game along the way.

So, if we can choose to rebuild our pyramid to suit our own hierarchy, what should be our Dominant Value? What happens if we value security first—or status? The three generations of wealth suggest that some values may be less effective at encouraging us to accumulate wealth than others. But why?

There are many different values people can pursue, and in many different areas of their lives. But if you want to have success you need to desire something more than everyone else.

A personal value is nothing more than a subconscious desire about an emotional state you wish to be in. But with the exception of one value, there is nothing inherent in the values *themselves* that is inextricably linked to the process of creating wealth. (In fact, it's important to note that not all wealth is *created* anyway. Wealth can be *taken* too.)

> "...**if you want to have success you need to desire something more than everyone else.**"

But in times past and under certain circumstances, valuing certain things *did* have the added benefit of leading you to perform activities that could increase your wealth. How did pursuing certain values once lead to wealth, why doesn't it anymore and what can we learn from this?

The different paths of different values

While there is something about creating wealth that is uniquely linked to freedom—and, as we'll see shortly, to valuing freedom—not too long ago people who pursued other values may have created wealth as a side effect too. But do those other values work as well now as they once did? Does desiring those things today produce the same results as in the past?

To answer these questions, we'll now look at the evolution of four traditional paths to creating wealth: the path of fame, the path of status, the path of power and the path of security.

The path of fame

Fame is a good Dominant Value to look at first, because as we saw in chapter 3 it's become a major driving ambition of a whole new generation. There have never been more available avenues for becoming famous than there are today, and it's also the most visible model we have of rich people.

In fact, it's one of the few 'positive' models we have of the rich. Celebrities are the 'good rich', while business people are often portrayed as the 'evil rich'. Everyone loves celebrities and hardly anyone loves their boss.

But before the days of mass media it used to be that if you were famous, it was *for* something. You were famous because you were a champion sports star, a famous author or a major industrialist. The only group of people famous for nothing was royalty!

Most people didn't know very many people outside of their small towns. If you managed to achieve fame you had to do something extraordinary to achieve it. You had to actually develop some skills.

And increasing your skills is one way to increase your productivity — that is, how much value you can create, and therefore how much wealth.

Back then, the desire for fame above all else may have paid off. With cinema came the rise of movie stars, but compared to today they were relatively few in number. It wasn't until recently that people even knew what their politicians looked like. With careful management of the press, Franklin D Roosevelt, the president of the United States in the 1930s and 1940s, managed to keep from the public an illness that confined him to a wheelchair. That's unimaginable today with politicians tweeting pictures of themselves hourly.

Reality TV, blogs, YouTube and Twitter now mean that if you desire fame you can have it relatively easily. You can have more fans than celebrities of old — without having to develop any discernible skill at all — all for the cost of a webcam and an internet connection! Now you can achieve the highest level of fame (for a brief period of time at least) without ever achieving any wealth along the way.

> **... fame today is a desire that is relatively easy to fulfil cheaply.**

So fame as a Dominant Value may not drive you to the great heights it once did. Although we are constantly presented with examples of the 'rich and famous', fame today is a desire that is relatively easy to fulfil cheaply, so if you are driven by a desire for fame you probably won't end up rich at all. And if you've been on the internet or watched reality TV, you may have noticed that sometimes people who have been consumed by a need for attention end up worse off as a result.

You may not be a millennial or, like Melissa, you may be part of the 50 per cent of millennials who don't have fame as a major value. There are some things you just know you don't value.

On the other hand, it's easy to *think* you value something only to keep finding that for some reason you never seem to end up getting the thing you think you value. That's because 'the things we value' are actually subconscious desires, and sometimes it can be hard to see them clearly ourselves.

A friend of mine, Andrew, is a great example of this. I met him through the gym after I'd been retired for a few years. We both had a health background so we hit it off immediately. Like me, he seemed to value being financially free, but as the years went by he kept working his job – although he always had a new idea or venture that he'd be pursuing on the side. I used to encourage him to 'quit and commit'.

He had a bunch of business ideas that he'd throw himself into; he'd set up the meetings, open trust funds and set up company structures with his solicitor, and have lunches with all the 'important' people. He'd get very busy, but for some reason the businesses would never take off and free him from his job.

In hindsight I've realised there are certain traps, or pitfalls, that come from not being free. The longer you've progressed along the 'work a job for life', 'climb the comfort ladder' path, the harder it is to shake off the effects those traps can have on your thinking. Earlier, I alluded to the fact that the way you earn money could influence what you value. I'll talk about that more in part II.

The effects of a regular job aside, my buddy worked for a major drug company as a rep, and they've got all sorts of tricks up their sleeves—such as company cars and laptops—to keep their reps addicted to the job. Who would have thought a drug company would be good at keeping people addicted?

To talk to him you wouldn't think anyone could want to be free more. He was right into working on his psychology: he even got a big tattoo on his arm of an eagle holding a banner with the word 'Freedom' on it. To be honest, I think it was partly so he could have an excuse to show girls his 'guns'. But still … that's got to count as commitment to being free, right?

One day we were catching up and I asked him, 'Would you want to be rich if you could only achieve that by starting a "vanilla" business? Something totally boring. That no-one else would even know about. You might do all your work from home or online, and your neighbours might assume you're a bum. Like, say, you're the paper king of Brisbane? You supply paper to all the paper stores. That's it. Would you be prepared to give up your corporate job and your company car, the inevitable promotions into management and the status of wearing a suit to work to do that sort of "no collar" business if it got you free?'

It wasn't an easy question for Andrew to answer.

Although fame may not function that well at making you rich if it's your Dominant Value, it can be something you achieve if you have it as a lesser value. The problem with fame as a Dominant Value is that people who primarily desire fame seem to have such a limited view of what it means to be famous. They look around them at those who already *are* famous and get their inspiration from there.

> **"We've all been raised on television to believe that one day we'd all be millionaires, and movie gods, and rock stars, but we won't."**
>
> *Tyler Durden in* Fight Club *by Chuck Palahniuk*

But those who go on to achieve great fame often do it by standing out in completely new ways, by treading paths that no-one has done before. Benjamin Franklin comes to mind as a good example. He's a guy who nearly everyone knows of even today, someone who achieved great and lasting fame. But it would be hard to argue that fame was his Dominant Value.

The path of status

Status is becoming more and more ethereal.

Once, you could display your status by having radically different things than most people could afford. The rich had cars, the poor didn't. As standards of living increased, it wasn't enough to have different *types* of things, you had to have different *brands* of things to differentiate yourself. Now, the whole concept of luxury goods is being challenged as more and more people can afford branded goods.

Once, if you wanted to have status, and if you valued it strongly enough, you may have worked harder than others so you could afford to buy more stuff. And while wasting your money on status objects may not be the fastest way to accumulate wealth, at least you had to be able to afford them first. And at least you still had the big home and the big car as a store of value, after displaying your status.

As status competition became more democratised, we shifted from buying big status objects to displaying high-status lifestyles too: eating at expensive restaurants, drinking boutique coffee and so on, leaving us with little to show for it. But now that we have easy personal credit, the cost of displaying status is not just that you waste all your money — it can mean that you end up in debt as well.

But that's not the end of the evolution of status competition. As you go from the third world to the first, the dividing line shifts from the more tangible to the less. Being higher status is not about whether you went to school or not in the first world, but which one. The struggle to display status shifted from different things, to different types of things, to different brands of things and finally away from the tangible altogether to displaying different behaviours and habits (food is no longer a luxury as everyone can afford to be obese. In primitive tribes you signalled wealth by being fat; now you signal wealth by showing that you can afford the costly habit—in terms of effort and time—of preparing good food and exercising).

But it's gone even further than displaying different habits—and has become even more intangible—to displaying different *beliefs*.

To understand what I mean you need to know that the path of status is all about signalling. A great example of signalling can be seen in the animal kingdom. In certain four-legged prey animals—several deer in North America, and more famously perhaps Thomson's gazelles and springboks in Africa—a curious behaviour called stotting has been observed. When a predator approaches a herd of prey, some of the prey animals break into a series of highly energetic leaps in the air. They just leap around on the spot, which seems crazy at first. Instead of running away or conserving their energy by disappearing into the crowd, these animals draw attention to themselves and waste precious energy doing this funny little dance. What's going on?

Evolutionary biologists have concluded that what the gazelles are doing is sending a message or signalling to the lions that are stalking them. Lions stalking herds want to pick out the oldest, the slowest or weakest prey to attack to guarantee

> **❝ ... the path of status is all about signalling. ❞**

the chances of a kill. What the prey are doing in effect is shouting out, 'Hey look at me, I'm so fit and full of energy that I can waste energy jumping around like a maniac and you still couldn't possibly catch me—so don't even try.'

But here's the catch—the signal they send has to be believed, which is why the gazelle developed a signal that involves so much energy. If stotting was easy and every gazelle started doing it, the lion would quickly catch on that some of them were faking; they might be acting full of energy, but some of them were actually old or slow. And the effort to jump around would only tire out these old gazelle, leaving them no energy to run when the lion attacked. Stotting effectively signals health because it comes with a real cost of energy, and only the fittest can afford to do it.

And so it often has been in the human world. You display wealth by signalling to others that you have more to spend. You can afford to 'waste' money on an expensive car, rather than a perfectly serviceable regular one, because even with all the money you wasted you can still put food on the table. Successful signalling involves cost. A signal is more believed the more it is seen to cost us. But in today's world with easily available credit, that signal is not as clear: has that person got money to burn, or have they just maxed out their credit card?

Status as a Dominant Value may not motivate you to accumulate much wealth anymore, and may in fact cause you to go into debt.

So if in our jostling for status we are starting to move away from having different stuff to having different beliefs, then what is the cost? In the past, status was found in owning things that the average person couldn't. In our cognitively stratifying society the greatest status concern for many people is to be seen to be more intelligent than others. (In chapter 5 I'll share one way that valuing 'seeming smart' directly costs you as an investor.)

One way to signal that you are smarter is with a better education, which nowadays comes with much greater cost than in the past, for less tangible gain. The risk–reward ratio for higher education is becoming less favourable. In the past, seeking out a degree often meant earning more money as a side effect of your pursuit of higher status. Today, with ballooning debt and a tight job market, that's often not the case.

On top of that, as more and more people now go to university, signalling you are smarter than others by having a degree is giving less cache and less status.

Another way to instead signal that you are 'more intelligent' and high status is to believe things that are counter intuitive. The average person believes what their lying eyes tell them, while the 'enlightened' person 'understands' the more complex reason why that which seems to be true, really isn't.

> ## " In a time of universal deceit, telling the truth is a revolutionary act. "
> *George Orwell*

So the race to gain status has moved on to signalling that you are more *moral* than others, that you have superior beliefs. As the status war heats up we seem to be rushing to adopt more and more extreme moral plumage to stay ahead of the pack.

'Moral exhibitionism' is the vice that cloaks itself as virtue. Signalling that you were smarter in the past may have at least involved getting a degree that may have had some value—but signalling that you are more moral than others doesn't require you to do or achieve anything anymore. So valuing status today is unlikely to lead you to *accumulate* anything either—other than Facebook likes.

You can be wrong more than you are right and you can still make money

As George Soros said: 'It's not whether you are right or wrong that matters, but how much money you make when you're right and how much you don't lose when you're wrong'.

This was an important lesson I learned early on in my investing career. Ask most people, 'What makes someone a successful investor?' and the answer 'making successful investments' comes pretty high up on their list.

Almost no-one says successful investors manage risk well, cut their losses early, manage their downside and maximise their upside. We simply aren't accustomed to thinking about the inputs as well as the outputs in our lives. I'll cover this further in chapter 9, where I explain why it is that we've all been trained to think exclusively about the outputs in our lives.

Nevertheless, the saying is true. You can make money simply by losing less money when you are wrong, and making more money when you are right—even if you are wrong more often than you are right.

Say you let your profits run and make $100 each successful trade you do, and you are strict about cutting your losses to $30 for each losing trade. You could be wrong three times as often as you are right and still come out ahead. In business, you could lose money on three items you sell as long as you make up more money in total on the fourth item. As an entrepreneur, you could start three businesses that fail to make it big if your fourth one takes off. But in teaching other people I've always found the difficult part of this truth is not in understanding it, but in applying it. Can you be wrong more than you are right and still make money? Phrased differently, can you stand to be wrong more than you are right?

Even if it could make you rich?

Most people can't. In economics and psychology there is a term called 'loss aversion', first demonstrated by Amos Tversky and Daniel Kahneman, that explains this tendency. Studies done on loss aversion suggest that we feel the stress of losses twice as strongly as we feel the pleasure of gains. Losing $100 costs you twice as much happiness as winning $100 would give you.

(continued)

You can be wrong more than you are right and you can still make money (*cont'd*)

Studies have suggested, however, that the effect of loss aversion is not as universal as first thought. So what motivation for being rich would allow you to persist with constantly being wrong?

If status was your Dominant Value — if you cared about being seen as a share-trading or property-investing guru, for example — you might find that your motivation for proceeding in the face of a losing trade or investment might wither.

If you valued being seen to be smart by others, then saying 'I was wrong four times this month but I cut my losses early and ended up ahead' may not sound as flattering to you as being able to say 'I picked it right again!'

Could valuing your freedom, instead of valuing being right, allow you to overcome your loss aversion?

The path of power

We live in a democratic age with equality as our guiding mantra. Doesn't democracy mean that the power is in the hands of the voters? Since everyone has the vote, aren't we all equally powerful? We elect 'leaders' but we can vote them out too, so surely there is no point in being driven by power anymore?

Nobody admits to being motivated primarily by power, yet nearly everyone can point to someone who is driven by this Dominant Value. Why is that?

There are two answers to that question. One is that power still exists today; it's just gotten cleverer at hiding itself.

So while we are supposed to live in a meritocracy, I'm not going to pretend that the only way to get ahead is to work hard, save and so on. Nor am I going to pretend that being connected doesn't pay off. But what I want to look at is how *well* does it pay, and does it pay as well as it used to — or are there better ways for you to become wealthy than by pursuing power?

I remember reading about a recent immigrant to the United States who was amazed that the president wasn't automatically the richest man in the country. His surprise points out an important truth: for most people around the world and for most of our history powerful people *were* the wealthiest in society and the accumulation of power was a paramount concern for most people.

So while power may not be as profitable a path as it once was, our instinct or desire for it is still there. The popularity of books such as *A Game of Thrones* and shows such as *House of Cards* or *Downton Abbey* demonstrates that we are still fascinated with power and those who wield it. And the world does seem to be getting less egalitarian, despite protestations to the contrary, while those who wield real power seem to be getting more flagrant in abusing it.

But even if things are not as free as they once seemed, we need to put today in historical, even evolutionary, perspective. And so, the second reason that people still value power is an evolutionary one.

For the vast majority of our history we didn't live in advanced civilisations. In fact, for the better part of 200 000 years we lived in small tribes and bands of people. For every 30 to 150 people there was a chief. Pull enough strings, push people in the right direction and the politically minded could arrange for their son to marry the chief's daughter, for example, and rise to the top of the status hierarchy in their world. Now, we live in countries with millions of people and the chance of manipulating your way to the top has become exponentially harder. It's like the path of fame in sports or movies where the top few spots now have millions of people competing for them.

> *"...while power may not be as profitable a path as it once was, our instinct or desire for it is still there."*

In fact, that's an interesting topic in itself. There's a concept proposed in the 1990s by anthropologist Robin Dunbar called Dunbar's Number that suggests that there is a cognitive limit to the number of people with which the average person can maintain stable social relationships. This concept has been used to help to design work environments that better suit our psychology: creating working teams sized to fit what we were designed to handle, counteracting to some extent the alienating effects of working in large, impersonal corporations.

Dunbar's Number is actually a series of numbers that vary depending on the closeness of the relationship between individuals—family, friends, neighbours, colleagues and so on — with an upper limit of people we can relate to of about 150, which incidentally is about the average number we observe in modern hunter-gatherer societies. What this tells me is that our brains are wired to do risk–reward calculations, and seeking out fame as the best hunter in your tribe, or power by aligning your family with the chief's family, was a reasonable goal in the environments we evolved in.

But the number of 'top spots' hasn't grown in proportion to the population today; we don't have a prime minister or president for every 150 people. And despite unlimited avenues for fame, there are only a handful of top celebrities and top sport stars for millions of people. And that's because the average person can only pay attention to so many celebrities at once!

But we didn't evolve a desire for power, or status, just for ambitious reasons. In the past, we depended on each other in a very real way for our survival against the seasons and the predators we shared the Earth with. If you didn't have some political skills, if you annoyed people enough to get kicked out of the tribe, you died. Today, socially awkward people can make

> **...wealth is a product of the networking of human minds.**

a product that millions, even billions, of people value. If the movie *The Social Network* is any representation of how socially awkward he is, a Palaeolithic Mark Zuckerberg could have found himself out on his own fighting sabre-tooth tigers instead of becoming a billionaire!

So in the past when we lived in small tribes, politicking may have delivered a much better return on investment, but the opposite was true too: innovating didn't pay off as well as it does today. In chapter 10 where we discuss cycles, and the nature of wealth, I'll introduce you to the 'Freedom First Wealth Creation Formula'.

The formula tells us that wealth is a product of the networking of human minds, but in prehistory there were only so many minds to network. We lived in a world where the network of minds that we have today — with hundreds of millions of people solving billions of problems for each other, and building on the trillions of previous advancements that have come before — didn't exist. So much of what we take for granted today are innovations that are built upon previous innovations; even a Leonardo da Vinci born in the Stone Age would have only been able to innovate so much. Before writing was invented, discoveries were often forgotten. When there were only 30 to 100 possible customers available to value your innovation, you could only grow so rich by creating something new.

And that's if you were allowed to keep what you created.

Rich doesn't always mean financially free

If, for example, the path to wealth you took was the path of power, your continued wealth may depend on your ability to support those who gave you power. In the old medieval monarchies one of the things the monarchs did to keep themselves safe from challengers to their power was to routinely visit those they had given power to.

A visit by the Queen and her entourage would be a costly affair that could last for weeks and cost lords or barons enormous sums of money as they struggled to host the royal court. Their wealth came not from any value they had created themselves, but rather was contingent on the blessing of the monarch. A title and all the income that was attached to it, was dependent on the goodwill of the ruler. To maintain their position, nobles were expected to receive the monarch, a duty that, while assuring their place at court, also served to drain them of money that they could use to raise support against the ruler, while the ruler also transferred the costs of maintaining their own household to their nobles. Quite devious. Thank goodness there are so many paths to wealth today that don't rely on you gaining the favour of someone in power.

In chapter 7 we'll see that while there is still temptation to choose politicking over producing in the workplace, getting ahead by politicking will make you less free.

Politicking is part of our nature. In this increasingly politicised world it can feel like you'd be a fool to ignore the need to be connected, to know the right people to get ahead. While power may like to hide itself, or at least it used to, it certainly feels like you can't hide from it. When it comes to building wealth, which path should you take? Should you value being freer over being more powerful, or should you value gaining power even if it costs you a little freedom?

The path of security

It's funny how we talk about the 'rich and famous' and the 'rich and powerful', but you don't often, or ever, hear people talk about the 'rich and secure'.

It's as if on some level we acknowledge that the desire for fame or for power is the desire to be 'greater' than, or to have more than, the average person. And the definition of being rich, of course, is having more than what is average.

While those other values may appeal to the very driven type of individual, security is something that most people find easy to value, and even value quite highly at different stages of life, for evolutionary reasons. And it's probably because of this that we are most often sold things by those in power, in the name of security.

But how effective is it at making us rich? Should you make security your Dominant Value? Do people who value security highly end up rich, and even if they do, do they end up financially free?

> **If money is your hope for independence you will never have it. The only real security that a man will have in this world is a reserve of knowledge, experience, and ability.**
>
> *Henry Ford*

I've noticed that with a lot of baby boomers who are retired, much of their conversation revolves around money: Where's the stock market going? Will housing continue to rise? Where's the best place to get a five-dollar steak, and do they do early dinner?

But seriously, some people have worked very hard their whole lives, and have done the right thing and funded their own retirement, only to realise at the end of it all that pursuing financial security doesn't necessarily get you financial freedom.

They may have finally had enough money saved up that they could stop working, but they are now realising that they wanted to stop working and be free to do stuff. And not be dependent on the market, on the pension, or constantly worried about money.

It turns out that, after a lifetime of prioritising security instead of freedom, security (to the extent that you even have it) doesn't feel that freeing. Who'd have thought?

Valuing security, however, is at the heart of 'responsible' financial advice.

In fact, the financial planning industry has its roots steeped in the value of security: the original financial planners started out as door-to-door insurance salesmen. 'Get security sorted first: get a good education, then a good, secure career, then make sure you've got a roof over your head, your health insured and your retirement funded, and then think about starting a business ... but only in your spare time—you wouldn't want to lose all that security!'

Not only is security at the heart of financial planning, but much of society revolves around the promise of security. I say promise, because what we often end up with is dependence and insecurity.

Education used to be a guarantee of a good job; now it's a requirement for any job, and a guarantee for none. Jobs used to last a lifetime; now industries don't last a lifetime. Work used to be full-time. Now, with more people employed part-time and even on 'zero-hour workweeks' (where your employer requires you to be available all week, but doesn't have to provide any minimum hours at all), a full working week isn't even guaranteed.

This insecurity has even been sold to us as 'cool' and is often referred to as the 'gig economy'. Taking boarders into your house, or acting as a taxi driver in your spare time might sound like something people did to make ends meet in the Great Depression, but in our Digital Great Depression the ubiquity of apps that allow you to do just that is seen as a positive sign as the economy becomes 'Uberised'.

The gig is up

According to the JPMorgan Chase Institute, in 2018 more than 3 million people in the United States made money from ridesharing apps alone. However, according to *The Wall Street Journal*, the average monthly amount that people are earning from ridesharing apps has fallen by half since 2013 as the number of people competing to make ends meet by performing these services has skyrocketed.

Pensions used to be 'defined benefit', where the benefit was guaranteed. Now, while we are still promised the 'security' of a pension, all the risk has been passed onto us, with pensions becoming 'market based' or 'defined contribution' only—which is a fancy way of saying the results aren't guaranteed, or secure, and that we carry the risk.

We are gradually being weaned off a secure life path, but despite this, we are still expected to buy into the illusion of security. We talk about retirement 'savings' even though most people are in reality retirement 'investors'. We take on greater risk, but are encouraged not to take on greater responsibility—let your fund manager or other 'experts' take care of that.

Which is why I say don't 'save' for retirement. On the one hand, you can't literally save by putting money in a bank with no risk and

...don't 'save' for retirement.

forgetting about it: inflation will eat away the value of your savings *over the long term.*

But in another important sense, you shouldn't 'save' for retirement because after a lifetime of working hard and putting all your focus on maximising your savings from your job, even if you do manage to accumulate a good amount of money, a retirement that depends on accumulated savings over a lifetime isn't secure. If something happens, even if it's just that you've wound up with less than you want to live on, it's a strategy that you can't simply repeat: it's not like you can go back to work and save for another 40 years all over again. On the other hand, a retirement that comes from *creating* wealth *can* be repeated — that is, wealth can be created again.

If you are someone who values security strongly, chances are you are not comfortable having a large portion of your money in the stock market. In fact, you probably want the security of guaranteed income in retirement and having your money in a vehicle that yields *variable* income each year wouldn't feel very secure to you at all.

Which is a shame, because as you approach retirement, you'll be confronted with the fact that if you want your capital to last, you are going to have to be invested in something that can at least keep up with inflation, which will be eating away at the value of your savings.

So that's strike one for security as a good Dominant Value, if you want to be rich. It may be a good value to motivate you to do the steps involved in 'traditional financial planning' — start saving early, live below your means and so on — but it's not a great value to hold if the end of that path involves committing all your life's savings to the stock market.

But, wouldn't it be great if there was a way to 'guarantee' with 100 per cent security that if you put your life savings in stock market-based investments and withdrew only a certain amount of money each year from your retirement savings (regardless of the actual interest or dividends your savings may be earning), your savings would still last as long as you want and not run out? Isn't that exactly what those who have security as a Dominant Value really want?

The real cost of security

Well, the good news is you can — sort of — by looking at long-term stock-market returns. A study on retiring early (based on data from the book *Irrational Exuberance* by Robert J Shiller) looked all the way back to

1871, and worked out what would have happened to your savings if you had retired at different points in time since then.

Looking back, you could compare how your savings would have performed from a worst-possible scenario—like retiring the day before the Great Depression—to a best-possible scenario—like retiring just before the market boomed. From there, you could work out how much money you could safely withdraw from your retirement fund each year, under even the worst possible conditions *historically*, and still have some money left.

That figure is 3.81 per cent of your *initial* retirement savings.

In other words, if you retired with $1 million, you could pay yourself $38 100 *each year*. That's an awful lot of savings for an awfully small income. That's the cost of being 100 per cent secure.

Clearly the cost of security is much higher than most people expect, or many people have planned for.

> **Wanting to be secure is not greedy; it's not even that ambitious. It seems crazy to me that people motivated by a simple desire to be secure, should feel they need to be rich first to do that.**
>
> *Matthew Klan*

As these figures sink in, let's fast forward the grieving process and skip from the denial stage straight to the bargaining stage—which is what many people do when they first realise they'll never save enough to live the lifestyle they want.

If you are prepared to accept a 2 per cent chance that your money might run out, then your 3.81 per cent initial drawdown can be increased to 4.01 per cent. With only 95 per cent security it increases to 4.33 per cent, and if you are prepared to accept a 10 per cent chance your money might run out, then your initial drawdown can go as high as 4.78 per cent, meaning with $1 million of retirement savings you could live on $47 800 per year.

Of course a 10 per cent chance of their retirement savings running out is probably terrifying to someone who values security. If you do 'run out of money' (or never manage to save up the tremendous amount that being 100 per cent secure requires), in most developed countries there is always the pension to fall back on (if you are old enough). However, for someone who values security, ending up dependent on a pension may not feel that secure either. With good reason too—with ageing populations and increasing debt it's uncertain how much longer the pension systems many have come to depend on will last. (I'll discuss the effects of the pension in more detail in chapter 7.) Watching your retirement savings decline while you hope the pension system will still be there at the end is hardly comforting, and not what most people who followed the 'safe and secure' path envisioned for their later years.

The cost of retiring young

Already, younger generations expect that when they retire, the pension as we know it will not be available to them.

Of course, if you want to be financially free and retire securely at a *younger* age, and therefore want your money to last longer than 30 years, valuing security the most may not be the way to do that either. The 100 per cent secure withdrawal rate gets *lower* (meaning you need a *lot* more savings to live off) the longer you want your money to last.

Needing to be 100 per cent secure means, in many cases, drawing out a very small amount of money from your savings to prevent a worse-case scenario that may never happen, and living below your means for many extra years before retiring, only to perhaps end up leaving behind more savings than when you started! (Sometimes vastly more: the safe withdrawal rate protects you against the worst possible outcome—but depending on what the market did after you retired, your $1 million retirement savings could have grown to $3.97 million in 50 per cent of cases, and in the *best* case scenario it could have grown to $11.13 million by the end of the 30 years.)

If only you could look ahead and see that the market is going to surge after you retire, instead of crash—you could retire with security years sooner!

Well, there is one way to do that (retire earlier and with less money), and that is to take the time to acquire some skills: anything you can learn—a hobby, some investing skills—that can earn you even as little as $5000 a year in retirement is worth $130 000 dollars in extra retirement savings ($130 000 of extra savings would give you, at a safe withdrawal rate, $5000 a year income). How many years of work would it take to save an extra $130 000, or $260 000, or $390 000?

So the flipside of these depressingly low secure retirement withdrawal rates is actually quite exciting: any small amount of money you can earn, or even better 'create', after you retire is worth *more than 20 times as much in retirement savings*. This is not 'continue to work in your retirement'. In fact, it's the opposite: it's stop work, and retire sooner.

> **" ... any small amount of money you can earn, or even better 'create', after you retire is worth *more than 20 times as much in retirement savings*. "**

Retire sooner

An old guy who lives down the road from me used to work in a high-stress corporate environment. To relax, he'd go fishing on the weekends. Eventually he'd had enough and quit his job. With time on his hands, he got certified and now has a part-time business taking people out in his boat to get their boat licences: a business that, because he already owned a boat, cost him almost nothing to start other than the time it took to get his qualification.

I'll show you in later chapters some simple investing skills you can learn, as well as why it's worth spending some of your time during your working years focusing on *your* growth, not just on your *money's* growth.

Retiring early to do something fun that makes a little money—rather than slogging away at your soul-killing-but-maximally-profitable career for more years—sounds smart to me. And if it turns out that instead of crashing, the market actually soars after you retire, then you won't need to make that $5000 a year anymore either!

Security as a motivator

The biggest problem I have with security is not the exorbitant cost that achieving a 'secure' retirement entails—my biggest problem with security *as a value* is that it's not a great motivator to accumulate that wealth in the first place.

Many people are motivated to *feel* secure, and as I'll talk about in chapters 7 and 9, there are certainly plenty of things that may make us feel secure, but feeling secure and being secure are not exactly the same thing. In this increasingly insecure world, feeling secure is often an illusion.

Dostoyevsky's Despair

Russian novelist Fyodor Dostoyevsky was motivated by security. He felt that pain and a lack of security were essential to his creative process. After the success of his earliest works he found that the material comfort and security he had achieved robbed him of his motivation to write. Being relatively secure, he had no urgent need to create anymore. Despairing at this, he gambled heavily and threw his newfound wealth away until, penniless again, he was finally able to feel motivated once more.

In fact, only a pathological need for security — never feeling you are secure enough — may actually drive you to accumulate riches. And even then, wealth made this way won't make you financially free, and it certainly won't make you feel that secure either.

> **Ironically, if you want financial security, you might be better off valuing something other than security.**
>
> *Matthew Klan*

If you think about it, within the desire for security can be found an embryonic yearning for freedom itself — for many people who 'want to be secure in retirement', what they really want is to be free from having to worry about money, from having to slave for it, from being stressed by it.

Instead of slaving *longer* for your money to reach a 100 per cent 'secure' retirement lump sum, why not confront your fear of not having enough, and embrace the desire to be free of worrying about money, using this desire to motivate yourself to master money instead?

When something is largely out of your control it's easy to worry about it, but *when you master something, it ceases to be a worry at all*.

A Quick Recap

While it's normal for people to value different things at different times and in different circumstances, people who become successful — that is, greater than average — do so by valuing something more than what is average. They have a Dominant Value. Different Dominant Values lead to different results, and not always the result you'd think. If you want to be financially *free*, you need to value the right thing.

CHAPTER 5
The path of freedom

Freedom: the perfect motivator.

W̲e live in a world where we're given a thousand different choices, all designed to make us as happy, contented and comfortable as possible. For many people, comfort can become a Dominant Value. Everything from ready meals, to escalators, to one-click shopping is designed to make our life easier. But at the same time we are living in a world that is rapidly cognitively stratifying. As manufacturing is taken up by developing countries, in the first world we expect that everybody should be capable of, and interested in doing, 'value-added' cognitive work instead.

The importance of motivation

While on paper this sounds good—working with our heads sounds easier than working with our hands—we are finding we are having to work harder and harder, and study longer and longer even for the simplest job. Electric lighting and caffeine have extended the hours during which we are supposed to perform at our peak. There is simply more competition and more demand for us all to perform at our cognitive potential for more of the time. And unlike with physical jobs, we are finding that we can't just shut off from cognitive work either.

Automation is now coming for professional jobs too: if you think you can go to university and get a good white-collar job and be safe from automation, think again. Repetitive mental tasks are *easier* to automate than labour is. There's a reason why we have accounting and legal software but no robot butlers yet. As all the 'easy' repetitive mental tasks get automated, what's left are the hard mental parts of white-collar work.

> **... it's more important than ever to be able to motivate ourselves.**

In light of all this, it's obvious that it's more important than ever to be able to motivate ourselves. To wring the best performance we can out of our grey matter. Yet in a lot of ways we're finding it harder and harder to do that. Managers and business owners, in particular, struggle with this problem: how do we increase employees' motivation when so much emphasis is put on comfort and ease in our culture? Doing anything other than the bare minimum can feel like a hardship.

I wouldn't describe myself as a particularly motivated person; in fact, I can be quite lazy. I almost called this book *The Lazy Way to Wealth*, but I didn't get around to it...

Despite this, it didn't require tremendous motivation for me to do some things that many people might wish they were motivated enough to do—like walk away from my job, with its guaranteed career path, to do something different. In fact, I found it easy. The idea of doing the same thing, working for someone else for the rest of my life, was repellent.

> **The first step towards getting somewhere is to decide that you are not going to stay where you are.**
>
> *John Pierpont Morgan*

And that's because there is a difference between *feeling* motivated, and *being* motivated to take the right action. The good news is that you don't need to feel motivated to be motivated.

What's important is getting the *right* motivation that *actually* motivates you to make the necessary changes that reality demands.

People say real change requires hard work, *but it's only hard work by the standards of an incorrectly motivated person*: hard work if you are fighting against your values.

We make the mistake of assuming everybody is the same. But they're not. People value different things: they have different time preferences, different levels of conscientiousness, and some people are more 'state oriented' and place more value on needing to 'feel motivated' than others.

Yet we just assume that if someone can't start saving early for retirement then they just aren't as motivated as someone who can, and we need to 'motivate' them more. But this ignores the reality that everybody tends to do what is easy for *them* based on what *they* value.

When we see that a lot of people aren't motivated enough by security to start saving for a retirement that is many years away, we decide to remedy their lack of motivation in several ways. Firstly we take a goal focus.

Goal focus

The traditional goal of financial planning—save enough money that you won't be broke or too dependent on a pension when you retire—is not particularly motivating. With a goal focus we try to get around this by trying to make the goal more inspiring.

Increase the pleasurableness of the goal

In the 1980s, when financial planners were quoting 17 per cent annual returns, it wasn't hard to believe that the magic of compounding interest could not just provide for a secure retirement, but make you rich too! But even with possible retirement riches as a goal, many people found it hard to start saving. Part of the reason for this is that the further away a goal is, the less desirable we find it.

Distant goals are less pleasurable—closer goals are more pleasurable

When increasing the pleasurableness doesn't work, we can keep the goal the same but bring it closer, so it's more pleasurable based on our desire to have things sooner rather than later (retire in 20 years instead of 30!). However there is a problem with this.

Why big goals alone don't work

While, sometimes, increasing the pleasurableness of your big goal can help you start to move towards it, sometimes it can backfire and have the opposite effect. The reason for this is that we are subconsciously very good at doing risk/reward, effort/reward calculations.

Big goal, big effort

When we imagine the big goal, we subconsciously take a guess at the effort required to achieve it, and assume that a big, pleasurable goal is going to require big, painful effort to achieve it: it can be so intimidating, or the path to it can seem so unclear, that people either give up, or indulge in wishful thinking. Everything has a cost in terms of the effort you perceive you must put in, *based on the skills you have today*, to get the reward.

> **From where you are today, it's impossible to predict how much you can grow and achieve.**

As we will learn in part II, humans are bad at predicting exponential growth. We base what we believe we can achieve on what we have done in the past, and then project forward in a straight line. But reality is curved, and you are not the same person you were a few years ago. You've grown and learned skills. From where you are today, it's impossible to predict how much you can grow and achieve.

So, if modifying big goals isn't enough, what can we do to help people achieve what they desire?

We try shifting from a goal focus to a process focus.

Process focus

A process focus attempts to get around the scariness of a big goal by breaking it down into a series of smaller steps or intermediate goals, to make the effort required to get to your big goal seem less painful.

You may notice that all 'responsible' advice seems to follow this format. To get people to *do* the desired action, whether it's to adopt a healthy diet and exercise regime or to save for retirement, these methods try to either make the goal seem more desirable than it currently is, or make the steps to get there seem less painful than they already are.

But this goal and process focus is on the 'right hand side' of what I call the motivation equation. *It presupposes that we are all the same and that pursuing a certain goal is going to be difficult anyway*, so we need to work on the process, or the goal, to make it less painful to get to.

Obviously, a much smarter approach would be to choose goals that align with a person's values, or better: align their values with their goals.

The polarity of short-term goals

Not every value is equally effective at motivating us to take action. We've seen that if comfort is your Dominant Value, you could choose a big goal that seems to align with your value (you could set a goal to be rich, reasoning that being rich would make you more comfortable), but no matter how much

> **... those first steps, those intermediate goals, need to be motivating by themselves.**

you break down the steps, for someone who values comfort, *any* change is going to be uncomfortable. So valuing comfort won't help you to get rich, *because it won't help you to take the first steps.*

What most people don't realise is that those first steps, those intermediate goals, need to be motivating by themselves, and represent the same things you value if you want to give yourself the best chance at success.

This radically changes how we think about motivation.

What is your ultimate definition of financial freedom? Picture that. Now, what is an intermediate definition of financial freedom, that, when you achieve it, will make you a little bit freer right now?

This is the step that most people miss, because they don't really value freedom. You may have defined freedom as having $1 million in the bank, but if you set that as your big goal and focus on that *number*, you could end up slaving away every year, tying yourself to a job you hate, taking on massive debt, trying to make/save that much money and end up less free along the way, and perhaps never arrive at your goal because your intermediate steps don't match what you value at all. You got stuck focusing on the number, when that number is just your best guess, from where you are now, of what financial freedom might look like, *in the future.*

Instead, if you think more about what freedom can mean to you *now* and start to really value it, you could start achieving the thing you want — freedom — sooner, with intermediate steps and shorter term goals, *that align with what you value.*

> **You can't know what the top of the mountain will look like until you get there.**

This doesn't mean you shouldn't have a big goal; you often need the big goal first, but really, the big goal is not at all important in the

45

beginning stages. You may have a goal to climb a mountain, but you can't focus on the summit at all in the beginning. *You can't know what the top of the mountain will look like until you get there.*

You have to have a smaller goal to successfully navigate the foothills as well, and your attention has to be on that, not on the big goal.

In fact, *your ideas about where you want to end up may even change as you progress.* You may find, as we saw in the section on the path of security in chapter 4, that you don't need as much money as you think to be financially free, if you learn some skills; or you may reach $1 million and realise that there are levels of freedom beyond that, that you want to achieve, so it's important to pick a first step that is *aligned* with your big goal, but is sufficiently self-contained.

If you can see that you *can actually get freer right now*, and that achieving that freedom puts you in a better place financially, then you can develop the confidence to continue on the path knowing that you're becoming financially free, without knowing 100 per cent what your final destination will be, and without being able to see all the steps at once.

For example, you may see how you can save some of your income, so you're not so trapped where you are. Once you're not as dependent on your current job, you might see how you could find a better job. Once you do that, you may learn some new skills. Once you have those skills, you may see how you can start a small business ... and so on. Each step you take that makes you freer helps you to build the skills you will need for the next step, giving you more choices and more *time* to capitalise on those choices. By aiming to be freer *first*, you set a goal you can achieve. This way, you don't give up in the face of a big goal that you couldn't achieve without *growing* yourself first, and becoming more skilled along the way.

Put your pain behind you

Nobody wants to make pain their primary motivator, but pain can be useful as something to put behind you. Pain has a purpose. As a former physiotherapist, I know that pain is only really a problem when it becomes chronic: when it invades our present with no hope of letting up.

With freedom as a motivator, not only will your first steps be more pleasurable to you, as they help you to move forward, but if you have something painful behind you that you've broken free from—whether that's debt or even being stuck in a job—you've now got a reason not to slip back. And who doesn't want to put their pain behind them?

Visualising freedom as a motivating value

The pain you leave behind acts as a backstop, while the small pleasurable first steps or goals in front of you draw you forward because they *align with what you value*, all leading you towards higher and higher levels of financial freedom.

Freedom, the perfect motivator

Freedom is unique among all the values we can hold that move us towards financial freedom. It is a 'homuncular' motivating force for creating wealth: the smallest part fully represents the whole. Freedom First means you get freer now, and continue to get freer. What you are motivated to become *is the same thing* that is motivating you each step of the way. It's self re-enforcing. The more freedom you gain, the easier it is to stay free, and to get freer.

A Quick Recap

There's a difference between *feeling* motivated, and *being* motivated to take the right action. Valuing freedom uniquely motivates you to become financially free because it makes each step you take towards your goal rewarding by itself.

CHAPTER 6
Putting freedom first

Making freedom your Dominant Value.

I talk to people who tell me 'I want to be rich', and so I share with them the financial planning path that, if you start along it early, and with a few tweaks, could allow you to at least retire with a good sum of money after many years of work. But then they say to me,

'That's too far away, I want to be rich much sooner.'

And I say,

'Okay, so you want to be rich, but only if you can do it quickly?'

Then I share with them an 'entrepreneurial path' that could see them rich in a couple of years. But they say to me,

'That sounds too risky.'

So I say to them,

'Okay, so you want to be rich, but only if you can do it quickly, and with no risk?'

Then I share with them an accelerated 'earn-save-invest path' that requires that they get the highest pay they can, do the most overtime, save the most amount of money possible, invest every cent and postpone any luxuries like a nice home, car or hobbies and, with only a bit of luck, they can be rich within 5 to 10 years with little risk. Then they say to me,

'That sounds too hard'

to which I say,

'Okay… so you want to be rich, but only if you can do it quickly, without any risk, or without too much effort… are you sure you really want to be rich?'

We saw earlier that values are subconsciously desired states or *feelings*, not to be confused with things that you consciously value having or doing. Because of this it's not obvious to most people what it is they value. I touched on this with Andrew, who consciously identified very strongly with wanting to be financially free, but seemed unaware of why he remained stuck where he was.

When I put my question to him about whether he could stand being his own boss, even wealthy, if it meant doing so in a 'low status' or anonymous business, what I was doing was a kind of values audit.

Values Audit

The process of asking questions to elicit answers which make it clearer what an individual truly values in a particular situation.

Identifying your hierarchy

I had done the same with Melissa when I'd caught up for lunch with her, and her answers were part of the reason I'd agreed to help her. I saw that, like me, she valued her freedom in a lot of situations where others might value security, but she hadn't yet made freedom a Dominant Value. It's hard to have trust in valuing something like freedom, when our whole society is set up to actively encourage you to value something different.

Even without having someone ask you challenging questions, you can often determine your own values by asking yourself questions, or listening to the way you speak.

Let's look at two people who feel that they would like to not have to work a job for life and are consciously interested in the idea of starting a business.

'I can't stand my job. I'd like to be freer, be my own boss; but I'm secure here and I need the salary if I want to save for retirement. Besides, that sounds risky …'

This person's values hierarchy might look like this:

1   security.

2   comfort.

3   freedom.

'I want to be financially free! Let's do this! I've got a job that pays well, but I could see myself running a successful company. I pride myself on hard work. But I don't want to start a small business; what if I got stuck working for clients and never made it big?'

This person's top three values might be:

1   status.

2   freedom.

3   comfort.

Values hierarchies are simply revealed preferences. Once you identify someone's values you can really start to see what makes them tick.

We established earlier that freedom is a unique value to hold to help you move towards *financial freedom* — by making each step you take rewarding in and of itself — so what should you do if you want to be financially free but you suspect freedom may not be your Dominant Value?

Start valuing freedom

If you don't naturally value freedom, that's okay — you're normal. I'm the one who's not! Here's how to start.

1. Recognise what you do value first

Identify what drives you. And what doesn't. You can't put your values in order if you don't know what they are. Introspection or a Values Audit can tell you if freedom isn't your Dominant Value, but it's also useful to identify the things you *do* really value.

One of the most powerful things you can do in life is to do your best to understand what really motivates you. We spend so much time and effort pursuing goals that we set far in our future, with little idea of what it is that we truly value. What do we really want? Do the goals we set even reflect that? Will pursuing those goals cost us more than achieving them will give us? What will really make us happy?

The Epicurean life

In 300 BC the ancient Greek philosopher Epicurus taught that the good life consists of three things: freedom, friends and an analysed life. Today, we've forgotten the lessons of Epicurus, and instead think he had something to do with buying luxury goods. To live an analysed life like Epicurus advised, you might have to find a little time and get a little freer, first. Sometimes you have to try something if you are going to develop a taste for it, and experience a little of something before you can really value it.

2. Accept that 'Freedom First' doesn't mean 'freedom instead of'

Freedom is unique in that, when placed first in your hierarchy of values, it allows you to have *more* of the other things you value too. Valuing freedom first means keeping your options open. Deprioritise freedom though, and as well as ending up less free, you may find that you end up with *fewer of the very things you desire more*.

For example, valuing comfort may mean you don't grow, progress or move forward much. After all, change is uncomfortable! However, anyone who is stuck in a rut will know that even the most comfortable rut eventually becomes uncomfortable. Humans just aren't meant to stagnate, we are meant to grow. So valuing your comfort too highly can end up making you *uncomfortable*.

Valuing security first may mean you give up a lot of freedom in the pursuit of it. Valuing security first may also make you less secure. While other people were taking on 'good debt', buying assets and pursuing financial security prior to the Global Financial Crisis, I was prioritising my freedom instead. Being free to develop skills allowed me to not only survive, but actually thrive during the greatest correction in most people's memories, and as a result I ended up more financially secure than I would have been had I pursued security in the first place. Freedom all by itself can meet other values.

Being free means you can't be fired, you are recession proof and you can be *more* secure about your ability to prosper.

3. Start to value it now

If freedom hasn't been a Dominant Value for you, there are probably things in your life right now that are holding you back, that you could get free from.

Think of all the little ways that you aren't free right now: the many little things that you just put up with. Build up your pain *as well as* your pleasure. Think of how great it would be to be free of a particular thing that is holding you back. Start to see how having more freedom *now* could greatly expand your choices. Imagine: 'If I had some savings put aside, could I tell my boss to take a hike?' What would that be worth to you? Finally, put a price on it. Start a savings plan like Melissa did that can only be used to make you freer. (We'll see more on how she did that later.)

4. Measure freedom when making a decision

Usually, when thinking about a decision that faces us, we measure every dimension of the outcome except how free it will make us. For example, when purchasing something, we think how pleasurable it will be to have, and maybe how much it will cost us in money — we may even occasionally think of what else we can't buy if we buy this thing: we compare this purchase to another potential purchase.

> **The cost of a thing is the amount of what I call life which is required to be exchanged for it, immediately or in the long run.**
>
> *Henry David Thoreau*

But we rarely think of how much freedom we must give up to have it. How much more we will have to work, how we will have to give up on certain opportunities if we take on this obligation. Buy things that make you happy — not things that will leave you feeling trapped in a job you hate, paying off debt that's enslaving you.

Another example is a promotion. Do you take the promotion to manager? Financial planning says yes: increase your income. But what if the income increase is very little and comes with a lot more commitment? What if what is attracting you to the position is the 'status' of the title? Some positions require that you increase your consumption to look the part, or the position adds stress and takes away what little time you had that you could have been using for something else. Look for opportunities to grow your skills, even if they don't always come with more money.

You are your most valuable asset.

5. Free yourself from social programming

Parents, politicians and product salespeople all want you to value security. Start to notice how well that's *not* working out for you. Find like-minded people. Start to hang with a different crowd. Changing your environment is one of the easiest ways to 'reset' and can make it easier to adopt new habits.

Be prepared to define things differently. Once you begin to think outside the box you'll notice all sorts of ways that society pushes us onto certain paths. Nowhere is this more obvious than the status we place on home ownership and the importance of getting on the housing ladder as soon as possible.

It's amazing how much the status of being a homeowner can cost you

I'd warned Melissa a month earlier when we'd met for coffee that I saw a correction coming, that even though she was working in real estate she shouldn't feel too pressured to buy a home straight away — especially when doing so would really stretch her financially and commit her to a job she didn't really love.

> **'Our houses are such unwieldy property that we are often imprisoned rather than housed in them.'**
>
> *Henry David Thoreau,* Walden

Looking back now, it's hard to remember just how strong the idea was that property would always go up and the grip it had on people's minds in 2007.

Which is why I wasn't really surprised by the topic of conversation when I next caught up with Andrew.

The last time Andrew and I had talked, I'd asked him the question about being the 'paper king' of Brisbane.

And it was clear he'd been giving it some thought. Did he want to commit to his part-time business with the risk that it might never be a huge success, or did he want to commit to the corporate path and the rise in status and income he hoped it would bring?

When Andrew told me he was thinking of moving to the coast to join another team and work for a promotion, finally committing to the 'job for life' path, I wasn't surprised. But I was surprised by how ferociously he was planning on committing to it. Convinced that property would double in value every seven years, Andrew confided that he was thinking of selling the unit he lived in and buying the most expensive house down the coast he could afford with the proceeds.

If he could scrape together enough deposit and stretch his borrowing capacity to the max (and beyond) he could maybe secure a property worth up to $1 million. While he would need every cent of his new salary (if he could get the promotion) and would be dependent on the job, if all went to plan he would be a millionaire in seven years … or so he believed.

Needless to say I had my doubts. And the thought of my friend taking out a massive loan at this stage of the game was worrying to me.

I'd lived through and directly experienced markets that went up, went down, and even stayed flat for years. You could say that by living outside 'the system' I was more in touch with the nature, or the seasons, of the economy. I had grave concerns about the demographic effects that the baby boomers retiring would have on a market that had been artificially inflated for decades.

I'd shared those concerns with Andrew in the past, when I'd thought the correction might come at the end of the decade. But after my experience with the stock market correction on the day I'd met with Melissa, my concerns were growing that it may come earlier. While stocks were still rising and everyone had forgotten the correction of two months earlier, I could see that volatility was rising — a worrying signal that often precedes major changes in the market's direction.

Instead of suggesting he abandon his plan, I put it to Andrew that he might want to sell his unit first, since prices were so high, and go back to renting while he contemplated his move and got to know his new market better, giving him a chance to perhaps shop for a better deal.

But he was dead set against the idea of sitting out of the market for any period of time, pointing out how much prices had risen and the cost that may come from waiting to buy.

Although he was technically right — sitting out of a roaring market could cost you money (provided you sold before the party ended) — I sensed that there was something else behind his reluctance to sell and rent for a period of time.

The status ladder

I've never really been motivated by traditional notions of status. But that's not because I care less about it than other people so much as I'm prepared to define it differently. People want to be able to evaluate others quickly, which is why when I first retired and someone would ask me what I did for a living, it felt weird and even pompous to say I invested for a living, while I was still in my twenties. After a while, though, I became comfortable with defying expectations, and I went through a stage where I would answer 'nothing' or even 'I'm unemployed', which was technically true because nobody employed me. It was a real eye opener to see people falling into a stereotype reaction.

There used to be one general social path that everyone could realistically expect to be able to follow, that would guarantee them a level of status and recognition in their communities.

Finish school, get a first job, leave home, get married, buy a home, have kids, get promoted, buy some investments and eventually retire.

Each level of the status ladder was a little higher than the previous one. A married person was considered more adult than a single person; someone working a job was a little more advanced than someone still at school. A home owner was better than a renter and somebody who owned investments like property was well on their way to being a senior person in society. In recent years it seems we've deprioritised social steps on the ladder, but the economic steps have become more important than ever, even as they have become harder to achieve. What I learned about status is that it is relative. It's different based on what culture or even time period you lived in. And in our culture it's still in the process of changing.

Status, property and tax

Not only does society reward certain paths, it rewards certain behaviours. In particular in the Anglosphere/Western countries there seems to be a particular obsession with home ownership as something eminently desirable. Because of this, we tend to find that governments reward home ownership and property investing with all sorts of incentives.

For example, in Australia we encourage people to own their own homes and pay them off by offering capital gains tax deductions for home owners.

- Home owners can't deduct their mortgage interest payments, but they can exempt all of their capital gains on the property when they sell.

- Property investors, on the other hand, can deduct their mortgage interest payments on their rental properties, but can only claim a 50 per cent deduction on their capital gains when they sell (and only if they've held the property for more than 12 months).

While the rules are slightly different among developed countries, the principle is the same. Most don't allow an interest deduction on personal loans, so countries that allow a home mortgage interest deduction have created exceptions to those rules.

Generally, people buy homes to live in before they buy homes for investment. And, in the past, most would have started doing this earlier in life, giving them more years to accumulate capital gains.

Australia's zero per cent tax on capital gains for home owners encourages people to 'trade up' their homes over time, starting a cycle of buying and selling for the rest of their lives.

On the other hand, most people don't get around to buying investment properties until later in life when they are earning higher incomes, so they are incentivised to buy investment properties with a deduction against their high incomes instead.

But what if you could get the best of both worlds, tax-wise, by not following the typical status path, and instead skipping ahead a few rungs on the status ladder?

Instead of starting out as a home owner, why not start as a property investor? If your first property is an investment, you can get on the property ladder *sooner* too. It's easier to buy a cheaper house *earlier* if you buy it as an investment property, than a house you might choose to call a home.

This is exactly what I did; the first house I bought was an investment, not a home — and so I shared with Andrew the six-year rule.

The six-year rule

The six-year rule allows you to treat a property that you have lived in for a period of time as if it is still your 'home' — or Principle Place of Residence (PPR) — for tax purposes for up to six years after you've moved out and started renting it out, as long as you aren't claiming any other property as a PPR at that time.

You can apply this rule to an investment property you own, as long as you have lived in it for a period of three months within any six-year period. And because it's actually an investment, you can deduct any interest you pay to own it.

Typically, the downside of owning an investment property in Australia is that when you sell it you have to pay capital gains tax (but only on half of the profit, provided you have owned it for a year or more), while the upside is that you get to deduct any net costs of running the investment property against your normal income, which is known as negative gearing. However, if you have bought your first property, lived in it for a few months, perhaps while you renovated it, then rented it out as an investment, the PPR allowance may apply. This means you can own an investment property, and although you may have rented it out for up to six years and deducted all the interest (just like you would with an investment property), you can still sell it and keep all the capital gains profit as well (just like you would with a home or PPR).

Another advantage of having an investment for a first property, is that if you are renting where you live and you run a business from home, you can deduct part of your rent as a business expense. Now, you can do that too if you own your own home and live in it (as a PPR) by deducting a part of your mortgage payment, but in that case you might lose your entitlement to claim the home ownership capital gains tax deduction in full, which is *the* major tax break for owning your own home.

So, in most cases, people who work from their home (that they own) are better off not taking a deduction against their mortgage for their home business so they don't lose out on the tax-free capital gains when they sell.

But this strategy allows you to make that deduction too: you end up making mortgage deductions (on your investment property), capital gains tax deductions (on your investment property, which is nominated as a PPR for the tax period), and the full home business deductions you are allowed out of the rent you pay on the rental property you actually live in.

Although you may have never heard of this strategy, I don't want to give the impression that the 'tax secrets' of the rich are special deductions or special techniques that only the wealthy have access to. There are plenty of highly paid salaried employees who **"Tax advantages tend to favour the free more than they favour the rich."** don't really have a lot of options when it comes to tax time, aside from negative gearing.

In fact, if anything, tax advantages tend to favour the free more than they favour the rich.

So I was able to convince Andrew to hold off on leveraging himself to the hilt. By not selling his property he would still have exposure to a rising market, and, by moving out and renting for a while and turning the property he owned into an investment, he would not only be saving on closing costs, he would be able to start to deduct his mortgage interest payments on his property too. Instead of giving up on his part-time business he'd be able to start claiming business expenses against his new rent and come out more than $8000 a year ahead in total, an improvement in his cashflow that made it that much easier for him to keep his options open.

While Andrew had contemplated pursuing *status that costs freedom*, perhaps now he would have the chance to instead experience how valuing freedom ahead of status could not only make him richer — as his increased cash flow was already proving — but by redefining *status through freedom* he might see that as a business owner and property investor he could meet his needs for status, without sacrificing his freedom at all.

Status *through* freedom

There's nothing wrong with valuing things like status, security, belonging, even to an extent power — we are, after all, socially evolved creatures.

The distinction comes in what relative importance we place on each of them. And how we *define* them.

If you find from looking at your own values hierarchy that you tend to be dominant in other values, for example status — even though what you consciously want is freedom — then you need to find a way that freedom *itself* can represent status to you.

You'd be surprised by how envious people are of those who are in the position of not having to answer to a boss, of being able to set their own hours. As work creeps further and further into our private lives, being able to control when, and how, and if you work, is a genuine luxury.

In fact, a very good case can be made that time is the only really limited resource in our lives.

In a world where the vast majority of people are employees, why are we all competing so hard to have slightly better jobs, when we could put ourselves in a totally different category from nearly everyone else by not having a job at all? Some people are sidestepping the 'status' of having a first job and going straight for the status of being self-employed; while others are questioning the need to enslave yourself to debt for the status of being a 'home owner' when you can start out with the status of 'property investor'.

Like the Red Queen's race in *Through the Looking-Glass* (where 'it takes all the running you can do, to keep in the same place'), in a world where people are working harder than ever just to stay the same, having more time and having more options is the new status indicator.

Why not set yourself free and leapfrog ahead on the status ladder?

Other applications of Freedom First: relationship and money conflicts

Once you begin to understand the power of values when it comes to motivating our behaviour, and the unique qualities that freedom has as a value, you can start to think of other ways you can apply this knowledge. Take, for example, relationships and money. Conflicts over money are said to be the number one cause of stress in a marriage, as confirmed by an American Consumer Credit

Counselling Survey, which found that 'Money is the leading cause of stress in relationships.'

Using our hierarchy of values framework, we can understand relationship conflicts as a 'different Dominant Values' problem.

If one partner values status, and the other values security first, then an inevitable conflict will arise when these values clash, as the topic of spending money reveals each partner's preference.

The person who values status, or pleasure, may be seen by their more conservative partner as jeopardising their financial security when they spend money, whereas they in turn might see their security-focused spouse as depriving them of fun.

You can't, and probably shouldn't, try to change your partner, but considering our values are subconscious it's pretty rare for people to end up with a spouse who by chance shares their hierarchy of values completely. What should you do if you find you have a different Dominant Value from your significant other that makes you conflict over money?

Rather than fight or argue over which value should take precedence when it comes to spending money, what if there was a third choice — a value that both people could learn to nurture first, that wouldn't require either partner giving up what they value? What if there was a value that both partners could learn to share as a team that *increased* the opportunity for each to have what they want?

Could they define status in a way that doesn't involve buying *things*, or financial security in a way that doesn't involve scrimping and saving every cent?

If both start to choose to value Freedom First together, then they can still have different hierarchies. Freedom is the only value that can increase your opportunities to pursue other values, and as we saw above, freedom is also unique in that it can itself *meet* other values.

It's better to recognise what you value rather than deny it.

Common ground can always be found through committing to getting freer together.

Finally, to really start to value freedom first, you may have to *get free first*. Sometimes you have to try something if you are going to develop a taste for it and experience a little of something before you can really value it.

In part II I'll explain the ways in which you are holding yourself back, without even realising it, by *not* being free.

A Quick Recap

Values are subconscious: you need to *elicit* your own hierarchy of values and take active steps to start valuing what it is you truly desire. Making freedom your Dominant Value can not only give you more freedom, but more of the other things you value too, such as security, or status.

To start valuing Freedom:

1. Recognise what you do value first.

2. Accept that 'Freedom First' doesn't mean 'freedom instead of'.

3. Start to value it now.

4. Measure freedom when making a decision.

5. Free yourself from social programming.

'*So what do you think is my Dominant Value? Do I even have one?*' Melissa asked.

'*That's a good question. The average person may change what they value over time, at different stages of life. Freedom is often dominant in the late teenage years as people get fed up living at home and want to move out into the world, make their own decisions and lead their own life.*

'*As people get older they tend to value security more, and so on. But even with those average trends most people tend to keep coming back to one or two values that dominate, and if there is ever a situation that forces you to choose, you'll see what's more dominant.*

'*It's really the situations you find yourself in and how you choose to respond to them that can show you what you really value. You said something the other week about having had a few jobs?*'

'*Yeah, I find I get restless if a job isn't going anywhere. I've never been fired — I work hard and I've always received great references; in fact, every new job I've taken has paid better than the last so I guess I'm doing something right. It's just that I missed out on the whole degree path. My parents were going through a messy divorce and by the time I was in senior school the situation was intolerable and I moved out of home, and any plans for uni fell by the wayside.*'

'*That sounds rough.*'

'*It's okay, I'm over it. But what it has done is left me feeling like maybe I missed out. Like I should go back to school so I can get a better job. But it's not like there's anything in particular I'm dying to study.*'

'*Since when does that stop anyone from going to uni anymore?*'

'*Ha, true. It's just this feeling that unless I'm signing up for the house, the mortgage, the career, I'm doing something wrong, I'm missing out.*'

'If you don't knuckle down, take on the "responsibilities" of debt and career you might fall behind...? Well you might be happy to know that the old paths and formulas, especially the "safe secure" path, are not what they once were.'

'Well that's good to know, because I've got something to tell you. I've quit my job!'

This is what I feared would happen when I shared my story — how I'd taken a safe, secure profession that I'd worked hard to gain, and walked away from it to pursue freedom instead. Had I encouraged Melissa to do something reckless?

'Okay, tell me what happened,' I replied.

'Well, I'd originally taken this job because the boss had offered me the chance to do marketing for the office and the chance to learn the buyer's agent side of the business. I'd just finished my real estate licence and was looking for opportunities to use it, and the buyer's agent side of things interested me — it was why I took this job,' Melissa explained.

'That's great, so you were motivated to take the job for the opportunities it offered you, and the freedom to apply what you'd learned and to grow. That's a good start, so what happened?'

'Well, not long after I started there the receptionist went on extended maternity leave, and they asked me and another office girl to cover for her at first, while still doing the marketing. Before long it became obvious that I was going to be solely covering for her, she was going to be on leave for up to a year, and any hopes of getting into working as a buyer's agent were permanently postponed. They did keep me on the same salary though,' Melissa replied.

'So they were prepared to pay you the same money, and technically the work you would be doing would be easier, right? And you quit. I hope you realise that that's pretty unique — I know a bunch of people who would choose easier work for the same salary if they could.'

'Yeah. But you had me thinking about what my values were and what I was valuing in a given situation. What I originally valued about this job was taken away, but did I value the opportunity to grow enough to do something about it?

'You said the secret to motivation is to put pleasure in front of you and pain behind you and not get comfortable. I could see that if I let it, I'd eventually get comfortable doing the reception work and forget that I originally wanted a challenge.

'And to be honest, the savings really helped. It's easier to build up your frustration with a bad situation if you're not dependent on it,' Melissa confided.

'It's interesting you say that,' I replied. 'You've just identified something very important — we've talked a lot about getting free but there are costs to not being free that most people aren't even aware of until it's too late ...'

PART II

The traps that come from not being free

David was a good friend from high school so I knew his background pretty well. Growing up when personal computers were a new thing, I remember spending hours at his place playing on the Commodore 64. As we got older, all that screen time saw David become a real whiz with computers—I remember when the second Terminator *movie came out with ground-breaking-for-the-time special effects, he was inspired: 'I really wish I could do that,' and off he'd disappear for weeks at a time alone with his computer.*

Out of all of us, David probably valued security the most. From an early age he expressed a desire to be a dad, and he was the first to marry after high school. Years later, an opportunity came up to move to the Gold Coast and study 3D animation for movies and special effects, but by that point life had got busy and his dream had become a hobby.

That wouldn't have been so bad for David if he hadn't gotten sick.

His ordered, settled life was thrown into chaos when, out of nowhere, he was struck with debilitating joint pains that would flare up intermittently, with no warning. After countless tests and no answers, it was finally discovered that David had an extremely rare autoimmune disorder. So rare, in fact, that only an experimental—and very expensive—treatment had been developed for it. It was such a toxic drug that he had to use a separate bathroom in his house to avoid poisoning his family with the chemotherapy-like by-products. Fortunately, the government covered the costs of the $2000-per-shot treatment. But even so, he was still off sick from work pretty regularly.

While his illness made him dependent on a drug, the prohibitively expensive nature of the drug made him dependent on the government. David's string of dependencies saw him trapped in a job that was getting worse and worse every day. His boss was starting to give him a hard time for calling in sick so often and David was feeling terrible about it, but he was stuck.

It's great that we have a social safety net, but the cost of that support is that you have to come under a certain threshold of income. David had already cut back his family's expenses to the bone just to qualify for the assistance in the first place—he couldn't quit this job and do casual work around his illness: he had a family to feed. And because of the expensive nature of the drug, it wasn't like he could just get a slightly better paying job and pay for it himself out of pocket—as soon as he went over the income threshold he'd have to get a job that paid substantially more before he could even hope to be back to where he started. Most people would be happy to see their salaries go up by 5 per cent a year; or maybe take a new job that pays 10 per cent more. But how many people realistically expect to be able to find a new job that pays more than twice as much as their last one? It's too big a leap.

But all of that was academic. The Dependence Trap was about to rob David of the security that he valued most. Because he couldn't continue to pay David a full-time salary if he was constantly off sick, his boss gave him an ultimatum: go off the full-time salary onto commission-only, or he would have to let him go …

CHAPTER 7
The Dependence Trap

There are costs to not being free. When you are not free the wrong things get rewarded.

A couple of weeks after Melissa had quit her job, she landed a new one. The interview process was actually fun, she told me later. She said she felt like, with a little savings and time on her side, *she* was the one doing the interviewing. She finally settled on a new job in real estate and unlike the last one this job also offered her the chance to grow, and would see her take on new tasks and responsibilities too. She'd be coming on board in a general office role, but on top of that, she'd be the in-house photographer for all the agents.

Most real estate agencies either outsource photography, or the agents take their own photos. The job appealed to Melissa because, years before, she had taken a photography course and had maintained a keen interest in the art in her spare time. In her new position, Melissa would also be a lot more independent—it would be up to her to organise her days and liaise directly with the agents to organise shoots, do her editing and so on. It was almost a mini business within a job; she had a lot more freedom.

You can be free of *dependence* on a boss long before you are *free* of a boss

This is one of the great things about valuing your freedom, first. When people have a vague, unexamined desire to 'quit work', it's all or nothing, whereas when you start to really value your freedom and examine the ways in which you are not free, you start to see plenty of ways you could get freer, even within a job.

The first step for Melissa came from building up some savings—when I first gave her the task to save for 'no-thing' Melissa thought it was a little strange. And she wasn't the only one: she told me later how she'd been talking to the girls from work, when the topic of saving came up.

The other girls were mostly saving for *things*: cars, a yearly holiday; one had just saved up a deposit for a home (no small feat considering this was at the peak of the market, right on the cusp of the GFC). They'd saved for tangible stuff, in other words.

Soon we'll look at how *income* is evolutionarily novel, but the fact is, even money is a pretty recent concept for our brains to handle.

It's much easier to save for tangible things, which is one of the reasons people have so much trouble saving for retirement.

Although Melissa had felt pressured by society to commit to the 'secure path', there would have been a cost to that: dependence. If she'd rushed to roll her savings straight into something tangible, like a house, and committed a chunk of her salary to a mortgage to the point where she was living week to week, she would have been stuck at her old job.

In fact, the one person in the office who had done the 'right thing' and saved for a house was an interesting case study. At only 20, she'd just got married—big wedding—and was now putting down a deposit on a house in an expensive neighbourhood. While Melissa took this at face value, I was more curious. We were at the peak of the market when housing was less affordable than it had been for more than a generation.

When I enquired further, Melissa admitted that it was curious that this co-worker had the title of 'Marketing Manager' (in what was quite a small office) despite no-one knowing what it was she actually did. On top of that she caught a lift in with one of the bosses each day—I wondered, was it possible she was receiving Economic Outpatient Care?

Helping your kids may be hurting them

Dr Thomas J Stanley and Dr William D Danko published a bestselling book—*The Millionaire Next Door*—in the 1990s based on their investigation into how the average 'millionaire next door' actually lived. Out of all the interesting insights they gleaned, one particular trend they noticed is very relevant to us today.

Stanley and Danko observed that more than 46 per cent of affluent parents gave *at least* $15000 to their adult children each year. The term that the two professors coined for the financial assistance that adult children continue to receive from their wealthy parents was Economic Outpatient Care (EOC). They found that, in addition to this, 43 per cent of millionaires with grandchildren pay for part or all of their private school tuition. And 59 per cent provide assistance for adult children in buying a home.

Had these researchers confirmed what we all suspected: that if you want to be rich you need a rich parent?

It seems not. The professors had instead stumbled upon something extraordinary: *the more monetary assistance adult children receive, the less wealth they end up accumulating.*

> **...the more monetary assistance adult children receive, the less wealth they end up accumulating.**

They looked across the various professions that the adult children of the wealthy worked in, and found some surprising results.

- Accountants who still received financial support from their parents as adults ended up having only 57 per cent of the wealth of accountants who received no support from their parents. So, if an average accountant at a given age would be expected to have accumulated a net worth of $100000, then the equivalent aged accountant receiving EOC would only have a net worth of $57000.

- Attorneys who received parental support only achieved 62 per cent of the wealth of their peers.

- Entrepreneurs achieved only 64 per cent of the wealth that other entrepreneurs, who didn't have financial support from parents, managed to accumulate.

In fact, the only situations where receiving financial support from wealthy parents didn't make the recipients *less* wealthy were in the cases of teachers and professors, while teaching was the only profession where receiving EOC made them wealthier than their peers.

This is startling. In any industry where your performance determines your income to some degree—retail, entrepreneurship, law—the extra $15000 *minimum* cash payment you receive each year (and that's on top of any housing assistance you may receive, or financial support your parents may give towards your children's education) has a negative effect: it decreases your wealth by more than the amount you receive.

Why is this? It could be because it lures you into a *status trap*—there is the temptation to accumulate the *trappings* of success that go with high performance. For example, a successful attorney may decide to 'signal' their success relative to their peers by buying a more expensive car or home, because people in this industry who are successful tend to earn more money. Teachers are in part immune to this trap because there is no such 'success differential' in teaching: successful teachers don't earn more than other teachers.

If you see a teacher driving a Porsche you don't assume that they must be a really good teacher … but you may assume that they have 'broken bad'!

Or it could be due to a *motivation trap*: EOC can rob the recipient of the motivation they need to produce wealth, incentivising them to 'politic' for money instead.

By 'politic' I mean do the things that get them the resources. Parents are most likely to support an adult child who is in need. You don't often hear of parents supporting children who have paid all their bills but don't have enough left to put aside for retirement.

The result of this is that instead of focusing on creating wealth—by looking to the market and solving the problem of what *other* people want and then devising ways to give it to them—the mind of the person trapped in dependence is instead focused on themselves and the problem of increasing their 'needs'.

> **Whatever the reason, the way we receive money has a profound effect on how we think about money, our motivation to earn it, and our ability to create wealth for ourselves.**
>
> *Matthew Klan*

Part of the problem with the negative effects of EOC may be caused by the affluent parents themselves. Like most parents, rich parents want to 'guarantee' as much as possible that their children will do well in life. Many of these parents try to 'buy' their children an upper-middle-class lifestyle by sending them to the 'right' schools and establishing them in the 'right' neighbourhoods.

These parents believe EOC will 'get the child going' but inadvertently they may only end up initiating a consumption cascade, as the children find they are then expected to buy more stuff to furnish the expensive house, to have a car that 'matches' their home, and to send their kids to private schools like everyone else in the neighbourhood, just to fit in.

It's important to know how to *really* help your adult children. There is nothing wrong with wanting to help, but for the wealthy parent EOC may fail to do what they hope it will. It doesn't make their kids productive or independent—and may even make them poorer than their peers.

The wealthy parent who wants to help their kid succeed in life may have to face the reality that *really helping requires a more hands-on approach*: teaching skills, and supporting the child with their experience, not just their money. If they can't find the time to do this, or perhaps don't know how to, they need to make sure that they are at least doing no harm.

What's the best kind of financial assistance to give kids?

There are ways of giving financial assistance that can help a child succeed in the world, but annual cash gifts are rarely one of them. Lending money for starting a business (provided there is a real business plan and perhaps even a history of repaying past productive loans) can help. But they should aim to free the child and not enslave them. Free them of interest on loans perhaps, but make certain that a repayment schedule is set up, and that no more money is lent to them if the loan isn't repaid! Lending for education—or, better yet, gifting an education —can help, but again only for an education with a business plan, not for a free four-year holiday to explore their inner selves!

When the housing market has been put out of reach of an entire generation, helping an adult child to buy a home is great if you can afford to do it, but be aware of not trying to buy your child 'status'. Helping them get into a house they can't afford is only enslaving them to a mortgage, and even if you buy a home for them outright, you may be starting a consumption cascade that cripples them as they try to keep up with the neighbours.

So why is all of this important?

The market for jobs, housing and education has changed radically for this generation.

- It is no longer just the wealthy who are helping out adult children. Now, post-GFC, 59 per cent of *all* parents are giving financial help to their post-university adult children.

- Half of the children of the affluent under the age of 35 receive annual cash gifts.

- One in four millennials making $75000 *or more* per annum receive help with groceries from their parents.

- One in 10 married millennials even get help with mobile phone bills.

- More than one in three millennials who are not in high-paying jobs receive regular financial support.

- One in five millennials live at home and don't pay rent.

- A study done by the Young Invincibles group in 2017 based on Federal Reserve data showed that millennials had a median household income of US$40581 and despite being better educated, millennials earned 20 per cent less than baby boomers did at the same stage in life in 1989 (US$50910 inflation adjusted). Their rates of home ownership were lower than that of baby boomers at the same age, their net worth was half, while their debt, especially for education, was much higher.

As a society we've got to create an economy that allows the young to start out with little experience and work their way up. Just because EOC doesn't help kids, doesn't mean we should fall back on advising them to 'knuckle down' and bootstrap themselves to success in cases where the odds are stacked against them.

As disheartening as it is that so many young people need support, what's worse is that many others simply don't have any support to fall back on.

When starter jobs have been outsourced, and even the most basic career requires a degree and the crushing debt and the wasted years that go with it, we have a structural problem we need to address.

Other people helping *their* kids can affect *you*

One of the things that Stanley and Danko brought to everybody's attention was that the wealthy don't always look rich; in fact, they could be living right next door to you. This means that if you are just starting out in life you may be working with people who don't obviously come from 'rich' families, who may still be receiving significantly more support than you are — especially in these tough economic times.

We have a very individualistic ethos in our culture, so it can seem at times that you're doing something wrong, when it looks like everyone around you is doing much better. When you look at your pay packet and wonder how others can afford things that you can't, it may be time to give yourself a break — maybe they can't afford them either!

This is where the combination of easy credit and the temptation to 'keep up with the Joneses' is a particularly dangerous trap (we'll talk about the Debt Trap in the next chapter) — *you have no idea what help the Joneses are really getting behind the scenes.*

Don't lose heart. And don't hate them; hate the system.

Financial support may help some people live slightly beyond what their income would suggest — but what it doesn't do is make them rich. And whatever they may gain in material comfort, Stanley and Danko's research shows that the recipients of EOC have more fears and concerns about money than their peers who don't get financial assistance each year, which makes sense when you consider that *they have less control over how they receive money than those who make it themselves.*

Finally, give yourself permission to walk to the beat of your own drum. While you will be hearing a lot more about intergenerational inequality in the years to come, we all have to survive in the system we find ourselves in. As older generations have had to adapt to the change from defined benefit pensions to defined contribution pensions — from one job in a factory supporting a family to two incomes being barely enough to make ends meet — younger generations are having to adapt even more. Doing so might involve making choices that seem unconventional or even risky to others, but attempting to follow a life path that others may only be following with a lot of help is a guaranteed way to end up in debt, or broke.

The retirement pension trap

So is the Dependence Trap something that mostly affects the young? What about those who've worked hard their whole life and gained 'financial independence'? How can Dependence Trap you if you've retired with a good nest egg?

One of the important ways that getting free makes you rich is by freeing your mind up to *create*. But dependence can also cause you to *destroy* wealth, not just be motivated to create less of it.

> **... dependence can also cause you to *destroy* wealth, not just be motivated to create less of it.**

When approaching retirement, people often plan how much savings they'll need based on how much income they would like to live on. Based on the low 'safe withdrawal rate' we looked at earlier, it quickly becomes apparent to most people that they'll need a lot of money to be secure in their retirement. But this is where the pension comes to the rescue! In Australia, you are currently entitled to a full pension at retirement if you have *no* savings at all, and you are *still* entitled to a full pension if you have savings up to an amount of $258 500 (not including the entire value of your house!).

So someone with no savings can retire with a pension income of $23 598 per year, and someone who has $250 000 in savings can retire with a slightly higher retirement income of: pension + 'extra income drawn from their own savings'.

If they draw down that extra income at a safe withdrawal rate of 4 per cent, then their new combined income would be $23 598 (pension) + $10 000 (4 per cent of their $250 000 savings a year) = $33 597.

But here is where it gets weird.

If you want to retire with any more than that in income—in other words if you'd like to retire even just a little 'rich'—you'll need substantially more savings to live on even one cent more in income. And until you reach that much larger amount of savings, any extra savings you have will actually decrease your income. Why?

Because for every $1000 extra you've saved above the $258 500 threshold, your pension income gets decreased by $3 per fortnight, or $78 per year. Let's say you save an extra $100 000: your pension would drop by $7800 per year; $7800 per year in income is 7.8 per cent of $100 000. So, if you valued security, any extra income you could safely draw down at 4 per cent from your $100 000 extra savings is more than cancelled out by the reduction in pension income — in other words, you're actually worse off!

So, if you value security and want to draw down money from your savings at the 'safe' rate, then there is no incentive to save more than $258 000; in fact, it's not until you've saved up enough money for your pension to be reduced to zero (between $560 000 and $840 000 depending on whether you are single or a couple), that any extra savings you might have start to add to how much income you can live on each year, at a safe draw down rate.

As we saw, what tends to happen in reality in the majority of cases is that people who retire with more than $258 000 become motivated to draw down more than 4 per cent from their savings per year — much more now that the pension reduction rate is 7.8 per cent. Some people, even if they value security highly, are tempted to 'blow' their excess savings altogether so that they can actually enjoy a higher retirement income for all their hard work saving — at least for the first few years (this is especially tempting for those who have a little more savings than the maximum amount you can have while still getting some pension. It's quite common to hear of retirees buying a brand new car — or whatever — to 'come under the threshold'). But this, of course, means that they may run through their savings quicker and eventually end up having to live on less income as they age, becoming more and more dependent on the pension as their retirement progresses.

Predicting consumer trends and profiting from the retirement pension trap

The effects of the pension on influencing consumer behaviour are so strong and predictable that you can forecast consumer trends and make investments based on being aware of this effect. In the early 2000s I predicted the continuation of a trend that was only just starting: retirees buying caravans.

As we've seen, a lot of retirees are technically asset rich and income poor, and the pension creates this perverse incentive for you to spend capital and still end up with about the same income, as your decreased savings result in higher pension income.

(*continued*)

Predicting consumer trends and profiting from the retirement pension trap (*cont'd*)

While some people use this as an opportunity to splurge, others find ways to spend the money that will decrease their cost of living as well, and a caravan does that: for an upfront capital outlay, you get to have cheaper out-of-pocket holidays in retirement.

Another trend that was predictable was the large uptake of solar panels by retirees. Not only do they attract government subsidies, but solar panels are a good way to take money that is in your savings column where it's 'asset tested' or counted against your pension and shift it into your home, the value of which is ignored for the purposes of calculating the pension. On top of that, solar panels decrease your outgoing expenses, helping with the 'cashflow poor' part of retirement.

While these options sound a lot more financially savvy than simply blowing excess cash in retirement, they are still a result of the pension Dependence Trap. There is no guarantee that money spent on your home or campervan would have been a good financial decision to make without the pension system.

Of course, all this talk of the dependence traps caused by the pension overlooks one type of dependence that even the richest retirees face: dependence on the markets to provide good income, and the constant growth of assets.

In chapter 8 I'll talk about some ways you can free yourself from dependence on the market.

There is more to dependence than you think

There is a negative stigma attached to the word 'dependent' that gets in our way when thinking about the effects that dependence can have on regular people. Not everyone who is 'dependent' is lazy, or a bludger—there are many ways that you can be very hard working and still be dependent.

You can even seem to be 'free' to most people, but still be dependent. Think of the small-business person who works very hard to get a government contract, and then works just as hard fulfilling it. Think of the author signed up to a major publisher churning out four books a year—very hard work! Or alternatively, the YouTube star who quits their job to create videos and play computer games full-time, making $100 000 a year working from home, which certainly sounds like a 'get rich' success story (these people exist!). How often have you heard 'quit your job and make a killing on eBay/YouTube/Amazon' (and so on)?

There is a reason we talk about Freedom First if you want to be financially free. All these people are making good money. The author or the YouTuber or the mum who quit her job to work from home selling on eBay may certainly seem free to most people. But how free are they really?

Many times during recent years people who thought they had it made on one of these platforms got a rude shock when the rules were changed on them. For example, when eBay suddenly increased its fees, or in the case of YouTube (which runs at a loss to this day), the amount of money that was paid to creators was cut drastically. YouTube stars pulling in $100 000 per year were suddenly earning half as much, and others who were making just enough to create videos full-time, were suddenly faced with having to quit altogether, or markedly reduce their output as they looked for other work.

A boss can't suddenly cut your salary in half. If they did, you could sue them. But there is no recourse if a big company such as eBay decides it wants to charge double, or if YouTube wants to pay you half of what it did before. Ironically, the YouTuber who quit their job to be more 'free' or independent may be in more of a Dependence Trap now than when they worked a job.

Platform dependence

The case of YouTubers and eBay businesses above is a good example of 'platform dependence'.

Author Nassim Nicholas Taleb, in his book *Antifragile*, warns that if you want to be resilient and secure you should avoid becoming too dependent on any one platform. So what's the attraction of placing all your bets on one platform in the first place?

The internet started out as a pretty decentralised, freewheeling, disruptive place, but has since consolidated into a handful of media giants. If you want to sell to the biggest markets, you need to be on eBay. If you want your video to reach the largest audience, you need to be on YouTube. There are always small sites that attempt to usurp the media giants, but the big sites have achieved an effective monopoly status: people use them because that's where other people are.

And these big platforms promise to make it easy: put your business on Facebook and people will find you—you won't have to market! Put your videos on YouTube and we'll pay you to make videos about whatever you want—you won't have to 'sell' anything, and you can focus on your content; we'll take care of the business!

Platforms can have their place, and this is where understanding your motivations is important. If big platforms seem like a secure and easy way to motivate yourself—whether it's selling online, or freeing your voice and creating content—then they can be a good place to start. I'm all for doing what will get you to take action, but see the platform or the gatekeeper for what they are: a way to get your message or your product in front of a large audience. Once you have started, then make sure you capitalise on that audience and don't become too dependent on one source for your financial independence.

> **...don't become too dependent on one source for your financial independence.**

The real risk with gatekeepers or platforms may not be just financial dependence. The cost of being reliant on any one source for income is that a good proportion of your creative mental energy ends up consumed trying to navigate the 'reward system' of that channel. For example, on YouTube many creators have shared what a nightmare it is trying to figure out what the algorithm rewards, and more and more of their time is spent navigating the system rather than creating content. Something that initially appeals to many people as a 'packaged solution' that makes things easy and doesn't require you to 'sell' can demand a lot more mental energy from you in the end.

Which brings us full circle for this chapter—the most familiar 'platform dependence' most people have is a job. Jobs are a great short-term solution to a long-term problem, and they promise to 'make things easy' in the sense that you just have to show up and work: you don't have to worry about finding the work. However, rather than spending our time delivering the best service we can, a good portion of our effort ends up revolving around satisfying the needs of a single person, a 'gatekeeper' (that is, your boss). But as we now know, you can be free of dependence on a boss long before you are free of a boss.

Dependence, independence, interdependence

Freedom from dependence doesn't mean you become an atomised individual, stoically cut off from all ties. In chapter 8 I'll talk about the difference between 'escaping' and 'getting free' and we'll see that getting free is about having more choices. And one of the ways to have more choices is to systemise things in your life: to have more networks, not fewer.

We're often encouraged to throw off all shackles of tradition in our pursuit of individual 'freedom'. But we still need connections to make life manageable. You don't grow all your own food, you outsource that. Which frees you up to do other things.

Freedom doesn't mean you never rely on anyone else for anything — far from it. It means you don't settle for just being dependent.

Dependence is being reliant on someone in a way that limits your choices. It's a one-way relationship where one party has all the power.

Independence is not being reliant on others.

But *interdependence* is working with others to *expand your choices* in a way that benefits both, without disempowering either. Dependence is relying on a judge to pick you on a reality TV show and give you a recording contract. Independence is booking your own gigs. Interdependence is partnering with other musicians/artists to promote your brands and both grow your audiences larger than you could on your own.

> *Six months after Melissa had left her old job, the effects of the GFC were starting to be felt. Through the grapevine, Melissa heard that the girl from her old office with the inflated job title had been let go. It wasn't clear whether it was a falling out, or if it was just that an office that had been able to take on a lot of fat in the boom times now had to cut back.*

If so, then that one office was emblematic of large swathes of the entire economy — many jobs contain an amount of 'make work' or 'politicking' activities. Through no fault of their own, many people have become dependent, perhaps on their boss, or more broadly on the current nature of the economy. What will happen to those jobs when we exceed our ability to forestall economic winter forever? What will happen to people who've spent their careers learning to be 'unproductive'? We will address this more in chapter 10.

A Quick Recap

There is more to dependence than most people think, and you may be dependent in ways you don't realise. Being dependent can limit your thinking and creativity, but being free of dependency doesn't mean being alone.

CHAPTER 8
The Debt Trap

Freeing yourself from dependence on debt.

Isn't it funny how the socially accepted ladder in life involves accumulating more and more debt, and more and more recurring expenses?

Get your first job — get a car loan! Get a higher education — get a student loan! Start your career. Get a first home — get a home loan! To make sure you can pay back all those loans, you had better get some income protection insurance, and car insurance, and home insurance, and finally death insurance for when you work yourself into an early grave! And on top of all those recurring expenses you had better start making some regular payments towards your retirement too. One thing after another, binding you tighter and tighter to your job, forcing you to work for a salary for the rest of your life.

In chapter 7 we talked about how being dependent can limit your thinking and creativity. Nowhere is this truer than with our reliance on *debt,* and our dependence on passive *growth.*

And not just individually: virtually the whole world — nearly every country — is addicted to debt too.

The illusion of stability at one of the most unstable times in history

Despite the familiarity of this life path and the centrality of debt to it, the past 100 years are actually quite historically abnormal. Over this time, the money supply has been consciously expanded, and since the 1980s the use of debt in particular has exploded, fuelling bubble after bubble and driving up the costs of some of the most critical things we need—giving rise to what is known as the FIRE (finance, insurance and real-estate) dominated economy, which has seen stagnant wages on top of ridiculously high house prices.

Except during war times, inflation in the past was essentially zero on average. One dollar in 1800 would buy you approximately the same amount of stuff 100 years later. From 1913 to 2018, however, the value of the dollar declined 96 per cent; what you could buy for $100 in 1913 would cost you $2529 in 2018.

In the past, periods of inflation would be followed by periods of deflation pretty regularly. While there have been periods of deflation over the past century—where the value of the average person's savings rose while the assets of the wealthy fell—these were few and far between and have been bitterly fought by central banks every step of the way. Which is curious, because *deflation literally decreases income inequality*.

In the past, the economy expanded and contracted, it grew and it had seasons. Then we decided to try to abolish those seasons and institute constant growth and constant inflation. The bargain always was that while people's wages and savings would buy less and less each year because of a deliberate policy of inflation, their salaries would rise even more to compensate for it.

But despite this implicit promise, everything that could be done to keep wages low has been done instead. Wages haven't inflated—assets have. I wonder who that benefits more, the rich or the poor?

Some economists have argued that rising asset prices make people *feel* wealthier—so they spend more—but as others have noted it's rising incomes, not rising assets, that encourage people to spend in any sustainable manner. And in real terms (adjusted for inflation), wage growth has stalled for decades. Incomes have barely changed in 40 years, which is bad enough for people who are working—but what about those who've stopped working and have retired?

When you stop working you still suffer the fall in purchasing power of your savings, but you no longer earn a rising income (if your income was rising at all) to offset it (assuming you're living on a fixed income). So after a lifetime of work, retirees can't just live out their days on the money they've saved: they have to invest their money just to keep up with the artificially declining dollar that we've mandated in our attempt to eliminate economic seasons.

> ❝ **A market can never be free, if debt bids the prices we see. Financialisation, has harmed every nation, it's why we're now hooked on QE.** ❞
>
> *Unknown*

In the lead-up to the financial crisis in the United States there was a small group of investors including Dr Michael Burry who, like me, saw what was coming, and by going against nearly everyone else at the time were able to make $1 billion profit when the market collapsed. There was a good movie made about them called *The Big Short*. It turns out what they were looking at was the rampant financialisation of debt in the United States. They could see that the loans against housing, which formed the basis of the new products Wall Street was creating and trading, were very unsound, but either nobody was paying attention or nobody cared.

While those investors close to Wall Street were predicting the crash based on debt, in Australia I was predicting the problems with debt based on looking at demographics.

No matter how cheap interest is when people reach retirement, they want to pay down debt. Debt only makes sense to most people when they are working and have the income to service it. The whole point of debt is to afford something that is too expensive right now, or to get leverage on your assets so you can grow them more quickly, and to build up enough equity to live off in retirement.

But with an ageing population facing retirement, and a younger generation facing stagnant wages while having the lowest workforce participation rates in recent memory, it no longer makes sense for people to take on as much debt. But, just like in 2007, while plenty of people are aware of this situation, almost everyone is in denial, and private debt levels are still worryingly high.

The end of passive growth?

We are starting to realise that debt itself doesn't magically create growth, and that piling on debt clearly isn't working anymore for our economy. But what about for us as individuals, as wealth creators?

For decades now the mantra has been 'there's good debt and there's bad debt'. But during the GFC we were living through a time of deflation, which meant that the value of assets wanted to fall while the value of our money or savings wanted to rise. On top of this 'natural' deflation, we had governments that were doing their best to fight it by rapidly increasing their debt and balance sheets. The result was a kind of disinflation, or period of prolonged anaemic growth.

Barring the correction in house prices that came with the GFC, on paper the Australian economy did okay—the aggregate GDP (Gross Domestic Product) continued to grow, a little. But that was achieved only through the highest rates of immigration of any Western nation. While GDP went up, GDP per person did not, and while property prices did rise again beyond their previous peaks, wages across the economy stagnated.

Was my advice to Andrew to *not* take on the most debt possible—buying the most expensive house he could, in the hope that his rising salary at his job would cover it all—wrong?

No. When the correction came, it was the upper end of the market that was hit first, and while the lower end of the market did okay, the upper end was also the slowest to recover. A decade later property prices in capital cities fell again. The era of endless growth was replaced by a period of increased volatility.

By following my advice, Andrew avoided getting caught in the pullback at the upper end of the market, turned his home into a modest investment, and increased both his cashflow and his freedom, so he was not only still exposed to the rising housing market, but in a better position to stay invested in it too. Not only that, but by avoiding tying himself to a mega mortgage and clinging to his job to pay for it, he was free enough to embark on a totally new venture as well.

So even though passive growth did continue to occur, it was much more selective, and leveraging yourself to the hilt to take advantage of passive growth in general, and counting on rising wages, was not the smart move.

Clearly such simple advice as 'take on good debt, to get leverage, to buy assets' is no longer enough.

" Everything popular is wrong. "
Oscar Wilde

In fact, most mainstream advice is usually outdated *at the time*. I remember in the 1990s, *after* the inflationary 1980s, financial planners were still extrapolating the double-digit returns of that period as if they would continue forever.

I remember hearing one say 'saving is for losers'! (Yes, someone actually said that! I'm sure they were only being half serious though, the implication being that if *all* you did was save money, and you never bought any assets, then the rampant inflation we were experiencing in the 1980s would see your savings fall in value while property was rising in value rapidly. So that *may* have been good advice—a decade earlier!)

When property is rising by double digits, holding property for passive growth, taking on debt and negative gearing seem to make sense. During the 20th century, real estate prices generally went up. But not always, and this was historically unusual: something that was driven at first by post-war demographics and compounded by governments easing interest rates and lending criteria. At the end of the 1980s the bubble popped, and a recession set in that saw prices flatten into the early 1990s.

Responding to this new, flat market, some began to advise not to hold assets for *passive growth* at all—hold them for *passive income*. By the time this advice became mainstream it was already becoming outdated, as prices again began skyrocketing and the passive growth party was back in full swing. However, there is a kernel of truth to this advice: ultimately assets aren't meant to grow passively—they are meant to yield returns. If a business, for example, increases its earnings, only *then* should the company's worth grow to reflect that.

> *"...with property in particular, we've come to expect that prices should always rise."*

But with artificially low interest rates, any asset that yields a decent income is quickly bid up in price by people desperate for a return, until the yield falls in line with the artificially low returns that have become the norm. And with property in particular, we've come to expect that prices should always rise. Lowering interest rates makes it easier to pay more for a property; but they don't make the property itself any more productive as an asset.

What worries people the most, though, is that we have been pushed into a world where all the old securities are being stripped away and more and more risk is being forced onto us. People are concerned, asking: Will my pension last? Will my retirement savings continue to grow? Will my house keep rising in value so I can maintain my standard of living, even as my expenses rise?

You don't want to work your whole life just so you can be independent enough to retire, only to find that although you may no longer be dependent on a boss, you are now dependent on a faceless market that's beyond your control: it can't be appealed to, you can't ask it for a raise and it certainly doesn't care about you, or how long you've worked to pay down your loans and save up your money just to invest in it. It's time to take back control.

Four levels of recovering from dependence on debt and 'addiction to assets'

The world has become financialised; as individuals there's no changing that. But we can work within and around this new reality and recover from dependence on debt and addiction to assets.

Level 1: develop a new view on debt

Each generation has had an overarching view on debt.

The so-called 'greatest generation' (who grew up during the Great Depression) viewed debt as bad. Having lived through hard times, they knew that debt could eat you alive, so they avoided it. Savings, on the other hand, really helped.

The baby boomers grew up with parents who valued saving, but coming of age during post-war prosperity, the baby boomers came to expect growth to continue — and as a result of their large numbers this was a self-fulfilling prophecy. At each stage of life, boomers created large consumer trends that drove prices up constantly. They came to see debt as something that, on one hand, could be bad if taken on for consumer products, or on the other hand, good if taken on for assets. The inflationary 1980s — when interest rates shot up sky high — are largely responsible for this. You could be seen to be sophisticated by simply taking on good debt. Taking on bad debt or just saving, by themselves, were seen as unsophisticated. The 'smart' people were taking on investment loans and negative gearing.

The generations that followed the boomers have seen assets rise and fall. They've seen interest rates at all-time lows, so debt has been tempting to take on; but the returns for taking on that debt have been diminishing too. The cost of things has continued to rise, and so debt has become 'necessary' for a lot of things that once were cheaper. Education is the obvious example.

Education has become increasingly expensive, and as more and more people get degrees, more and more people need to get degrees than ever before. At the same time the returns from higher education are diminishing: with wages stagnating there is even less certainty of a secure job at the end of it. (For millennials, not only has college debt increased, but their income relative to previous generations has also decreased.)

On top of all this, the jobs we do get are rapidly changing so that not only are the degrees we get obsolete in no time, often the industries we work in can become obsolete too.

To keep the party going, to ensure asset prices continue rising well beyond their intrinsic value, we're enticing people into debt slavery and also doing everything we can to stop wages rising in value. We're even doing away with the idea of full-time work itself. People need income to service debt, and we can only lower the interest on debt so far: can you see why it's easy to predict that this state of affairs can't continue?

The lifelong consequences of student debt

Recent studies have found that there is a negative correlation between student loan debt and the establishment of small businesses.

What this means is that young graduates with a crushing student loan debt are encouraged to avoid the risk of starting a business and instead reach for the security of the 'stable income' that a job promises.

Student debt can also affect credit ratings, making it harder to get a business loan. Our over-credentialised world with inflated education costs is causing fewer of our youth to start businesses—yet small businesses create the majority of new jobs. It's a catch-22: debt makes people desperate for jobs, but in the process suppresses the entrepreneurialism that creates jobs.

This is a terrible side effect of the student loan bubble all by itself—stunting our growth at just the age when most people are likely to be willing to take risks—but the consequences are longer lasting too.

People are paying off student debts for more of their life now: the average length to pay off those loans has risen by 80 per cent.

(continued)

The lifelong consequences of student debt (*cont'd*)

This is having a major impact on the ability of our youth to create 'lifetime wealth'. Research has found that households without any student debt obligations have about seven times the typical net worth of households headed by a young, university-educated adult with student debt.

Not only does this debt delay the ability of graduates to start building wealth, it also has a fundamental and profound effect on other markers of lifetime happiness and success, for example it can significantly decrease the long-term probability of marriage by a significant amount as well.

If all that wasn't bad enough, an article in *The New York Times* on this new 'debt slavery' described how students were being encouraged to sign away their rights to future income in exchange for investors' help with their tuition. This is literally serfdom.

Instead of lords and tenants, we have financial elites and students/employees.

Instead of dealing with the runaway credentialism and the bloated administration that is fuelling the education bubble, we're taking an inherently unstable 'asset' (higher education) that is maintaining its inflated 'value' only through more and more debt, and we've started bundling and packaging up all this 'bad debt' in a way that is eerily similar to the mistakes made in the subprime crisis.

New views on debt

Our views on debt have changed over the generations:

- *pre boomers* — 'Debt is bad.'
- *baby boomers* — 'There is good debt, and bad debt.'
- *post boomers* — 'There are costs to debt regardless of whether it is "good" or "bad" debt.'

To ascertain the true costs of debt we need to ask ourselves:

- What does this debt cost me, in terms of money, but also in terms of opportunity? What stage of life am I at? Do I want flexibility to pursue opportunities? Do I want the security of low debt levels for times when my income is uncertain? Could I find a better way to get this thing I want without taking on debt? (More on this later.)

- What is the return on this debt? If I'm relying on something big to happen that's out of my control—rising asset prices, job market booming—should I take on this debt, even if it's 'good'?

- Beyond good debt or bad debt, what is the amount of debt?

Having lived through several market crashes as an active full-time investor, I can tell you that maximising your leverage through debt is nuts. It's way more important to survive the many seasons than it is to try to maximise your harvest in any one season.

Always go into a deal with some equity so you can ride out any corrections. If you've got at least 20 per cent equity, in most cases you'll be fine; less than that and debt can kill you. Even 'good' debt can be bad.

> **"Our over-credentialised world with inflated education costs is causing fewer of our youth to start businesses — yet small businesses create the majority of new jobs."**

After the GFC there were many stories of people who had maximised their 'good debt' to buy several investment properties, only to end up homeless, living in makeshift 'tent cities' in the United States. Besides that, even in the best-case scenario, cranking up your debt to the max ties you to your primary source of income—your job—at a time when jobs are less secure than before because income is needed to service debt.

As you saw, part of having a new view on debt is being prepared to question what everyone else is doing, and resist the temptation to take on the same debts as everyone else. This can be as simple as not going into massive debt for a degree with no guarantee of a job at the end of it, or as sophisticated as the example I shared with Andrew, where taking on a manageable amount of investment debt made more sense at his stage in life than taking on the more massive debt he was contemplating for a home.

Renting versus buying

One piece of conventional wisdom almost nobody questions is whether it is better to rent or to buy a home. You've probably heard

(continued)

Renting versus buying (*cont'd*)

'Rent money is dead money,' 'If you rent you're just paying the landlord's mortgage' or even 'You can't live in a share/stock.' I don't want to get bogged down in comparing renting and saving versus just buying a home and paying the mortgage, because ultimately, for most people buying a home is a stage-of-life issue, a security issue and a family issue, and not a financial issue at all.

Nobody buys a home for purely economic reasons, though we often tell ourselves that's why we are doing it. But by convincing ourselves buying a home is the *only* smart decision, we risk rationalising going into massive debt early in our lives, or spending way more than we would otherwise on a home, in the belief we are doing the right thing.

I saw a comparison recently that went into the actual numbers comparing two hypothetical people: one owning a home, the other renting and investing in shares. The study was done in Canada, using all the relevant transaction costs and historical growth trends of property and stocks experienced there. The conclusions were interesting and illustrated several things.

Firstly, after 25 years, the guy who bought a home, who stayed in it and paid off his mortgage, ended up accumulating $681 000 in net worth. The second guy, who rented the entire time and invested the extra take-home pay he had left after paying rent, ended up with $578 000 after 25 years.

Open and shut case, right? It's better to buy? Well, not so fast. No-one knows how well either property or shares will do—better or worse than their long-term averages—over a period of 25 years. So already trying to prove which is better is looking shaky. But even if you assume both assets stick to performing in line with their long-term averages, some small changes can turn out to make a big difference in outcome.

For example, if the renter never bothers to start investing in shares, clearly they do much worse. Most people are aware of that, and some people even admit they bought a home because it was the only way to get themselves to save.

But what most people wouldn't guess is that all it took for the home owner in our example to do worse than the renter/saver, was for the owner to move house only twice in the 25-year period. If it's unrealistic to expect people to rent and save, how realistic is it to expect most people today to buy one home and stay in it for 25 years straight? Most people don't realise what a chunk transaction costs take out of your pocket when buying and selling a home. Our economies are heavily dependent on getting people to buy a home and take on debt and then slugging them with outrageous transaction costs.

One final thing that I noted was that the comparison overlooked one critical aspect that most comparisons between buying versus renting and investing overlook.

In the example, the home buyer put down a $50 000 deposit and then borrowed a lot of money to buy a house.

The renter simply used their savings to buy $50 000 worth of shares. By taking out a loan to buy a more expensive asset, the home owner was using the power of leverage. Without leverage, let's say you buy a $200 000 home versus $200 000 worth of shares: based on long-term averages the shares will grow more.

But that's not what the example compared. It compared a leveraged asset (the home with a mortgage) versus an unleveraged one. If our renter/saver had simply borrowed some money to buy more shares in the beginning, like our home owner borrowed money to buy more 'house', then our renter/saver would have come out far ahead. *They wouldn't even have had to borrow as much.*

When you realise that the passive returns from housing come largely from the leverage associated with it, it's an eye opener. (This is not the only advantage of investing in property; property allows you to add value easily, but that's an active investment strategy I'll talk about later.)

So whether someone who rents actually saves, whether they take out a small loan to give themselves some leverage, or on the other hand whether the home buyer moves or stays in one place for 25 years, all affect the outcome. It's not a clear case of one being better than the other.

But how realistic are either of these scenarios? People move all the time, and without a savings plan most people fail to save. And it's

(continued)

Renting versus buying (*cont'd*)

normal to want different things at different life stages. Tying yourself down to a mortgage at a young age when the transaction costs of moving are so high may cost you important opportunities when you are young. However, as you get older and you've settled into a career or established a business, renting will be far less attractive than the security of owning your own home.

Owning a home is not just a financial decision, it's an important lifestyle decision. It's a social issue, a family and community issue. It's built into our psyches, but that doesn't mean that we can't occasionally choose to step outside the 'normal' box and do something different.

Level 2: leverage rising assets without debt

If leverage is the reason for the success homebuyers have had, are we doomed to have to take on massive debt so we can get the leverage we need to grow our savings for retirement, now that we need larger and larger amounts to be able to stop working?

Most people's first experience 'investing' usually involves buying stuff. They buy their first home, or rental property, or even some shares. I'll talk about why that is in chapter 9, and how we can break free of this 'consumer' mindset. But there are ways you can capture the profits from rising assets without taking on massive debt to buy them at all. And this is important to realise now that we know assets won't always rise like they have during the past 30 years of unprecedented expanding debt.

The reality is, that even in a booming market most of the gains occur in only a few months of the year (I'll discuss this in chapter 10). In chapter 9 I'll show you a technique you can use to earn income from your shares during those months of the year when they are going nowhere, instead of just paying out interest on your debt to hold them while they go sideways.

Beyond just lessening the costs that come from taking on debt to buy and hold assets, what if we could get *leverage without any debt* at all?

At the beginning of this book I shared with you a trade I did, based on my short-term view that the market would rise over the next few weeks. If I had simply bought shares to capitalise on that view, I would have had to buy $1.16 million worth of shares—just to make the same amount of money on the one trade that,

> **"...even in a booming market most of the gains occur in only a few months of the year."**

instead, only cost me $24 000. Even if you had borrowed money to buy the shares, you would have had to come up with a lot more money than that, just for a deposit. (And that's just the 'long' trade I did. The short spread I had done the previous day actually paid me money upfront—though I did have to have margin available to cover the position.)

Okay, so at first glance this stuff seems confusing. And I'm not entirely sure that that isn't deliberate on behalf of the financial sector. But really, financial instruments such as options are not that hard to understand. At their heart, financial instruments are just pieces of paper that can be bought and sold, just like shares can be bought and sold. Not too long ago the idea of being a share owner was completely foreign to most people, but now, since we've financialised our economy and actively worked to erode people's retirement savings, everyone who puts something aside for retirement has been forced to become an investor. This is not necessarily a good thing. *But if you are being forced to become an investor, it pays to at least be a better informed investor.*

Options and other derivatives are essentially contracts that give people the right to do something, often the right to buy something, without having to own that thing first. You may have heard of how rich executives sometimes get paid in stock options? These options give them the right to buy shares in their company at a certain price—let's say $10. If the executives can do a good job (or get lucky) and drive their company's stock price higher, then these options will be worth more. Being able to buy something for $10 that has risen to $20 is very valuable! It's like a discount coupon. A discount coupon is worth more the more it can save you. These types of options are called 'call options'. How much would you be prepared to pay to have the right to buy Apple shares for $1 today?

The other option that people are familiar with is when a Hollywood writer gets their script 'optioned'. What that means is that a movie studio buys the 'rights' to a script for an amount of time. They don't actually own the script, the writer still does. But for a period of time they have the sole right to make a movie out of it. If they don't make a movie in that time frame the option 'expires', but the writer gets to keep the money they were paid and are free to sell another option on their screenplay to a different studio (this can be a good strategy to make money too: selling options. I'll talk more about how you can do this later). This example is great because it shows that an option is a way for people to 'reserve' something for a period of time, to control something without owning it.

Control but not ownership

> **Once you understand that you can profit from something without owning it, you open yourself up to unlimited possibilities for making money without having to go into debt to do it.**

The wealthy realise that there is more to investing than just 'purchasing' assets. Control is often more important than ownership. Once you understand that you can profit from something without owning it, you open yourself up to unlimited possibilities for making money without having to go into debt to do it.

Here are some examples of 'optioning' something that don't involve shares or options! Say you decide to buy a property, but the owner wants more money than you are prepared to pay for it. You can walk away or you could offer the owner a deal: you'll meet their price if they will meet your terms.

- You might write into the sale contract that you want an extended settlement. That way, in a booming market you benefit from the growth of the property before even settling on it.

- You could ask for terms that allow you to access the property or do certain repairs before settlement. In a flat market that allows you to start adding value to the property before coming up with the money to buy it.

- You can add in clauses that allow you to transfer or on-sell the property before it settles allowing you to make your profit and never have to buy the property outright!

- You can even get the seller to agree to what's called vendor financing, where they lend you the money to buy their property!

The opportunities for creativity in property are endless, which is part of what makes it such a great active investment.

Understanding the importance of control and getting over the mindset of ownership is a big step towards freeing yourself from dependence on debt and buying assets in the hope they'll rise in value.

Finally, in the example I gave earlier, if I had bought $1.16 million worth of shares and they had gone down only 10 per cent in value, I would have lost more than five times the amount that I actually put out there to control the shares instead. Control, not ownership gave me the ability to put a small amount of money out there and potentially capture all of the 'upside' (if the shares had doubled in value I would have kept an extra $1.16 million) while limiting the downside. This is something Taleb calls 'optionality'.

Optionality

Whenever you enter into any deal in business or life, you want to look for the opportunity to limit your downside risk, while maximising your upside profit potential. This was something Donald Trump learned early in his career. By personally taking on massive loans to finance his developments, when the market turned against him he ended up almost $1 billion dollars in debt. He famously joked to his wife that any old bum on the street was worth $1 billion more than he was at the time. While he was eventually able to turn it around, Donald learned an important lesson. Minimise your downside while maximising your upside.

Many of the newer buildings that bear the Trump name aren't even owned by him: groups of investors pay him to licence his name, so there is no downside for him, and he often takes a percentage of the upside as well. Control, not ownership.

So to round out this section, what other ways can you think of to get leverage without debt, or to put a small amount of money out there in exchange for a large potential upside?

Once upon a time, when higher education was cheap and skilled jobs were in high demand you could invest a small amount for education that would yield a large amount of extra earnings. While that is turning into a worse and worse deal, there are still community colleges or strictly vocational degrees that fit the criteria: less money, higher return. However, 'qualification' and 'education' are not synonymous; while colleges still hold a monopoly on granting pieces of paper, sites such as YouTube now make 'education' essentially free.

While you might still need the piece of paper to get a job in the corporate world, all the skills

" Time is an asset, just like money. "

99

you need to start your own business are freely available. You can teach yourself almost any human skill you can imagine for next to nothing if you have the drive.

The final way to get optionality is time.

Time is an asset, just like money. You can invest it and it doesn't have to cost you anything. That's the ultimate definition of limited downside: risking losing nothing but your time.

Finding the time to learn a new skill, start a small business, teach yourself to invest, and so on, is possibly the best investment you can make.

Which is why I say *if you want to be financially free you need to get free first*—and this may simply mean you need to buy yourself some *time* back first.

Level 3: make money from assets even if they are falling in value

Once you realise you can make money from assets without owning them, you can actually start to make money from assets that are falling in value too!

We're so conditioned to *buying* things that we hope will then go up in value, that most people don't realise that you can make money when things go down in value too. You can 'short' stocks, or even buy contracts like the options I described above, that make you money when stocks go down in value.

Instead of giving you the right to buy something at a certain price, a different type of option—called a 'put option'—gives you the right to sell something instead. If you can lock in a price to sell something for, say, $10, and that thing falls in value, then the contract you have is worth more than when you first bought it. If that sounds complex, don't worry, you're already an expert with this type of complicated financial product ... after all you have insurance, right?

An insurance contract is a piece of paper that you pay for, that allows you, for a certain period of time, to 'sell' an asset at a certain price. Most of the time the insurance contract expires worthless: you paid a premium, but eventually when the year ends and your house hasn't burned down or you didn't crash the car, the contract is worthless and you have to pay a premium again for the next year—*and you're happy about this!*

However, if your car did rapidly fall in value (because you crashed it) your insurance contract would be 'worth' a lot more. You would call up the insurance company and 'cash' it in for a lot more money than you paid for the contract initially (your premium). When it comes to shares, put options and other similar derivatives work the same way. You can buy them to insure shares that you own, or you can simply buy them with the view to selling them later for a profit, if the shares in question fall in value.

Wouldn't you like to have been able to insure the price of your retirement portfolio before—*or even during*—the stock market crash of 2008? It's not like it happened overnight either—*it went on for over a year.*

Why is it we are all being nudged/pushed/forced into becoming investors now, but no-one tells us we can insure our life savings? It's almost like it's more profitable to sell us managed funds than it is to teach us the skills to protect our wealth. During the 12 months of the GFC not only was I able to protect the value of my shares, but I was able to make more than $50 000 per trade as volatility soared and the markets fell. When the market finally bottomed, because I didn't believe in taking on much debt to buy assets in the first place, I wasn't eaten alive by the margin calls that forced so many others to sell their shares at the very bottom. Better yet, I had cash to invest.

Level 4: don't be dependent on assets rising or falling— create assets!

You don't need to be dependent on assets rising or falling. While it's important to know that there are ways you can get around the financialisation of our economy by using more sophisticated tools than the average person, in a way that's adding complication to an already overly complex problem. Since when did we all have to become investors just to stay in the same place?

This last step is the step that really excites me. Most people, if they ever get around to it, will only own assets. Some will learn how to control assets. But real freedom—in contrast to going into massive debt just so you can buy assets and then pray they'll go up—comes when you realise that you don't need assets to do anything at all.

You can create assets yourself.

Own → Control → Create

Another way to think about creating growth could be called *active growth*. Active growth is the opposite of passive growth. Passive growth is where you work hard at a job, pay tax, then buy an asset and hope that it will rise in value passively. The era of easy passive growth may be coming to an end. Active growth is where, instead of being dependent on the market going up, you guarantee your profits *upfront* by creating equity. (Getting profits upfront is important, not just to free you from dependence on passive growth, but also so you create the capital you need to do the next deal, making it easier to take the next step—getting freer so you can get freer again.)

With property investing, neither 'passive growth' nor 'passive income' make getting your next property any easier straight away. (See chapter 14, where I introduce the term 'Freedom Escape Velocity.)' In the next few chapters I'll explore the importance of working for equity instead of just income, but for now let's look at a few examples.

Property

Doing a renovation on a property is one way you can actively raise the value of a property, so regardless of whether the market booms or not you can build in equity straight away (if you're smart about it and use this strategy at the right time). However, while renovations are an example most people are familiar with, they may not be the best strategy, depending on your current market.

There are many better ways to create equity that the average person may be less familiar with.

Bargain purchases are one. Developments are another: the best development transforms something from one category into another that has higher market value. Splitting blocks, or securing a re-zoning are examples of this. Even bargain purchases can be used to get active growth. You can't control what the market will be prepared to pay for a property, but you can control what you pay for it. Strategies for buying 'below market' are an essential way to guarantee you some profits upfront, regardless of what the market does. (I'll share an example of a bargain purchase made using an awareness of cycles in part III.)

Lastly, while most people are more familiar with shares or property when talking about assets, there are two assets that give you the *most* leverage and the *most* potential to lock in active growth upfront.

Business

Most people only consider going into business if there is the possibility of making more money or income than at their current job. But the real value of a business is that for the same number of hours you work, you not only are getting paid income, like in a job, but you are building an asset too.

Your job is not an asset. Retire at the end of a life working for someone else and your income stops and that's it. Retire after building a business and your income may continue if you've leveraged yourself out of the business; but even if not, you'll have an asset that has real value too.

On top of that, depending on when and how you sell your business, you may be able to bank up to $6 million tax free too (more on this later).

Finally, the second asset that we can actively 'create' that nearly everyone overlooks, is *yourself*.

You are an asset

Most people are pretty passive about how they grow this asset—we go to school, let others train us for the job market, then any other 'upskilling' we do is often left up to our boss. But by taking charge of actively growing yourself—learning new skills, even taking up new hobbies—you can exponentially improve your wealth-building ability.

One skill or hobby that you enjoy doing in your retirement might earn you only a couple of thousand dollars a year, but as we saw earlier, it could free you from having to save over $100 000 in retirement savings. That's one way to end the 'addiction to assets' and free yourself to retire that much sooner.

Getting free of debt

Debt can create a horrible feeling. It becomes one of those things that we just don't want to think about. We want to ignore the situation.

Unpaid bills. Letters in the mail that you are afraid to open. You throw them in a pile and they glare at you. Once the pain has built up enough, people can be motivated to take action. And the results can be amazing. Plenty of books have been written on how to get out of debt, and who needs to explain why? The pain is clearly motivation enough. Like putting your hand on a hot stove.

But who wants to have to be motivated by pain alone? Or to only be able to dig deep when your back is against the wall? We have all experienced the amazing amount we can get done when there is a deadline looming. For ages beforehand, we may not get much of

> **"...who wants to have to be motivated by pain alone?"**

anything done, then within the space of a night we can do more in a few hours of pressure than we could in the weeks prior.

When people do face and start tackling their debt, they often experience a surge of energy—a new sense of purpose.

They are tackling something that was causing them real and immediate discomfort. They are making progress that they can see, and that sense of getting free from something is a powerful motivator. But what happens after that? The crisis has passed. The immediate pain has gone. Traditional financial advice may be good at providing the tools you need to get out of debt but it's not great at tapping into the motivation you need to get rich.

I've noticed with those in debt that it's not unusual to tap into the desire for freedom when you are being crushed by something. Freedom is such a powerful motivator precisely because it is something we usually only ever tap into when we've lost everything else.

"It's only after we've lost everything that we're free to do anything."

Tyler Durden in Fight Club *by Chuck Palahniuk*

But while the average person may not really value freedom on a day-to-day basis, the average person doesn't end up rich either.

So how should we approach getting free of personal debt?

Let me first say that there are a lot of great books and resources that are full of tips and techniques you can apply when you've made the decision to free yourself of personal debt. Things like calling your bank and asking to speak to the debt resolution team. Most countries have a banking ombudsman and have mandated that consumer lending be accompanied by many safety nets—for example, you may find that your bank is willing (or obligated) to freeze the interest on your credit cards for a period of time, or roll your balance into a card with a lower rate, or eliminate your fees if you contact them for help. These are all things that you should take advantage of immediately, but how should you go about actually getting out of debt?

There are several schools of thought on this, but I'm going to break them down into two categories: the mathematically efficient, and the actually effective. What do I mean by that?

Well, some financial planners advocate for a payment strategy called the debt snowball—Dave Ramsey is a famous proponent of this strategy. The way it works is, let's say you have three personal finance debts: one credit card with a $500 balance on it, another card with a $5000 balance and let's say a personal loan or a third card with a balance of $10000. Now let's pretend that the largest amount, $10000, has the highest interest rate, while the smallest amount has the lowest interest rate. How should you begin paying off all this debt? You probably have to pay a minimum amount towards each of them each month, but should you then direct, say, 10 per cent of your salary to pay a little off each of the loans each month? Or should you pay off one of them first while making your minimum payments only on the other two?

The debt snowball guys say to pay off the smallest amount first because that will create emotional momentum. Once you've paid off the small amount, you've eliminated one debt entirely, and can now direct the 10 per cent of your salary that you're using to pay off your debts towards the next card, but you can also add to that the minimum monthly payment you were paying off on the first card too, creating a 'snowball' effect.

On the other hand, the strict, mathematically efficient approach would say no, you should start to pay off the amount that has the highest interest rate first because that makes the most financial sense, even if it's the larger debt and will take much longer to pay off. Who's correct?

Well, surprise: it's not the mathematical literalists. While they are correct that paying off the loan/card with the highest interest rate is the most efficient way to go about it, and will save you money overall, it will only save you money if you actually go through with it and keep paying off your debt.

Testing the debt snowball technique

A Kellogg School of Management study with over 6000 participants was conducted to test just this hypothesis to see whether the debt snowball technique worked. They found it was more effective to have people pay off the smallest amount of debt first, as people who did that were more likely to persevere and pay off all their debt than those who didn't.

This goes for other tempting strategies too. Why wouldn't you just roll your personal debts into your mortgage if your bank lets you? Surely paying only mortgage interest of, say, 5 per cent beats paying credit card interest of 17 per cent? But even if the interest is higher, *if you actually pay off your credit card debt,* you'll come out miles ahead of where you would be if you simply added that debt to your mortgage at a lower rate and it never got paid off. And if you do that, what's to stop you racking up credit card debt again?

In trying to be efficient, people sometimes miss the chance to be free. And it's getting free that makes you rich.

> **In trying to be efficient, people sometimes miss the chance to be free.**

So what's the lesson? Being mathematically *inefficient* is okay if you're tapping into the right motivation. And without realising it, the debt snowball guys were tapping into the power of Freedom First. Getting free first, in this case ridding yourself of one debt entirely, helps you to feel freer. And *feeling* freer is something you can begin to value.

Escaping versus getting free

> **People spend more time 'escaping' from work than they do trying to get free from it.**
>
> *Matthew Klan.*

Freedom First tells us there is a difference between escaping and getting free.

People who want to escape from pain are often powerfully motivated — in the short term. But wanting to escape from prison, and being able to stay free once you get out, are two different things. There's no point getting out of prison if you're only going to end up back inside again.

Getting free of debt isn't about doing the right thing after doing the wrong thing. You can do the right thing and still end up crushed by debt. We saw this with the housing crash: people who watched their expenses, avoided consumer debt and took on nothing but 'good' debt in an attempt to grow their wealth by adding leverage ended up financially ruined. Which is why we need to stop defining debt as 'good' or 'bad', and instead ask, Does this make me more free, or less free?

The reason to get free from debt, is so that you can do more. Having debt hanging over your head is not just painful, it's *restrictive:* it fills up your mind; it ties you to income to service it; and it stops you from breaking away, creating and trying new things.

When you start to really value your freedom, you'll come to see 'getting out of debt' as not just a way to avoid pain, but as a way to *free up your mind*, as well as a way to *give yourself more choices*.

This is why I suggest doing something else that's also mathematically inefficient while you're paying off debt...

Save for your freedom.

You can start saving *while* you're still paying off your debt. At first this makes no sense—why would you put money into a savings account earning nothing, when you could be using that money to pay down your debt, which could be costing you 12 per cent or more in interest?

There is wisdom in achieving something positive while undoing something 'negative': it helps you to transition away from an 'escaping' mindset to a 'getting free' mindset.

If you wait until you have paid off all of your debt before you start to think of ways to create, to invest, innovate or start a business, you will be waiting a long time. If you start saving for yourself while you are paying off debt, your mind is better able to start thinking of all the positive changes and choices you could make.

What if you could stop thinking about your debt straight away—even before you've paid it off? Free your mind from debt, before you free your balance sheet from debt?

In part III, I'll show you not only how to do that, but also how to free yourself from ever having to worry about bills, groceries and all those other short-term expenses that fill up our minds and stop us from working on something bigger.

Obviously, getting out of debt or avoiding debt can make you freer; in fact, it's also one of the many ways that getting freer *directly* makes you richer. Every dollar of personal or credit card debt you pay off is like earning 17 per cent on your savings, *after tax.*

Some people find that the act of saving for something rather than buying on credit not only saves them interest on every purchase, but also means they buy less stuff that they end up not really wanting. Which may be one of the biggest advantages of going debt free.

However, *Freedom First isn't about going without.* It's about being free to have everything you *really* want.

The real cost of debt is not the interest. Using debt causes you to miss the relationship between purchases and costs. The real cost of debt is what you're tempted to give up when you spend now and pay later. I'll talk more about the relationship between how we earn and how we spend in chapter 9.

If debt is bad because it can cost you your freedom, then there is one trap worse than debt that *no-one* in personal finance is talking about.

And it's the reason that we get trapped into using credit in the first place.

Credit exists. The genie is out of the bottle. And he's a bad genie. But what tempted us to listen to him in the first place and believe that he could grant all our wishes with a quick ride on his magic plastic card?

Before we had the temptation of easy credit we had the temptation of safe, secure, regular, predictable income.

Before we became slaves to credit cards, we had already become slaves to pay cheques.

Without the illusion of reliable, repeatable payments *coming in*, we would have never felt tempted to take on the debt that locked us into regular payments *going out*. And now the whole world is stuck in the Income Trap, addicted to the regular hits of income, just as the supply is starting to dry up...

A Quick Recap

Debt is a big part of what traps us into short-term thinking and working a job for life. We need to evolve beyond thinking in terms of 'good debt/bad debt', and think about the *costs* of debt, especially in terms of our freedom. You don't need to slave your life away, servicing debt in the hope that you will one day have enough assets to retire—you can get leverage and create wealth without debt. You don't need to be dependent on the market always rising, and you can even create assets yourself. Getting free of debt isn't about 'righting a wrong'; it's about giving yourself more choices.

CHAPTER 9

The Income Trap

How you receive money shapes the way you think about it, and affects your ability to create wealth.

> " **No God has commanded worshippers to their pious duties more forcefully than income, as it subtly directs the fabric of our lives.** "
>
> *Gregory Clark*

I remember vividly when my parents retired; they had a decent amount of retirement savings—just enough assets that they didn't qualify for a pension. My mother, an intelligent, professional woman, said to me: 'But what will we do for income when I stop working?'

I looked at her quizzically.

'I need money each week to pay for the groceries,' she explained.

The answer may seem obvious to you (or if not—hang in there), but the fact that it didn't to my mother was a real eye opener. I was used to living outside of the Income Trap, but after a lifetime of working for a salary, she wasn't.

Starting retirement should be the high point of a person's savings in their lifetime. Sadly that's often not the case for many people, but even for those people who have saved a nest egg, the transition from the regular comfort of a pay cheque to going without one can be a shock. I pointed out to my mother that they hadn't really been living pay cheque to pay cheque before, so why did she think they would suddenly start doing so now?

She looked at me curiously, so I explained: 'You shop weekly for food at the moment right? But you get paid fortnightly? How are you able to shop on the weeks when you don't have a pay cheque coming in?'

Before she could answer I continued cheekily, 'So your ability to spend money isn't really tied to when the money comes in—if it was, you'd have to receive a pay cheque every day just in case you had to duck out for something mid-week or pick up something on the way home from work.'

She reluctantly conceded my point, but still seemed to want an answer: where would the money that they would spend actually come from?

This thinking is why many people in retirement are tempted to convert their entire assets into annuities. But longer retirement horizons mean the need for the comfort and perceived security of income is literally making people poorer. Getting free of our need to be paid in income literally makes us richer.

> **Getting free of our need to be paid in income literally makes us richer.**

It was this incident that brought home for me for the first time just how serious the Income Trap was, and how pervasively a lifetime of earning a salary could affect our thinking.

Income is evolutionarily novel

For the vast majority of our history on this planet, people didn't work jobs. So salaries and income are evolutionarily novel. Most people don't have to go back more than a couple of generations to find ancestors who farmed the land, and in evolutionary terms farming itself is relatively recent.

Just as 'the way we earn money affects how we think about it' is the theme for part II, the way our ancestors acquired food has had a profound effect on the way our minds work too. Agriculture began in some places up to 9000 years ago, but research has shown that as recently as 3000 years ago we were still undergoing a multitude of genetic changes to adapt to the relatively 'recent' change to our diet that agriculture and settled communities had brought.

But the era of mass 'salary man' employment is much more recent than that—we haven't had long to adapt to earning a consistent income. Why is that important?

Compare working a job today, to farming. Farmers don't get paid each week. They don't get paid for each hour of work they do, including overtime. In fact they may not get paid at all. And they may not find out they're not getting paid until the end of the season.

Farmers have to have different time horizons. They have to plan for the future because that's how they earn their living. And prior to agriculture we spent the vast majority of our history as hunter-gatherers. While, in some ways, gathering is similar to a job—you get up each morning and go to work securing the food you will eat that day—hunting certainly isn't. Hunting requires planning, patience and organisation. It may be days or weeks between kills. And it's that uncertainty of reward that means that when you do get the chance to strike, you have to make sure you bring home enough food to last until the next opportunity to hunt presents itself. Compared to a job, even gathering has more of this 'resource management' requirement built in—different things are in season at different times.

Jobs, and the regular income we earn from them, are not just evolutionarily novel, they are also a type of 'supra stimulus'.

What is a supra stimulus?

In nature, salt and sugary tasting foods are relatively rare. Sweet fruits were only in season for a brief time. Most animals were lean, and so fatty tasting food was pretty rare too. Despite the scarcity of fat, its calorie density—as well as the fast calories of sugar and the critical importance of salt for the functioning of the human body—meant that those of our ancestors who developed a taste for these things were more likely to work harder to acquire these relatively rare resources in the ancestral environment. These ancestors then had an evolutionary advantage over those who didn't, which is why we crave sweet, fatty and salty foods so much.

Fast forward to today and the rare foods it was once an advantage to crave are now abundant. And that's bad enough for our waistlines. But on top of that we've gone one-up on nature and created sweeter sweets, and richer food than our ancestors could have ever dreamed of. These foods are 'supra stimuli', in that they are much more potent, distilled versions of the things we crave than we ever evolved to cope with. And because we weren't designed to handle them, for many people they have become literally addictive. Once you understand the concept of a supra stimulus you'll see there are a lot of things in modern life that can fit this description. Social media jumps to mind: we all crave community and validation, but in the past you had to work for these things. Now validation can be had with the click of a mouse and the snap of a selfie, and an endless stream of likes from strangers can quickly overwhelm our primitive minds and addict us.

> "Once you understand the concept of a supra stimulus you'll see there are a lot of things in modern life that can fit this description."

Our ancestors lived in an uncertain and dangerous environment and they craved regularity and security. This made them hyper sensitive to patterns. Our brains are designed to detect patterns, so much so that we are considered to have what's called 'overactive causality': we tend to see patterns where they may not even exist. We used to see spirits in the winds and gods in the thunder clouds.

While the cost of seeing patterns that *didn't* exist was low in the past, the rewards for noticing patterns that did exist were huge. If you failed to notice that animals tended to go to the watering hole at a certain time, or that winter followed autumn, you would starve.

So why is income a trap?

The reason we find income so attractive in the first place is that it seems secure.

The regularity of salary income is especially addictive. It comes in frequently and reliably, like clockwork.

> **Over the long run income is more powerful than any ideology or religion in shaping lives.**
>
> *Gregory Clark*

It's addictive even when we know our jobs are not actually secure and that we can be fired. If you have ever been fired, think back to that time: how many weeks in a row did you get a regular pay cheque in that year? How many weeks in a row were you fired? Ignoring how long it may take to find a job in the first place, once you've got one, the odds are that you'll be paid by that boss more than you'll be fired by that boss, obviously. You only get fired once! Chances are you may have held the one job for 50 weeks in a year and only got fired once. Flip a coin 50 times and if it comes up heads each time even I would be tempted to check both sides to see if it wasn't heads on both. Even though it is possible for something to happen that often and still not be a certainty, there is a flawed statistician in each of us. We can't help but think that something that happens that regularly is secure—our brains were selected to latch onto patterns.

Not only does the regularity of income lure us into a false sense of security, but it comes in *identical sized small doses*. It's regular and it's constant. The same amount at the same frequency. Like a rush of drugs, it's just enough to temporarily ease the fear of not having enough. Just enough to let you feel like you've got a handle on the problem of your expenses—for now.

And like morphine it dulls your senses. You'd like to find a better solution for making ends meet but, well ... you've at least got some sort of solution in place for now. And one that feels pretty secure and reliable. Of course, you would be tempted to look up from the grindstone for a complete solution. If you could have a big win, that would solve the problem of expenses forever, that would interest you enough to give up the security of the regular, predictable solution that you have right now: a solution that may not even be working for you. So, you can see one reason income can be a trap is because it can lead us into chasing the 'big win'.

There are other aspects of income that are evolutionarily novel too. Modern salaries create a disconnect between our direct actions and our results. You can have a bad week at work and still get paid exactly the same amount, or you can work hard and outdo yourself and still get paid exactly the same amount.

On the one hand, you may eventually get fired; on the other, if you constantly outperform there is a chance you may get recognised and promoted. But the direct connection between what you produce and what you earn is severed. The feedback from your actions is dampened.

We experience very little control over our salaries if we work a job, which means we don't tend to think of money itself as something we can use as an input to produce with; instead we think of money more as an output of the work we do, that we can then consume with. This lack of experience 'productively investing' has

> **Modern salaries create a disconnect between our direct actions and our results.**

a direct impact on our ability and willingness to invest our money.

The only direct connection between our effort and our income is the *time* we work.

Money is simply the reward for time spent. This can make it hard for people to be willing to spend any time or effort creating a new business or product that doesn't immediately reward them for the time they've spent.

Finally, this relationship between the time we put in and the money we get paid blinds us to another reality too: the value of money is constantly changing. As we saw in chapter 8 we've tried to engineer a world where there is constant growth. The cost of this meddling is that the value of our money is constantly being eroded. But when you exchange a set number of hours each and every week for a set number of dollars it's hard not to feel that the value of our money is constant.

And, when our efforts are rewarded with a fixed rate—dollars for hours—it can seem like our value is relatively constant too. People find it hard to conceive of earning vastly more than what they are used to earning, and underestimate how much value they could provide for others by doing something different, and how rich they could become as a result.

Income encourages its own consumption

I've touched on a lot of the effects that the Income Trap can have on our thinking, but the last insidious effect of earning an income that I want to explore is how it encourages us to spend right up to it. This explains how we all fell for the Debt Trap in the first place.

It always struck me as weird how very different people, with different sized families, different hobbies, diets, lifestyles and also very different incomes could all end up equally poor at the end of the month. Mathematically, it doesn't seem to make sense that with so many different variables and inputs, different people could all arrive at the same figure: zero.

According to a 2009 *Sports Illustrated* article, 78 per cent of former NFL players became bankrupt or were under financial stress within two years of retiring and it is estimated that 60 per cent of former NBA players are broke within five years of retirement. The answer obviously is that the regularity and the apparent security of money coming in encourages some people, regardless of the amount they earn, to spend up to that amount.

As we saw in the previous chapter, debt only compounds this tendency. Before widespread consumer debt became available (and it didn't become available until after the historically unprecedented era of the 'salary man' arose), people could spend all of their earnings each month and at least they would only be back at square one.

Now we live in a world where people aren't just at risk of spending all of their pay cheque, they are at risk of committing all their pay cheque to regular, outgoing payments. We don't buy stuff with cash much when we can put it on credit, and the real evil of credit is it allows us to spend more than we have, in exchange for committing to minimum monthly payments. At least in the past when you 'splurged', you only wasted this month's money—now when you impulse buy you'll be paying for it for months or years to come.

" Spend all of your money and you're broke, but commit all of your money and you're enslaved. "

Matthew Klan

Debt and income create a vicious cycle: you have the income so you can afford to take on some debt and monthly payments. Now that you have debt you need regular income, or how will you pay the monthly payments? It's a catch-22.

Of course, it's not just the debt that traps us into regular payments, it's the income itself.

It seems every business has cottoned on to this tendency of income to 'spend itself' and nowadays everyone wants you to sign up for regular payments. Why would companies risk having you not buy their product every month, when instead they can lock you into easy payments, or a monthly plan? I remember the days when you could visit a gym when you wanted to and only pay per visit—and it was affordable to do so. Now they are set up to lock you into a plan in January while your New Year's resolutions are still warm!

Debt and income (and the weekly cycle of expenses) condition us to think short term. But creating wealth requires long-term thinking. We ask people to save for retirement yet we bill them weekly and pay them weekly. The problem is immediate.

" I've always said that a job is a great short-term solution to a long-term problem. "

Matthew Klan

I'm not anti-job! But while we get charged interest weekly, the loan lasts a lifetime. And so do the rest of the expenses we have in life. We focus on solutions that help us meet the problem of the weekly payments, but ignore the problem of the lifetime-sized debt, or lifelong expenses. We need the freedom to break out of the short-term cycle of 'earn enough to spend, and then earn again' if we want to be able to think long term.

So how do the wealthy get around this tendency that income has of encouraging its own consumption?

In researching how the wealthy manage their finances, Stanley and Danko found more than half of all millionaires operate on a strict annual budget.

They account for every expense and plan every cent they are going to spend. While that may not be much of a surprise to many people, the thing I found most interesting was that almost half of all millionaires *didn't* operate on a strict annual budget.

What's going on here? Some of those millionaires may have inherited their money, while some earned so much money that they could spend wildly and still have enough left to be technically wealthy — at least while their income lasted. But these were only a minority of the millionaires surveyed. The majority of the non-budgeters invested their money first, and then spent what was left. There were only a couple of lines dedicated to these people in the book while there were pages devoted to the minutiae of budgeting that the other group of millionaires did. This is a shame, as it gave some readers the impression that millionaires are just tight old people who count every penny and never spend their money.

But what I wanted to know was what was going on with these other millionaires who didn't budget? How had these guys managed to not only stay rich, but grow richer, without the discipline of a budget stopping them from wasting their money?

Because that's what a budget is. It's a control that people impose on themselves to stop them doing something that they would otherwise do. Which is precisely why people hate budgets just as much as they hate diets. If only there was some way to make yourself want to eat healthy food rather than fight against your desire to eat bad foods.

Had these millionaires discovered a way to want to spend their money productively, to invest first and spend later?

Money as an input as well as an output

In a job, money is always just the reward, so of course the temptation is always to spend it. You put work in and you get money out. Money is only an *output*: you put in hours working, and you get back money. But you can't use that money as an *input*: you can't invest some of your salary this week to increase your salary next week.

job → **money is *earned* and used for *consumption***

You can't use money as an input, or control what you earn to any real extent. Once you get out of a job though, money can start to become something else altogether.

Job versus small business

It's worth starting a small business — even if it's not so different from what you do in a job.

small business $\rightarrow$ money is created, and it can be used for consumption or production

Some people say it's not worth starting a small business because you're just 'buying yourself a job'.

For a start, you're not buying yourself a job — you are creating a job for yourself, which is certainly better than being dependent on someone else to give you one.

But the concern seems to be that on the outside some small businesses can look a lot like a job, with many hours serving customers and doing the sorts of tasks that you may already be doing in a job. However, scratch below the surface and approach a business not with the thought of 'earning an income', but instead with the thought of creating an asset and you'll soon realise that not all of your time will be spent working *in* your business at all. Some time will be spent working *on* your business. And that will create the need to spend money on your business, and all of a sudden money isn't just the reward you get for working a job that you 'deserve' to consume, but suddenly money is something you can *invest*, and you can use it to *produce*.

Then money isn't just the *output*, it's also the *input*.

You have a choice: you can spend the money on yourself, or you can invest in yourself/your business. In a job you don't have that choice of reinvesting your earnings back into increasing your production capacity.

If you work for a salary, you may be able to invest in upskilling by doing extra education/training that *may* result in a pay rise — but that will always feel like a risk if you are dependent on a boss recognising your 'investment' and choosing to reward your investment by paying you more. Your input of money (investing in educating yourself) isn't directly linked to your output of money (salary), which is why we tend to want to get our bosses to pay for any training we do.

And that's a shame because you are your own greatest asset. *Nothing you invest in can show better returns than investing in yourself.*

Education, a smart investment?

You can invest in your education in an attempt to increase your remuneration at your next job. In fact that is the way a lot of people 'rationally responded' to the financial downturn: dropping out of the workplace and going back to school in the hope that this was a short-term correction and that the market for jobs would pick back up where it had left off. And they'd be able to make up for the lost wages and cost of their education by stepping back on the ladder at a higher rung. But what if the correction lasted longer than average and the cost of the education was higher than in the past? And what if the next boom, when it comes, comes from an entirely different sector of the economy? That's quite a risk, which is why any direct feedback you can get from investing in yourself is so important.

So any investment you make doesn't get directly linked to your income when you are working a job. In a small business, however, the link between what you spend your money on and what you earn is obvious: money spent (wisely) on marketing will lead to new customers. As demand rises, investment in new stock or new equipment can directly increase your income in a way that you can measure. The money you earn is no longer just the reward for hours worked: suddenly it has the potential to be capital that you can invest to directly affect your bottom line. Money is no longer something to just consume with, it's something you can produce with too. One of the reasons people struggle to save to invest is that for most people, investing is such an intangible thing—it may change something vaguely in the future, but right now you can't see a positive result for having invested your money instead of spending it on stuff. Learning to see money as an input is revolutionary.

Your experience of money

I can totally understand people who say 'I wish I could live in a world without money.' I don't agree with them, but they are expressing a feeling rather than a prescriptive policy anyway. For most people, money is something you only really think about when you spend it, more so than when you earn it because anything that is regular and consistent tends to fade from our mind, while unique and variable things catch our attention. Likewise, things we can't see get noticed less, while things we can see stand out more to us. Which is why we stop thinking about our salaries, which are usually the same every week and are paid directly into our accounts, but we pay much more attention to our expenses, because they are often out of pocket, much more random, and often unpleasant.

And when we do experience pleasure spending money we often buy things with credit cards and don't see the payment happen, but later we get a statement in the mail that feels negative. I believe a lot of the advantage people find from going to an all-cash budget is that you tie your reward to its cost—so the pain of handing over cash is balanced out by the pleasure of the thing you're buying, instead of the pain waiting in the credit card statement leaving you depressed a month later.

So what those people who say that they would like to live in a world without money are really saying is that their experiences with money in the modern world feel mostly negative.

David was offered an ultimatum: if he wanted to hang on to his job he'd need to go onto commission. Without any real choice in the matter David was forced out of the Income Trap as his regular predictable pay cheque was now gone. His boss would no longer pay him a weekly salary—only a commission on jobs done. But while things seemed to be getting worse, something amazing began to happen.

For the first time since working for a salary, David had gained control over his inputs, and any actions he took could affect his outputs too. David was always a good worker, but the freedom to work as hard or as little as he liked lit a fire in him.

From fearing when the next flare-up of his illness would rob him of mobility, his focus could now shift to what he could control: what he did with the times he was well. His productivity soared. When he was healthy he was outworking not only his former salaried self, but all the other guys at the shop too.

He later confided in me that earning his income in 'lumps' instead of regular income meant for the first time it was easy to save. When he had a fixed income it was too easy for all the money that was coming in to be allocated ahead of time, but with a little uncertainty, which came from breaking free of the Income Trap, David discovered something that I and the 'other half' of millionaires that Stanley and Danko surveyed had learned.

While a strict budget may be necessary when earning an income, once you get control of your productive capacity, paying yourself first is a much easier and more natural way to accumulate wealth, without the restriction of a budget.

This newfound freedom and greater sense of control had unforeseen consequences too. For the first time in ages David's flare-ups became less frequent, and his illness entered into a partial remission. There is a connection between mind and body: being at the mercy of an illness, constantly waiting for it to next lay you low has a negative effect, but looking past the illness to the next healthy period that will allow you to kick into high gear again, can completely reorient your focus away from dreading disease to anticipating health. (Many people report a similar feeling when they break free of the Dependence Trap.)

And while David was still sick occasionally, he was now finding a new energy when he was well; he started bringing in a lot of new work to his boss's business.

If David's story ended there, that would be awesome.

He was starting to save, he was feeling healthier, was sick less often, and when he was well he was on fire.

But it wasn't to last…

The Income Trap affects *how* we invest

Of course, you can always invest your money in someone else's business if you work a job (that's simply investing in shares or managed funds) but you can't increase *your* returns from your personal efforts at your job by reinvesting in and expanding your job. You can't expand your productive capacity.

It's because of this that employees tend to approach investing in stocks or property with a consumer mindset. Because in their primary economic activity money is only an output — something to consume—they approach investing like they are 'buying' an asset. Some people even coach people to 'buy assets, not liabilities'. While that can be good advice, it reinforces a passive mindset.

A consumer who tends to think of buying assets will often fall into the trap of waiting for the 'best deal', delaying in fear of 'buying the wrong thing'.

Another trap for consumers who think in terms of the best deal, is to rely on past performance. It's easy to look back and see that you should have bought VHS instead of Betamax, or Blu-Ray instead of HD-DVD. One product clearly won out. Likewise it's easy to see that over the past few years property did better than shares, or vice versa, and that tends to either lure the consumer–investor into buying assets at their peak, or to endlessly putting off investing at all.

Which is a shame because assets don't have to be purchased; they can be created, often with little or no money at all. And the best time to get working on creating an asset is now.

Big risk investing

Earlier, I talked about how a job is a great short-term solution for the problem of expenses. I also pointed out that having a short-term solution in place can sap your motivation for seeking a better solution. But another side to earning an income is that there is a direct cut-off point for the utility of savings. What do I mean by that?

We've seen that thanks to credit cards, people often don't even bother to save up for stuff anymore, but even before the rise of mass consumer credit, the illusion of secure incomes and jobs had a negative effect on savings, which is why I think the Income Trap is more insidious than the Debt Trap.

Someone who has embarked on a career, and feels reasonably secure that they'll always be able to get a job, sees little tangible benefit from accumulating savings beyond a certain point. A few thousand dollars of savings could represent a holiday, or a nice present; a few tens of thousands of dollars could represent a nice new car; a little more money could represent a deposit on a house.

> **... the Income Trap is more insidious than the Debt Trap.**

But beyond that, savings have little direct utility. For most people, once they've got the house, car and annual trip sorted out, the next reason to save is for retirement.

Retirement is so far off and requires such a large jump in savings that many people never get started on it, but for those who do, their savings represent a big temptation. Say you've got $100 000 saved. That's not really enough to retire on for most people, so there it sits in your retirement account. It has no present utility to you. Add to it long enough and you may have enough to traditionally retire, but whether it is in your account today or not doesn't actually change your life right now one bit. If it was a smaller amount, say $20 000 and you didn't have a car then that money would have utility: you wouldn't want to waste it because there is something you could use it for right now. If it was a larger amount, say $1 million, you could also use it right now by retiring, which would certainly change your life.

But when you work a job—when your day-to-day expenses are met by your salary—then there is always the temptation to take that money and go for the big win: $100 000 may not have much utility right now but if you could decuple it (times it by ten) then you could quit work for good! But what if you lose it? Well, you'll still have your job. You'll be sad, but your day-to-day life won't actually change.

This takes away an important balance to investing. A good investor doesn't need to shy away from risk, but a good offence should be balanced out with a good defence.

In other words, as we saw in chapter 8, you can take on debt mindlessly, justifying it as 'good debt' or 'buying assets', but a sophisticated investor asks, What is the *cost* of this debt? You take on debt only if you have a plan for how it will make you freer.

When you are no longer an employee working a job and saving for retirement, and instead are running your own business or investing your own capital, your savings have utility again. Because money can now be an input as well as an output: that $100 000 could be used to expand your business, or invest in a property to renovate. But more importantly losing that money has a real cost: if you burn through all your capital you might have to go back to a job.

Overtrading to replace income

Another trap that people supported by the security of a job often fall into when they learn to trade stocks, is the temptation to 'overtrade': doing too many small trades in an attempt to replace their weekly income.

Aiming for smaller amounts of profit doesn't make you any more likely to profit.

It's like our ancestors trying to hunt for small meals every day. You can't force the game to be there just because that suits you. You hunt when there is something to catch, and then make sure you catch enough to last until the next hunt.

Straight line thinking

Straight line thinking is the reason the vast majority of people get into investments too late in the boom and stay invested too long.

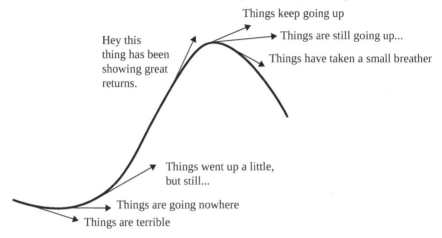

There are a lot of things that can contribute to straight line thinking, but being paid the same salary every day, every week of the year, is a big one. The regularity and consistency of debt payments going out, or interest earned on savings coming in, is another.

The tendency to think in straight lines is only enhanced by most people's experience with investing, and it's in investing where the costs of straight line thinking can be highest.

For many, their experience of owning investments is mostly passive. In the case of things like mutual funds, most people only pay attention to what their fund is doing when they receive a yearly statement. Because of this, subconsciously at least, it's easy to imagine that the returns their fund made this year were made in a straight line, just like a savings account.

Most people, happy to see that they made, let's say, an 8 per cent return for the year, will look forward to a similar return the next year. However, this 'annual return' could blind them to a much more important reality: growth doesn't occur in a straight line. Their fund could have grown by 16 per cent early in the year, but by the end of the year the tide could have turned and the market could have started falling in value, finishing only 8 per cent up for the year. So it's easy to see why people end up staying in an investment too long. The same happens in reverse too: faced with negative news, or negative returns, it can be hard for people to realise when the market or their assets have begun to recover.

When things start to rise in value (perhaps after a downturn) it takes a while for people to feel confident that the trend will continue. Most people want to see a straight line—prices going up consistently—before they feel confident to buy in. But prices go up in trends—three steps forward, and countertrends—two steps backwards. Due to loss aversion, those backward steps shake people's confidence: people take a loss much more emotionally than a similar-sized gain. This is another reason the average investor struggles to get in on a new trend until it's too late.

Finally, while it often takes overwhelming evidence to get people to commit to an investment, once they have, it can become like a bad relationship, requiring only the smallest positive confirmation to stay invested in, despite perhaps overwhelming proof that it is heading in the wrong direction.

The Income Trap affects *why* we invest

Income thinking not only affects the *way* we invest by making us want to *buy* assets (rather than control or create them), it can also affect why we decide to invest in the first place. One obvious example that comes to mind is how people with a high income are often tempted to take on an investment for the deductions they can claim from it. But buying assets for tax reasons is a terrible idea. Buying an asset for the losses it makes now, and then relying on passive growth to somehow happen and make up for that, is not only making yourself dependent on the market, but it's also losing one dollar to make back 30 cents. I've said it before, but the tax secret of the rich is not tax deductions. (I'll show you what it is in part III!)

Investing for income

Investing for income is very tempting for retirees who have spent their lives working for income. Things like stocks or even property that have irregular income—and can rise and fall in value—can seem less secure, while things like bonds or annuities that offer predictable income can seem more familiar and more secure. Unfortunately, as we saw in chapter 3, with longer retirements and the rising costs of healthcare, the price of security is higher than most people will ever be able afford: and that's if they invest in things that grow!

Choosing assets that mostly return income, instead of a mixture of growth and income, or selecting assets with higher income while overlooking the risk to capital (because income is what you are most familiar with), is a sure way to ensure that your assets won't last as long as you do.

An example of the lure of passive income is what happened to investors in Australia during the mining boom. The Australian economy was powering along prior to the GFC, fuelled by a mining boom as we furiously dug stuff up out of the ground to sell to China. This mining boom, in turn, drove up housing prices and rent. In some places—mainly small mining towns—you could find positively geared properties that were renting out for double digit rental returns.

When this happens, you have renters effectively paying more to rent a house than it would cost them to own it. Why would they do that?

Investors didn't care: these returns really appealed to those who were hungry for income—but there was a hidden cost. At the height of the boom these properties in the middle of nowhere were eventually selling for up to $1 000 000. But after the boom those same properties plummeted in value to $200 000 and less, as the once prosperous mining projects were wound up. What's more, not only did investors lose capital, but the formerly lofty income these properties were yielding dried up too. Perhaps the renters weren't so 'dumb' after all? *An awareness of cycles, and freedom from 'income thinking' could have prevented this from happening to these investors.*

The allure of income

The Global Financial Crisis was the classic example of promising the security of 'higher than bank interest' passive income while ignoring, downplaying or outright hiding the risks. Cunning investment houses took something that was inherently insecure (high-risk loans to borrowers at risk of defaulting) and then packaged those mortgages up and sold them to large institutional investors such as schools and pension funds, who were looking for nice secure 'passive income'-style investments for their conservative clients (but ones that paid higher income than 'boring' fixed-income investments!).

(continued)

The allure of income (*cont'd*)

The rating agencies were complicit in giving these bundled high-risk mortgages the veneer of security too. But as we all now know, that 'secure' income was an illusion and it brought the financial world crashing down.

If some investment or opportunity raves about its income potential, pause and ask: *If I'm being sold on the income from this investment, who is making the profits or the growth?*

This can be important to ask even with common financial products such as reverse mortgage arrangements and annuities that people facing retirement come across every day. What are you giving up for the 'security' of income?

Instead of sacrificing growth for 'packaged' passive income-style investments, there are plenty of ways you can go about actively increasing the income from your retirement assets. With property, for example, you can add value for your tenants to raise your rental returns, seek out bargain purchases so that the rental return is effectively higher, or use tax strategies such as depreciation to turn a cashflow neutral property into a positively geared one.

You can even learn to create active income from a share portfolio.

Covered calls

Out of all the assets you can own, shares are one that you seem to have the least control over. You can control when you buy them and when you sell them. But you can't easily add any value to shares. To get higher returns out of a share portfolio, people either try to buy low and sell high, or they buy higher risk shares in the hope of higher returns or greater passive income.

But there is one strategy that allows you to own the more 'secure', large cap shares for growth, and still generate more income from them, in effect 'renting out' your shares. Imagine being able to get started generating active income from an asset that only costs $10 000—much less than it would cost to own an investment property!

We saw earlier that an option, whether it was an option on a book for a movie, or an option on a property, or shares, gives the person who buys the option the right (but not the obligation) to do something—often to buy something (like shares) in the future—in exchange for a small amount of money now. We know why someone would take out an option on something: by controlling it instead of owning it they can get leverage without outlaying large sums of money or taking on large amounts of debt while they add value to it or wait for the asset to rise in value. So an option may make sense to buy, but why would anyone want to sell one?

For the money of course!

The best analogy to explain this is to think of a rental property. If you own a rental property and you sign a tenancy agreement with someone, you are giving them the right to 'control' or use your property for the period of time agreed to. If you've owned a rental property you'd probably agree that while the tenants have all the rights, the owners have all the obligations! Why give away control of your house to someone else to the extent that you can't even enter the premises without notification? Because you are being paid rent, of course!

Selling options on shares you own works the same way. If you own 100 shares in a company you may be able to write a 'covered call' (or sell a call option) against them. For example, you might 'option' your shares for $11, even though they are worth $10 today, and pocket the income—let's say a couple of hundred dollars per option. On some shares you can potentially do this each month.

So instead of chasing higher returns and 'passive income' from the share part of your retirement portfolio by investing in perhaps 'riskier' shares, you can still have your large cap blue chip shares—which, while not as exciting, are generally more secure—and instead increase your yield by writing covered calls against them. You are actively generating income on top of the income that the shares may passively provide you in dividends. This allows you to choose the best shares to grow your retirement savings, rather than jeopardise your savings chasing greater passive income at more risk to your capital.

(continued)

Covered calls (*cont'd*)

Many people actually consider writing covered calls a passive income strategy. While it's true it can be done with not much more than a phone call a month, in chapter 10 I'll take you beyond income thinking and teach you why, if you really want to profit, you shouldn't think of this as an income strategy at all!

> **...the rich pay people salaries and income, but they get paid in profits, dividends, equity and capital appreciation.**

But with all this focus on income it is important to remember that the rich pay people salaries and income, but they get paid in profits, dividends, equity and capital appreciation.

Obviously the rich can also get paid salaries—the difference is that they aren't *dependent* on them. They aren't stuck in the Income Trap, and because they aren't reliant on income; they are freer to think in curves, see growth opportunities, work for bigger rewards and not get stuck thinking in straight lines.

Getting free first

Taking action that will make you freer now is critical.

It takes time to find a good property, or a profitable trade or deal. One formula for finding a good property says you have to look at hundreds of properties, physically inspect a dozen, and put written offers in on several, just to find one good deal. All of this takes time, which is why buying yourself back this time with your very first deal is so critical.

You can do this by ensuring you look for deals that allow you to lock in your profits upfront, rather than ones that require you to wait for the market to rise before you can afford to do the next deal. For a similar reason, if you like the idea of buying investments that return you higher income, with the goal of eventually buying enough of them that your investment income can replace your job income, you may be better off looking for a deal that will reward you with more time now so that you can use that time to leverage yourself into the next deal, and then the next, accelerating you towards your goal, and allowing you to quit your job much sooner.

In part III, I'll introduce the concepts of Freedom Escape Velocity and Perceived Income Level Lag (PILL) and show you how even just earning income that is variable instead of linear can help you to break free of the Income Trap, save and invest more easily, do away with budgeting and even pay less tax.

> ## The more regularly you need money, the more expensive it is.
> *Matthew Klan*

Something as simple as a little savings can make you less dependent on a salary, and if you can get free of short-term thinking, you will be able to start thinking bigger picture, working for opportunity and focusing on growth—of yourself, your career, your business—and your wealth-creating potential.

A Quick Recap

There is no greater unacknowledged addiction in the modern world than the one we have to income. Earning an income encourages us to consume, rather than produce. Regularly exchanging our hours for dollars can put a limit on what we think we are worth, as well as give us the illusion that the value of our currency is stable. It conditions us to think short term, when creating wealth requires us to think long term, and it can cause us to see money as only an output, when seeing it as an input can be life-changing.

CHAPTER 10

Growth, cycles and the econosystem

Getting in touch with the network of minds.

Previous chapters in part II explored the traps that are holding you back from being free. This chapter will give you a glimpse of life outside the Income Trap, free of short-term thinking. When you are free of the nine to five, when you don't need to go to work tomorrow to put food on the table, what does that look like? Why is that so important, and what are you free to then do? You are free to grow, to look for opportunities instead of short-term fixes, to get in touch with the econo-system and to tap into the power of the network of minds.

> **Live each season as it passes; breathe the air, drink the drink, taste the fruit, and resign yourself to the influences of each.**
>
> *Henry David Thoreau*

Whether it's shares, property or business, in this chapter we'll explore how wealth is created, and how being in touch with, and aware of, the seasons of money can make you rich.

The Freedom First Wealth Creation Formula

What is 'wealth'?

> **"It takes two minds to create wealth. One free to create, the other free to value."**
>
> *Matthew Klan*

Seems like a pretty important question to ask if you want to get rich! But, too often, we spend years of our life aiming for something without really understanding what it is.

Well, if you get right down to it, wealth is an emergent property of the network of minds.

What does that mean? Simply, that wealth doesn't exist without humans. Wealth is something we create in our minds. It can seem like wealth is 'something out there': assets, gold — tangible stuff. But if all the humans disappeared off the face of the earth tomorrow, all 'wealth' would evaporate too. Even though there would still be gold in the earth, it would have no 'value' without people to give it value.

In the 20th century we saw some simple-looking formulas that have explained complex phenomena—such as $E=mc^2$, which describes the relationship between energy and mass. But more than that, the application of these simple formulas has unleashed tremendous energy.

If you are a budding wealth creator or entrepreneur and you'd like to unleash the unlimited energy of your mind to create wealth, then the one formula you need to know is what I call the 'Freedom First Wealth Creation Formula'.

1 mind free to produce, multiplied by 1 mind free to value = wealth creation

Like $E=mc^2$ this formula looks pretty simple. But can it tell us anything useful? Let's break it down and change some variables to see what we learn.

You might remember from school that if you multiply something by zero, you get zero. So, if you have one mind that produces something but there are no other people to value what you've produced, you've created zero wealth.

1 mind to produce × zero minds to value = zero wealth

Imagine you are Robinson Crusoe and you are stranded on an island. You may build yourself an awesome treehouse, but have you created any wealth? No. But you have created something of value to yourself.

This teaches us an important lesson: *Do what you love, that other people will value.*

Often, in this era of unlimited choices, we are told: Do what you love! While on the face of it, this sounds nice, I'm often reminded of our ancestors who lived in small villages, where

> **Do what you love, that other people will value.**

every day was a struggle for survival. The choice of careers for most people throughout most of history was very limited, but they still managed to find meaning and purpose in what they did.

I remember growing up, being told 'You can't make a living playing computer games.' Well, the truth is, we are so fortunate today that you actually can make a living playing computer games! (In fact, the top two YouTubers of 2017 both ran video game channels, making $16.5 million and $15.5 million respectively.)

It's a great idea to do something you love: in part III I'll show you how to turn a hobby or a skill you didn't know you had, into a business that can set you free. But even the guys who play computer games for a living know that the other half of the Freedom First Wealth Creation Formula is important too: you need to do something that other people value. These YouTubers are not just doing what they love; they are filming, editing and narrating their gameplay so that other people can value it too.

What if we play around with the formula some more?

zero minds to produce × 1 mind to value = zero wealth

Just like before, multiplying by zero gets us zero. Of course, there are not too many situations I can think of where there are zero producers in real life. But this does illustrate an interesting point: *in the modern world we have the balance between producers and consumers completely out of whack.*

Everywhere you look, we are being encouraged to consume, consume, consume. In some cases we've become such sophisticated consumers, some people are afraid that what they produce could never meet their own high standards, so they never embark on a creative endeavour.

On the production side of the equation, small producers are being gobbled up by bigger producers flush with cash in this easy money economy, which ultimately decreases the number of producers in total.

Governments love consolidation of producers too—a few big businesses are easier to regulate, control and hand out favours to. That's why you see so many big businesses down with whatever is the latest political trend. You didn't really think your bank cared about the environment, did you?

While we are all consumers by default, if we want to balance the wealth-creation equation and unleash prosperity, we need to encourage people to produce. A society with only a handful of producers who think in lockstep and aren't really free to produce, plus a population reduced to being consumers, is not a winning formula.

> **In the modern world we have the balance between producers and consumers completely out of whack.**

While people do technically produce at least as much as they consume (unless they are in debt or receiving welfare from state or family) their habits and thinking are defined overwhelmingly by consumption because it is as consumers that they are free to make the most choices.

We have seemingly unlimited choices of things we can buy, see or do with our money. But, by and large, what people produce is decided by someone else: a boss, a teacher and so on. (This is where the 'free to produce' part of the formula is important.)

When we consume, we get in touch with the network of minds. We form the yin to the yang of wealth creation: someone else creates a product or service freely, from their mind, then as consumers we are free to choose to give value to their creation—we decide what we are prepared to pay, and whether we value the new creation enough to buy it at all.

But that is only part of what creates wealth, and it really is the secondary part. So when it comes to creating wealth, thinking predominantly as consumers makes us run the risk that we will view 'getting rich' like we view everything else—as something to 'get'. We want to consume our way to wealth!

Think like a producer

Wealth isn't created by consumers. Consumers value the products that producers create. If they find no value in them, then no wealth is created, but if producers don't produce something to value in the first place, there can be no wealth either!

A *consumer-minded investor* 'buys' a property, for example, because they believe it is the best purchase they can make and it will be better than other purchases such as shares.

A *producer-minded investor*, however, thinks about what they have the skills and experience to produce, and also what others will value.

If the property market is in a downturn, the consumer-minded investor may be fleeing the market, while the producer-minded investor may see that while people are not paying up for the standard three bed/ two bath property, they still need to live somewhere. Maybe people will choose to rent more, and smaller units will do better held for cashflow instead of capital gain. The producer-minded investor may extrapolate out and realise that more renting might lead to more need for storage between moves and invest in storage units instead. They might take the large house that has fallen in value and convert it into several dual key residences, for example. They will be aware of the changing needs of the market because they are in touch with the market. When you put on your producer hat you begin to think 'What will other people value?' The more you can tap into what other people will value, the more wealth you create and the richer you become.

Using the Freedom First Wealth Creation Formula

There are two ways to tweak the Freedom First Wealth Creation Formula to increase the wealth you create.

The first way is to increase the multipliers by.

- *appealing to more consumers.* Instead of multiplying by '1 mind free to value', what if you could have hundreds or even millions of consumers value your product? Would that make you wealthier? Some businesses may be 'service oriented' and feel they are limited by the number of hours in a day, but what if some part of your business could be 'virtualised' and sold online where it can reach the whole world? How to do this comes under 'specialising so you can systemise', a concept we'll touch on in part III.

- *sidestepping the gatekeepers.* An important question to ask when starting a business is 'Who are my customers?' The answer is not always the visible consumers; sometimes it's a gatekeeper, someone who seems to be in a position to deliver your product to many consumers. If a gatekeeper is your real customer then you are down to just '1 mind free to value' your product or service—the gatekeeper themselves. And they may not even be that 'free to value' your product in the first place! It's tempting for a small business to seek out government contracts or the patronage of one big customer, but don't overlook the danger of the Dependence Trap. While there are only a handful of gatekeepers, most of your competition is focused on competing for their attention, leaving you to go directly to the consumer and the market.

- *networking with other producers.* Instead of having '1 mind free to produce'—usually yours—what if you could multiply your productivity by forming strategic partnerships with other producers? You can multiply what you produce and increase the wealth you create.

The second way is to increase freedom, which is an important part of the formula.

It takes two *free* minds to create wealth. As well as increasing the *number* of producers or consumers in the formula, we can increase the *freedom* each has to perform their roles. This can be done by:

- *being a better consumer.* If you are too busy to make effective decisions as a consumer, you'll end up trading money for worthless stuff and decreasing your wealth. People only buy something when they perceive that it's of greater value to them than its price in dollars is. Having the time, or the freedom, to think about what you really value, helps you to make good purchases. Having time on your side is the best way to be able to negotiate as a consumer: buying out of season, buying in advance and buying in bulk can all save you lots of money, but only if you are free enough to be able to do those things.

- *increasing your scope for producing/making yourself freer to produce.* How free are you to produce? Even within a salaried job you can look to increase the amount of freedom and scope you have to produce: you can take on a project that you have a greater degree of control over, for example. You can also look to take a job that gives you more than just a wage; look for work that allows you to develop a skill that you could use outside of work, perhaps in your own business. In chapters 12 and 15 we will look more closely at how you can profit from an increased scope for production.

Finally, you'll notice one thing that's not in the Freedom First Wealth Creation Formula: cutting costs. Finding better, more effective ways to deliver your product or service may be boring, but it can be a legitimate part of 'producing' when it comes to creating wealth. If you create a better *system* for delivering the same product and level of service to your customers, then you are creating something new that's of value, but if you just cut corners to cut costs, you may increase profits in the short term, but you're not creating wealth.

Finding ways to artificially drive down the costs of labour to keep unproductive businesses chugging along is not only as old as slavery, but it's a sure sign that a company, or a country, is no longer able to create and thrive.

Cycles

Now that we've introduced the concept of the network of minds, we can pull back and look at the bigger picture: what happens when you take the small nodes and local connections we've looked at so far, and scale up to the entire world? The network of minds starts looking like an organic system, an ecosystem of wealth creation that I call the econo-system where billions of people make trillions of connections with each other, and just like nature, this econo-system has seasons and cycles to it, and being aware of the organic nature of wealth creation—being aware of these cycles—can make you money.

Many people are aware of consumer cycles: we've all heard of winter sales (though how many people plan ahead based on such sales, as opposed to just using them as a pretext for buying something now, is up for debate). There are even weekly cycles you can track for things like the price of petrol. But cycles exist in more than just consumer products. Cycles exist in markets too: in stocks, property and business.

Lifetime cycles

Probably the biggest cycle that affects all markets, is what I call the lifetime cycle. The lifetime cycle can be understood broadly as the study of demographics. Seen as a group, people do similar things at similar times throughout their lives, on average. We all go to school at the same age; we start our first jobs at similar ages, get married, buy a home, earn more, have kids and save for retirement at roughly predictable stages throughout our lives. These consumer spending cycles allow us to predict what people will be doing and spending at different ages.

Earlier, in chapter 8, I told you that it wasn't debt so much as demographics that allowed me to predict that there would be a significant downturn at the end of the decade. The problem with credit default swaps and the debt bubble itself was just a proximate cause. It turns out that in the United States and other first-world countries we have an ageing population. What that means is that there are more older people than younger people. Now imagine the average older person: are they moving into bigger and bigger houses as their family grows? No, those years are behind them and they are instead likely looking to downsize their homes now that the kids have left and they're getting older. Entering retirement, people not only earn less money, but they often spend less too—except in some areas, like healthcare. So it was relatively easy to predict that the baby boomer generation, which was the largest generation in history (especially compared to the preceding generation, which created a wave-like demand effect as it passed through each stage of life) upon reaching retirement, would have a big impact on many sectors of the economy. We saw not only the price of houses fall, but the cost of healthcare soar.

Decade cycles

People tend to look back on their life in terms of decades: their teens, twenties, thirties and so on. It seems natural for us to think and plan in decades and it turns out that businesses are no different. Businesses tend to plan aggressively for the decade ahead, expand, then once a new decade rolls over they tend to take stock and consolidate. Each decade has been marked by different trends in fashion, music and so on, but it takes time for everyone to decide what the next cool thing will be—what this decade is going to be about. Since it's businesses that sell the fashion and the music, they tend to tread water at the beginning of the decade too. That's why, in the stock market, another name for this cycle is the decade hangover cycle.

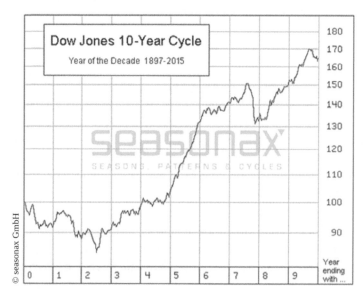

From 1900 to now, only one half of every decade has been responsible for nearly all the gains in the stock market for that 10-year period. It's usually the mid to later years of the decade (1995–99 and so on) that see most of the gains, while the first couple of years of the decade tend to be flat. In fact, almost 40 per cent of the entire gains for the decade tend to happen in the '5' years, on average.

You'll also notice that the '7' years also tends to have a negative return. If you'd simply stayed out of the market in the first two years of each decade, and also skipped the last part of each '7' year, you could have avoided some of the worst corrections and bear markets in the past 100 years (1907, 1920–22, 1930–32, 1937, 1940–42, 1960–62, 1980–82, 1987, 2000–02). The GFC, of course, also had its start in late 2007. (If you'd stayed out of the market from 2000 to 2002 and then got back in, you would have caught one of the biggest booms in history from 2003 to 2007. When the market fell from late 2007 through 2008 it 'only' fell back to where it was at the end of 2002.)

The decade following the GFC didn't follow this cycle closely, but then it wasn't exactly a 'historically normal' period of time following such a once-in-a-lifetime correction. Often it takes one such 'substandard' cycle to pass before the pattern re-asserts itself again.

Yearly cycles

So we've looked at cycles that span years, but there are even predictable cycles within each year, with certain times of the year reliably performing better on average than others. Just as we saw that the vast majority of the gains each decade come from only half of the decade, it turns out the majority of the gains each year come from only a handful of months. The worst months each year tend to be February, June and October in Australia. (They tend to be February, May and September in the United States.)

According to the Hirsch Organisation (www.stocktradersalmanac.com/Strategy .aspx), investing for just the half of the year that has the best months— 1 November to 30 April (February corrections tend to be mild compared to the other two negative periods)—and missing out the worst months, you could have turned US$10 000 invested in 1950 into US$467 103 today, instead of losing US$77 if you'd only invested in the other half of the year!

Just as the decade cycle was based around businesses spending, the yearly cycle seems to be based around other predictable activity too. There is a saying in the market: sell in May and go away. May/June tends to be a negative time in Australia because individuals and fund managers tend to sell their losing stocks before the end of the financial year to lock in a tax deduction. Some mutual funds have their redemption dates or their fiscal years ending in autumn in the United States, which coincides with the yearly September/October period for corrections. However, this only explains a portion of why September and October tend to be historically bad months: some of the worst crashes in history have happened at this time and even stock markets can get superstitious sometimes!

Presidential cycles

Not only do markets respond to when companies plan and spend money, they also react to when governments may spend money.

In the United States there is a fixed election cycle of four years and another stock cycle can be observed in response to this. When a president is heading for re-election, starting in the third year of his term when the campaigning really kicks off, the markets expect and often receive a boost from all the promises of extra spending from both candidates.

On average, 88 per cent of the time, the third year of a presidential term sees an average stock-market return of 16 per cent that year. The first two years of the next term often experience a 'hangover' as the reality of all the promises sets in.

Civilisational cycles

The last few cycles we've covered were stock specific, but of course there are many more cycles that affect all sorts of things—all the way up to civilisational cycles. We certainly are living through historically significant times! Alexander Tytler had a theory of civilisational cycles that says nations pass through predictable stages in their progress from growth to decline:

'From bondage to spiritual faith;

From spiritual faith to great courage;

From courage to liberty;

From liberty to abundance;

From abundance to selfishness;

From selfishness to apathy;

From apathy to dependence;

From dependence back again into bondage.'

This further supports the notion that there is a link between freedom (or liberty) and wealth (or abundance), while reminding us that valuing freedom or liberty takes courage and is something that has to be nourished or it will be forgotten.

Seeing cycles can make you rich

Now, using what we've just learned about cycles, you can see how I was able to predict two major events that many people felt were unpredictable well in advance.

Trends helped me predict an end-of-decade bust in 2002

Using the decade cycle we can see that if there has been a correction at the end of the previous decade, the first two years of a new decade are likely to be flat. From 2000 through 2002 markets trended sideways as we recovered from the Tech Wreck. Knowing that the baby boomers had a few good years in them before the oldest would start to retire, it wasn't hard to see that the next few years from 2002 onwards would see good growth—possibly great growth.

Looking ahead with the decade cycle in mind I knew to be wary of late 2007 (the yearly cycle supported this too), but if the boom didn't bust then, we might have had until as late as 2010, which would be closer to the boomers retiring. Therefore, to my mind, 2003–07 at least would be a fantastic five years to make hay while the sun was shining.

After the GFC, a historic correction, the next 10 years would not be so easy to predict. My best guess at the time was that this would not be a correction we'd bounce straight back from; we could easily see a decade of flat growth following it. No amount of stimulus would make up for the decline in consumer spending, and in fact that stimulus would only increase the gap between the rich and the poor. And sure enough that was what we saw, a decade of stagnating wages and flat growth, while assets in the United States at least were eventually reinflated.

But aside from the price of stocks, big corrections have other, more important effects. Sometimes stock corrections trigger recessions, even depressions. And these affect the average person more than the changes in the price of stocks, as most people are employees and not full-time investors. Stocks falling might hurt their future retirement funds, but losing their jobs affects the food they are putting on their tables now.

In fact in the years that followed, it was these larger effects that to me became easier to predict than the market itself. After the bankers had seen their businesses saved, and Wall Street and rating agencies had gotten away without a single person held accountable, cracks had started appearing in the system. At the time of the GFC, the bank bailouts were opposed by 75 per cent of all voters, regardless of party.

After the Great Depression in 1929 there were huge changes in geopolitics. Wasn't it obvious that coming out of the GFC, a financial crash of historic proportions, as well as the decade after it, during which the average voter was still feeling the effects of the crash, would make political change more likely, rather than less?

Cycles helped me predict the unpredictable election

The 2016 US presidential election was regarded by many to be one of the most historic and unique elections in living memory—and also the one that the greatest number of people failed to predict.

Looking back though, it surprises me that anyone was expecting things to continue along the same path. At the very least, people should have expected some change. The movement that came to be known as Occupy Wall Street, for example, should have alerted people that business as usual wasn't going to be tolerated for long from either side of politics, especially when, for the 2016 election, it looked like the two major parties were planning to offer the electorate Clinton versus Bush Round 2—the definition of politics as usual.

Predicting elections

While the smartest way to take advantage of a presidential election may be to hedge your stocks accordingly based on the four-year presidential cycle, what most people are interested in is can the elections themselves be predicted?

Two of the most accurate predictors of presidential elections are independent models by Professors Allan Lichtman (30-year track record) and Helmut Norpoth (20-year record), which take into account things like: Has the same party held the office of president for two terms? Is the economy good or bad? These models ignore all the usual things you are supposed to think are important—such as polls and policies—and in fact just these two factors (incumbency and flat economy) by themselves heavily favour the challenger to win.

But, larger political cycles aside, what also encouraged me to take a position on the 2016 election was what investors call a 'market mispricing'.

Market mispricing

Stock markets and other markets rely on good, accurate information to help people judge what an asset should be worth. Sometimes, for various reasons, the markets get bad information. This bad information leads people to value something for less (or more) than what it should be worth. When this happens, it's often not long before the correct information gets out and the asset moves back up in value to a price that more accurately reflects what the asset should be worth. Think of a property that everyone says is full of mould, is falling apart, and there's a rumour that it's about to be condemned: all this information would cause people to put a low value on it. But once people actually go and look at the house, maybe run it by a building inspector, and find out that there is actually nothing wrong with it, the price should shoot back up.

So what I noticed occurring with the Trump candidacy was what I considered a market mispricing. News outlets had Trump's chances at winning the primaries, and the election, at irrationally low odds. I planned to take advantage of that by placing a 'trade' prior to the conclusion of the primaries. I was sure that once Trump won the primary, people (the media) would finally realise his real chance of winning the election had to be close to 50 per cent—after all there are plenty of people on both sides who will vote for whoever the 'official' candidate is, as long as they have the R or D after their name—at which point, if I wanted to, I could have made a nice profit before the election was even held, by selling the contracts that had been mispriced early on, for closer to their 'true' value.

But rather than reflect this, the polls and the markets stubbornly kept Trump's odds low. Some had him at a 5 per cent chance of winning *after* he won the nomination. This was insane. But it was the kind of insanity I was familiar with leading up to the GFC. Rationality had been banished, emotions and wishful thinking took over and a bubble of disbelief was created from every news outlet, keeping his odds low and necessitating that I hold my position. In the end, I made $100 000 from predicting the 'unpredictable'!

The strangest thing about the whole experience for me wasn't the worldwide media attention I received as a result of the trade, but the angry reaction of some people. These were people who knew that I had predicted the housing crash years before, and even profited from it, without for a second feeling like I *caused* it.

We are living through revolutionary times and, looking forward, I predict that things are going to get crazier before they get calmer. Old political labels will become meaningless. This period of division will resolve, however, and a new equilibrium will eventually form. These political re-alignments happen quite regularly throughout history, but it can be hard to recognise it's happening after a lifetime of familiarity with the same two major parties.

Whatever your political views are right now, this message is for everyone: as the world changes around us everyone deserves a chance to be financially free, to live their best life and to make their own highest contribution.

> **If liberty means anything at all, it means the right to tell people what they do not want to hear.**
>
> *George Orwell*

I suggest you don't spend too much time at first worrying about multi-decade, political or civilisational cycles: in fact, getting lost in the big picture is a distraction if your mental horizon is consumed by the short term—if you are living pay cheque to pay cheque.

Get started noticing trends

You don't need to be able to predict a once-in-a-lifetime correction to profit from an awareness that there are trends, cycles and seasons to the econo-system. Realising that your industry might be changing, that the era of reliable retirement pensions is ending and that higher education does not guarantee the prosperity it once did are all trends to be aware of that can greatly impact the course of your life.

Beyond passive income: applying what you've learned

In chapter 9 I shared with you the covered call strategy, which in some ways is the 'perfect' almost-passive income strategy. At least that's how it's often promoted. I prefer to think of it as an active income strategy, or better, an active dividend strategy.

In certain situations, it pretty much is a risk-free way to actively generate some extra income from an asset with very little time — and far less money outlaid than for an investment property, for example. The way writing covered calls works is this: if you own 100 shares in a company, you may be able to write a covered call against them.

We learned earlier that when someone buys a call option they are buying a contract that gives them the right (but doesn't obligate them) to buy a parcel of shares, at a given price, for a set period of time. The reason they would do this is because they believe the shares are going to rise in value, and they'd like to 'lock in' a price they can buy them at in the future, if they go up. If they don't rise, at least they haven't forked out a lot of money to buy shares that then fall in value. You can buy these contracts through a broker in the same way as you buy shares.

However, if you are someone who owns a parcel of shares, you might want to write or 'sell' these contracts to buyers, giving them the right to possibly buy your shares in the future, in exchange for some 'rental' income right now. Again, although this sounds tricky, it is something you can just get a broker to do for you.

When you 'write' an option (you don't have to actually write anything, you just choose one) you can choose how long the option will last for, what price it will allow someone to buy your shares for and how much you want to sell it for.

If you own shares that are worth $10 today, that you'd be happy to sell if they ever go up in value, you might 'option' your shares for $11, and pocket perhaps a couple of hundred dollars of income for doing so. On some shares you can do this each month.

Each month that your shares stay flat, you keep the income and the option expires. If your shares go down, well, at least earning some income helped offset that. If your shares do rise in value, say above $11 by the end of the month, you may be 'forced' to sell them. (You don't have to sell your shares; you can always simply buy back the option contracts you sold, however this may cost you more than you got paid for the contracts initially.) After the month has finished you can write another option the next month, perhaps at a higher price if the shares have risen.

Imagine being able to generate 0.5 per cent, even 1 per cent, of income per month. That would be an extra 12 per cent return per year—on top of the dividends you already receive! Some people go so far as to claim you can generate even more per month (you can, but there is a cost to this which no-one explains).

The hidden risk with this strategy is that it could cost you some growth: markets move in cycles and most of the gains that occur even in good years tend to happen in the space of a few months. If you are forced to sell your shares (that were worth $10) when they rise in value, you might be selling shares for $11 that have actually risen higher than that in value. For some passive investors who are perhaps well into retirement, this doesn't bother them: they are happy to receive the extra income from writing options, as well as the capital gain that results from selling their shares for a little higher than what they were worth. But everyone else who wants their money to grow over the long term should be aware of this. Because this 'cost' is invisible (while the income is visible) most people never notice it.

What bugs me is that some people sell this covered call strategy as a passive income strategy, appealing perhaps to people stuck in the Income Trap, when with just a little awareness this can actually be a much more profitable active income or active dividend strategy.

Pitfalls of being passive

The worst part is when these people appeal to greed and advertise that you can make 1 per cent, 2 per cent even 3 per cent per month! You can make more money from writing covered calls, the more 'in the money' you write them. When you are giving people the right to buy your shares for $11—as in our example (while your shares are currently worth $10)—you are writing what is called an 'out of the money' covered call. The share would have to rise above $11 for you to get exercised (and have to sell your shares).

You can make higher rental returns, though, if you instead write an option that is 'at the money' or 'in the money', giving someone the right to buy your shares by the end of the month for $10 or even $9*. However, encouraging people to do this passively every month just means they will get exercised and forced to sell their shares all the time. Staying stuck in the 'income' frame and trying to increase your returns in this way will just end up costing you money.

*If your brain is going 'Hang on, who would want to sell the rights to buy their shares for less than what they are currently worth?' stop right now—don't panic, you don't need to understand this. This is just an example of how we can apply principles we're learning to even 'sophisticated' strategies. The truth is though, that this stuff is much easier to learn than you'd think, and I've successfully taught many people to get their heads around these concepts in a matter of days.

Making a good strategy great, with an awareness of cycles

We saw earlier that a share strategy that involved buying shares and holding them during the best half of the year, and selling everything and sitting out during the worst half of the year could be a very profitable use of an awareness of cycles. However, it would involve the transaction costs and tax costs of selling all your shares every year.

By using options instead, you could write 'in the money' call options, 'renting out' your shares for much higher premiums only during the months that the market is likely to be flat or declining, and abstain from writing calls during the months the market is likely to rise—maximising your earnings, while minimising the chance you may have to sell your shares and miss out on growth. You could even add to this strategy by going the other way and writing puts during the best months of the year, when it's most likely shares will rise! (I haven't even touched on writing put options. We discussed how you might buy a put option to insure your shares, but did you know that you could write a put option and get paid money to buy shares? Once you start learning this stuff, the possibilities are endless.)

By unplugging your mind from the Income Trap, becoming aware of seasons and taking a more active approach to generating income, the covered call strategy can be an excellent way for you to actively generate extra returns from your shares, without giving up the growth.

Don't worry if this section seems confusing at first: what I wanted to show with this example is that straight line thinking and the allure of passive income, can blind you to growth, while an awareness of cycles can see you generate higher active returns without giving up your growth at all.

Why is this so important? Well, first we need to understand the power of growth, as well as take a glimpse into how billionaires think about growth, which those stuck in the Income Trap can learn from.

Growth

The stories surrounding chess go back almost as far as the great game itself, which current estimates place at over 1400 years. From the earliest days of chess it was more than just a game; it was also a teaching tool that captured people's imaginations, and was often used as a metaphor to help transmit complex ideas, such as the power of growth.

One chess story from India involved a king and a travelling sage. As a gift to the king, the sage invented for him a novel new game called chaturanga, or what came to be known as chess. So impressed was the king with the new game that he offered the sage any reward he could name. The sage thanked the king profusely and said, 'All I would ask of your majesty is a single grain of rice for the first square on the chess board, two grains for the second, four for the third and so on — doubling each square.'

At first the king thought this too modest a request, but the sage insisted and being a man of his word the king assented to the request. However, he quickly realised that he could never fulfil it. After doubling for several squares the amount quickly grew so large that all the rice in India, and indeed the world, would not be enough to repay the debt: the 20th square alone would require 1 000 000 grains of rice, and the 40th square 1 000 000 000 grains. By the 64th and final square the king would have to have given the sage over 18 quintillion grains of rice, more than enough to cover the entire surface of the earth several inches deep, or enough to create a pile of rice larger than Mount Everest! Just as the king was trying to think of how he could repay his debt (or have the impudent sage killed) the sage revealed himself to be Lord Krishna himself, who told the king he could repay his debt over time. And so the tradition of serving Paal Payasam to visiting pilgrims was said to have started, and the immensely powerful concept of exponential or compounding growth was also illustrated in a way people could understand.

Tech billionaires and growth

If anyone should understand the power of growth, it's PayPal co-founder Peter Theil. Peter is not only famous for starting PayPal, he was also the first outside investor in Facebook, buying a 10.2 per cent share in the company for $500 000. He later cashed in the majority, but not all, of his holdings for over $1 billion. His success as a venture capitalist in Silicon Valley is legendary. A character called Peter Gregory in the hit TV series Silicon Valley was even based on him and his unique approach to investing.

So, considering Peter's skill at growing a small company into a giant, and spotting other seedling companies that were about to grow huge, I found his answers to the following questions quite revealing.

Peter did an 'AMA' or Ask Me Anything session on the website Reddit where, for a few hours, he fielded questions from all over the internet. One user (called 'papabearshoe'—where do they get these names from?) asked him what was the worst investment he'd ever made and what lessons he learned from it.

Now, if you are like most people you would expect Peter to answer with an example of an investment that lost him money. But here's what he said:

Biggest mistake ever was not to do the Series B round at Facebook.

What Peter is saying here is so important if you want to understand the power of growth. The worst investment he ever made was not something he invested in that lost him money—or even an investment that he didn't make. We all can look back at investments we should have gotten into.

No, the biggest mistake he ever made in investing was not to take the opportunity to invest more money in Facebook when he had the chance to, in the second round of funding. Most people would be happy turning half a million into well over $1 billion dollars, which is what Peter did with his first-round investment in Facebook. But by not adding to his initial investment, he missed the chance to multiply his money more than 2000 times.

How many failed investments could you do where you lost 100 per cent of the money you put out there, if one investment grew your money over 2000 times? That one missed opportunity was as costly as doing thousands of investments where he lost 100 per cent. But as humans we are prone to want to avoid losses at all costs, and we find it hard to wrap our straight line thinking brains around the power of growth.

Another user called 'byalik' asked Peter what had been the most difficult mental barrier to his success.

Peter answered:

Even when one understands that exponential growth and exponential forces are incredibly important, it is still hard to internalise this.

At the time of the launch, PayPal was growing at 7 per cent per day. Peter continued:

We did not fully fathom the rocket we were riding.

Growth is far more powerful than loss. What Peter understands is that *if you plant a seed, and it doesn't sprout, you've only lost a seed. But if you plant a seed and it grows, it can grow into a mighty oak, a million times the size of the little seed it came from.*

We referred to this, in chapter 8, as optionality: the ability to put a small investment — of your time, or your money — into something where what you have to lose is limited, but what you stand to gain is potentially unlimited. The heart of optionality, the secret to how it works, is the power of growth.

Beyond compound interest

If you've ever read a financial planning book, you might recognise this 'power of growth' as a concept called compound interest.

> **The best investment you can make is in yourself!**

But compound interest is simply one example of the deeper law of growth. In fact, applying the power of growth to savings, while you work a job your whole life and never touch the savings (you have to start early to really see a good effect from this) seems to me to be the least exciting way you can harness the power of growth, and the most boring way to tap into the power of savings too!

Rather than rely on your money growing passively while you work to feed it, there are much more direct ways you can tap into the power of growth: out of all the possible assets you could have, the one that has the most potential to grow is you.

The best investment you can make is in yourself!

Growth versus fixed mindset

Dr Carol Dweck of Stanford University believes that most people adhere to either a fixed mindset (where they mistakenly believe that their abilities are fixed) or a growth mindset (where they believe they can grow their capabilities by way of effort, struggle and failure).

While I don't agree with Dr Dweck that we can sort people into either a fixed or growth mindset, I do think that there is tremendous power in opening your mind up to opportunities and possibilities for growth.

In fact, if exposed to the right conditions, anyone, regardless of mindset, can and will begin to grow. For example, most people have experienced how much you can learn and how rapidly you grow the first year in a new job or business.

If you want to unlock your potential to grow, it can be as simple as getting freer first. Get free of your comfortable rut, put yourself in a position to grow and connect yourself to the network of minds.

> **...if exposed to the right conditions, anyone, regardless of mindset, can and will begin to grow.**

Why is it so important to have a growth mindset and be open to learning new things and growing?

Because wealth isn't earned, it isn't found — it's created, and grown.

Plugging into the econo-system

> **Being aware of cycles is one thing, being in touch with them is another.**
> *Matthew Klan*

The final trap that comes from not being free is the 'lack of feedback trap'. You don't get the same feedback from the network of minds when you are insulated from it by the boundaries of your job. You may work with customers, but the network of minds includes all the producers, suppliers, customers and clients that the business you work for deals with. As an employee, you may listen to what customers tell you, but it's not until you can measure all the costs and see for yourself what customers are prepared to pay for that you will truly know what they value. Lack of feedback extends to the cycles and seasons of the econo-system too. Jobs, salaries and passive investing all shield us from direct and timely feedback from the market. While we are all aware of the seasons in nature, there is a reason why you should ask a farmer what the weather is going to do, and not an office worker.

David had become freer to produce. His boss had put him on commission, because he was often sick and had missed so much work that he didn't want to pay him a regular salary. But the freedom that came from being able to control how much he worked had unleashed the fire in David. Not only was he making more money than before, but his illness had stopped flaring up so often.

However, this new productivity came with a cost. David's boss started to get almost resentful of the money he was making (despite the fact that he was making the business more money too). Clients were coming to the shop and asking for him by name. His boss started to pay him later and later. Things were coming to a head. Would David retreat from his new freedom back to a salary, perhaps with another boss? Or would he double down and shoot for even more freedom now that he'd had a taste of it?

One day the decision was taken out of his hands, and David lost his job. Realising that his security (or at least the illusion of it) was gone, initially created a panic—over the course of a weekend David got busy registering a business name, cleaning out an office under his house, and on Monday he picked up the phone with trepidation and made his first 'sales call': someone he'd done good work for repairing computers in the past.

He later told me how terrifying that first call felt, but it was a success—he landed some work and his first client.

David didn't do everything perfectly at once. But what's amazing was how something simple—getting free and getting in touch with the market—actually started to lead him in the right direction naturally.

At first he had done what many people starting a small business do: he started out as a generalist. (When you are not used to living outside the Income Trap it's tempting to want to try to be all things to all people to get as much work as possible early on. In part III we'll look at why you want to specialise so you can systemise.)

But then something interesting happened: the market told David what to specialise in if he wanted to prosper.

In his old job, David had done the work that the boss had given him. But in his own business, David was in touch with the network of minds. He knew first-hand what it was that consumers were willing to pay for, and what he could produce with other suppliers at the lowest cost. More and more people came to him wanting to get their mobile phones fixed, and the computer repairs he was initially doing took a back seat.

The market had led him to find a niche business.

Maybe it was because of a downturn that more people were repairing rather than upgrading their phones; maybe it was because the constant increase in features that phones had had since smart phones first burst onto the market, was reaching diminishing returns.

The point is, David didn't sit at home while working a job, researching current trends in an attempt to predict what the next niche business would be before starting his business. He started his business first, and got connected to the network of minds. With a mind open to growth opportunities, he let the market tell him what to focus on, and it told him to specialise. And that's when his business really took off.

A Quick Recap

There is a 'nature' to the economy that being stuck in the previous traps can isolate us from. Getting in touch with the network of minds, applying the Wealth Creation Formula, and observing and responding to the cycles and seasons of the econo-system can unlock our potential to grow and to find what we love doing that other people will value.

PART III

Getting free first

CHAPTER 11
Free from the short term

Specialise so you can systemise. The power of savings.

'I've got some news for you. Can we meet for lunch?' Melissa asked, touching base for the first time in months.

'Sure,' I replied.

I wondered what surprise she'd have in store for me this time. She tended to decide on something and act on it, and I'd been filling her head with all this talk of freedom, and building up the pain of the 'job for life path' the past few months. Not that she needed much encouragement to get sick of working in one place for long anyway as she'd proved the last time we'd met, surprising me with news that she had flexed her new-found freedom and quit the job that had promised her much, but was going nowhere.

'I think I'm going to quit my job,' Melissa informed me.

'Oh, you're telling me in advance this time?'

'I've been thinking and I don't really want to just replace one job with another one this time. I think it might be time to be free of a boss for good!'

I guess I should have seen this coming. But with the GFC only just starting she still caught me by surprise.

'Oh really, what are you thinking?' I asked.

'Things are getting pretty tense at work… I thought I could start a photography business. Every so often the office gets a flyer or some marketing from local photographers looking to pick up some work. I know I can do the photography side of the business to a good standard. I've had plenty of experience, and to be honest, looking at some of the marketing we get, I'm pretty sure I could do that to a similar or better standard too.

'Remember how you told me if I saved up some money in a freedom account, I'd start to see ways that money could be an input as well as an output? Well, when I started doing photography for the agency I had a professional camera already. I think it was part of the reason I got hired! Anyway, after starting work I quickly realised that I'd need a wide-angle lens as well if I wanted to produce the best possible photos. The boss was already getting me to use my own equipment at work, so I put it to him that if he didn't want to invest in an office camera he could at least go me halves in a new lens for my camera. And he agreed.

'That was one of the first things that I "invested" some of my freedom savings in. I didn't have any plans at the time, just a feeling, but now that I'm thinking of starting a business, I've already got a lot of the equipment covered.

'The thing is, though, I'm not really sure how to actually start, or even what I should exactly be doing. I'm pretty sure the boss will be quite happy to continue to work with me as a contractor—it'll solve one of his problems by having one less salary to pay—and most of the agents at the office would continue to use me, I think, but of course there isn't enough work at just this office to support doing photography full time. So what should I do? Should I look into other types of photography I could offer, to get more work, like weddings or baby photography?' Melissa asked.

'Wow, it sounds like this idea has been building for a while. And, good question. Should you be a specialist or a generalist?' I replied.

'I totally get the temptation to start as a generalist,' I continued. 'Starting a business and stepping away from a salary and the Income Trap can be liberating, but part of the reason income can be so addictive is that it provides an illusion of security. Going without that at first can be a shock, and for most people who've spent their life in

the Income Trap their first instinct can be to quickly fill up their time with bookings to "replace" their income. Starting as a generalist is often what people do to attempt to quickly fill up their days with work.

'But we know that freedom leads to wealth — so don't be too quick to fill up your hours — it's better to invest time in creating a system that delivers a lot of value to customers than it is to spend your time "getting busy", trying to please everyone and satisfying no-one, just so you have "income". But if you think about it for a second, it's actually kind of selfish to be a generalist too.'

'Selfish? How do you figure that?' Melissa replied.

'Remember the Wealth Creation Formula?' I asked her. 'Your job is to produce, and it's the consumer's job to value. So, you want to produce the maximum value you can for consumers, if you want to create wealth.

'When you are thinking of being a generalist you are focused on yourself, and getting yourself as many customers as you can. You're not focused on providing the best possible value to a customer. The saying goes that if you are a jack-of-all-trades you'll be a master of none. You want to be a master,' I explained.

'Well it's true that even though I was trained in photography, after doing real estate photography for a while I can say that the quality of my work definitely improved. I imagine it's the same for other types of photography as well,' Melissa observed.

'Exactly. So being a specialist works better with the Freedom First Wealth Creation Formula and it may help you detox from the Income Trap by forcing you to focus on creating a system and not just chasing income. In fact, this second point is one of the most important reasons to specialise.

'You want to specialise, so you can systemise.'

Specialise so you can systemise

Choosing to specialise, so you can systemise, is an important principle if you want to get financially free, regardless of whether you are starting a business or learning an investment skill (we'll look at an example with property investing later). But for most people, their first chance to really experience the power of systemising comes while working a job.

There are many disadvantages to a job, one of which is how little freedom you have to control the inputs, as we addressed earlier. But the one redeeming feature of a job is also its biggest selling point—the regularity and 'predictability' of income. It does at least allow you one area that you can control: what you choose to do with the outputs.

You could say that a job is designed to turn hours of your life into income. And, while chapter 9 explained the downside of that, the regularity of income does allow for those who value their freedom to get their first experience with the power of systemising, and its ability to set you free.

Systemise your savings

For the one year of my life that I worked a job as a salaried professional, one of the first things I set up was an automatic savings account. I wasn't used to wage income, so I found it novel to play around with systemising my income. Many places suggest that you should 'pay yourself first' and set up an 'emergency fund', where you opt to have a portion of your salary go straight into a bank account separate from your normal transaction account.

This is all good advice as far as it goes, but I was always motivated more by freedom than security, so when I realised I could get my boss to direct my salary to different accounts, I wondered how I could take advantage of this to free myself from more than just 'emergencies'. In the end I had my salary split and paid into five different accounts: freedom savings, freedom from debt, freedom from bills, freedom from expenses, and freedom for fun.

1. Freedom savings account

If you only do one thing from this section, do this: set up an automatic money transfer that directs *at least 10 per cent* of your salary into a separate account (you can ask your employer to do this on your behalf, or you can usually set up your online banking to do it too. If all else fails you can do what some people do and revert to an envelope system, cashing, and then dividing up your pay cheque as soon as you get it into separate envelopes).

As a young guy, I was directing 30 per cent of my income into this account. I didn't have debt, or dependants, and I had a different view on saving than most people. I didn't envision working a job for the rest of my life, nor did I have any desire to live below my means while scrimping and saving forever either. There's a reason why I call this a freedom savings account—not just a savings account. It's because, as I've pointed out before, siphoning off some savings from your salary is an excellent first step for getting freer, and a good *short-term* strategy. Constantly saving while working a job for the rest of your life? Not so much.

Working and saving in Australia

A Members Equity Bank survey found that almost two-thirds of Australians saw no increase in their incomes in the last financial year. Also, one in four people had less than $1000 in the bank, with half of those people having less than $100.

But what about emergencies? Should you set aside an emergency amount of money first, before saving for freedom?

Putting aside money for emergencies is great. In fact, it's the little emergencies that tip a struggling family, living pay cheque to pay cheque, over the edge. But it's not the 'unforeseen emergencies' that are really the problem: accidents and emergencies strike everyone.

The problem is being stuck in the short term without the freedom to respond when life throws you a curveball.

Free yourself from the short term

If you are poor, you don't need to be saving for retirement. I'd even say you don't need to be saving for emergencies.

You do need to be saving to buy back some time now, not in 30 years. Buy yourself some breathing room — you need to be freeing yourself from the short term.

People think that the biggest improvement in their lives would come from just having more income. But there are plenty of people with higher incomes living pay cheque to pay cheque, as well as plenty of other people with lower incomes who have more freedom from the short term.

> **The biggest improvement comes when you go from having no economic freedom to having even a little economic freedom.**

The biggest improvement comes when you go from having no economic freedom to having even a little economic freedom.

There are a thousand ways that living on the edge, stuck in the Income Trap, makes life more expensive without ever encountering an emergency. Maybe you'd like to buy stuff in bulk at better prices, but you've only ever got enough money to make do now. Maybe a great opportunity comes up, but you can't afford a sitter to watch the kids so you can't take advantage of it. Just being able to live a little beyond the day to day opens up huge opportunities to save money. Not to mention the opportunities to make money that appear when you free your mind from the short term, step back from chaos, and survey the big picture. Besides, if you free yourself from the short term you have already given yourself a buffer against many emergencies.

Saving for emergencies, *without saving*

One problem with an emergency account or fund is that the money needs to be available instantly. This means that most people end up putting a chunk of money into a standard bank account to have it instantly accessible. The downside of this is that you could have a few thousand dollars sitting idle in a transaction account, earning no interest, for the off chance that you might have an emergency. This is where a credit card can be useful if you have no debt problems. A credit card with a zero balance is like having thousands of dollars sitting there ready to be used in an emergency, and you won't be punished by low interest on your savings.

You can instead direct your freedom savings account money straight into an investment account like an online savings account or an index fund or shares. Having taken care of the emergency with your credit card, you then have time to transfer money from your freedom savings account (where it's earning higher interest) and free yourself from the short-term debt.

Psychologically, having a separate credit card for emergencies can work well to stop you dipping into your 'emergency' fund for anything that isn't really an emergency. (You might even put it behind glass in a picture frame with the words 'break glass in emergency' written on it!), and it also leaves you free to view your Freedom Savings as just that: savings to be used to free you.

When it comes to emergencies, what most people end up doing is overspending on a category I call variable expenses. Then come bill time, they find themselves short of money, so they dip into their emergency account. A bill is *not* an emergency. Don't worry, in a minute I'll show you how to free yourself from ever having to worry about bills again.

> **A bill is *not* an emergency.**

2. Freedom from debt account

This is a second account you can direct your salary into for the purpose of paying off your debt. (We talked about how to prioritise paying off your various debts in chapter 9.) Once you've paid off a debt, the money you directed into this account can be redirected towards your freedom savings account. Just setting up an automatic payment plan to tackle your debt won't free you from debt instantly, but it will free you from constantly worrying about debt for good.

Freeing your mind from the short term is important. By systemising where your income goes you can free yourself from debt, and free yourself to dream.

But there is still the day-to-day drudgery of worrying about bills, the tedium of budgeting, and the constant worry about spending too much on fun things and ending up short.

When I was systemising my salary I didn't want to obsess over the minutiae of a budget; I didn't want to spend every fortnight wondering if there was enough money to pay the bills and I didn't want to go out on a Friday night worrying about spending the rent money ... so I wondered if there was a permanent way I could solve these problems and not have to think about them — so my mind could be free.

3. Freedom from bills account

How great would it be to never have to worry about paying a bill again?

To never worry about making the rent or mortgage payment? By setting up a freedom from bills account you can do just that.

If you think about it, expenses in life are either predictable, or variable. Your freedom from bills account is set up to deal with the *predictable expenses* that don't vary based on your activity. Debt repayment plans can come out of here too if you don't want a separate account (keeping it separate can help you to see the progress you are making). This is an account that will take care of all the 'big' expenses that come up regularly and frequently — such as rent or mortgage payments — or infrequently — such as insurance and registration. These big expenses often end up overdrawing people's accounts.

To set it up you can deposit the first couple of weeks' savings you make in your freedom savings account to 'seed' this account. After all, freeing yourself from worrying about bills is a pretty good use of freedom savings.

Some people choose tax time to start this account and use their tax refund to seed it instead.

The reason you seed the account first is that you might get a rush of these bills all at once; by putting a little money into this account first, you'll be able to cover these.

Once it's seeded, sit down and tally up all the annual expenses you can predict: rent, mortgage, insurance, phone plans, registration, services, memberships— everything that you spend money on that is a predictable amount.

Divide the total yearly amount by 52 to come up with a weekly payment — or 26 if you get paid fortnightly — to work out a freedom-from-bills amount to deduct from your pay and direct into this account. Simple, right?

Then there are the variable expenses. Most people lump all variable spending into one account, but I like to separate it out into two categories, which I think is important psychologically: freedom from expenses (the boring stuff that's variable) and freedom for fun (the fun stuff that's variable).

4. Freedom from expenses account

Boring expenses that are variable can include groceries, fuel, work lunches and so on: stuff you spend money on each month that's not fun, but varies based on your consumption. For this account, you are going to have to estimate how much you spend; keeping your receipts for a few weeks can help with this. (Some bills that do vary based on your consumption, like your electricity bill, technically can go in here, but being a big bill that only comes a few times a year you might choose to estimate the average amount and put it in your freedom from bills account instead. I like to think of the freedom from bills account as the one that covers all the big stuff that you don't actively buy. You actively buy your groceries each week — and therefore can more easily control how much you spend — but you don't 'buy' your electricity in any meaningful sense.)

Note that I'm not asking you to budget at all here. When I set this account up for myself I wasn't poring over my grocery shopping receipts and eliminating things, or taking a bag lunch to work. I was trying to simply separate out what I was actually spending, on average, on mundane stuff and have that amount available in a separate account.

When I worked out a weekly amount to cover this I allowed a little margin, and if I went over I had to dip into the final account: the freedom for fun account.

5. Freedom for fun account

Finally, how good would it feel to know that there is an amount set aside you can spend with no guilt, however you want, without fear that you won't be able to afford to eat or pay the rent?

This is the beauty of a freedom for fun (or freedom to spend) account. Many people happily spend money on stuff that's fun, and run out of money for the stuff that's not, until they can't even enjoy spending money on the stuff that's fun anymore! But, with this account, you can spend this money however you want, and if you blow it all before payday—no worries!

The objective, in setting these accounts up, is not to budget but to simply systemise *the money you are already spending*. Once you have a set amount of money to spend on fun, with no risk of cutting into other necessary spending like rent or food, it starts to become natural and automatic to think more carefully about what you spend your money on. Unlike traditional budgets, you're not denying yourself luxuries so you can pay for boring necessities; you are instead learning to choose what luxuries—which fun stuff—gives you the biggest bang for your buck. You learn to really ensure that you get enjoyment out of the money you spend, which is a much more positive skill to learn than denying yourself pleasure out of guilt.

The good thing about separating out the boring variable stuff from the fun variable stuff is that without thinking about it, it becomes natural for most people to start to want to spend carefully on the stuff that really doesn't give them pleasure either, like making sure you don't overpay on fuel, or overpay on groceries. If you overspend on boring stuff, it directly eats into the stuff you really do enjoy spending money on. And if you spend more wisely on shopping you can end up with a surplus that you can put into your fun account! You might find you want to examine some of those fixed expenses we mentioned earlier too, if doing so can directly lead to a surplus in your freedom from bills account that you can do something more pleasurable with. You could shop around for a better mortgage rate, or insurance, or subscriptions and so on.

In fact, a lot of people find that something else even more powerful starts to happen: having started to enjoy seeing their savings grow in their freedom savings account, they often become motivated to find surpluses in their other accounts and *direct those to their freedom savings account*, and not just to the fun account.

The most important step by far is to automate the savings. Once you see that savings amount grow, for many people the rest starts to take care of itself. Once you see that this money can be used for bigger things—like investing, starting a business, getting qualifications or buying equipment you can use to generate extra income—you naturally start to lose interest in just 'consuming' stuff all the time. The vast majority of financial planning advice is based on the assumption that you are an employee who just wants to consume. The best cure for over consumption isn't to try to deny and punish yourself, or 'hide' your money from yourself, but to discover something better you can do with your money, discover the power of producing instead of consuming, and start to see how money can be an 'input' instead of just the 'output' of your job.

At some point, all this systemising of your salary can be like organising deck chairs on the *Titanic*—there are bigger issues. But what's most important, is that while the act of budgeting is fighting against your values, systemising your spending like this can help you to change what you value.

> **Once you establish the correct value for money it becomes natural to save it and to want to see it grow.**

Freedom First is about developing a *healthy* view on money. Money is valuable, it shouldn't be something you try to ignore, but you shouldn't obsess over it either by feeling guilty or 'punishing' yourself. You want to appreciate that money can give you choices. Having the freedom to choose, to not waste money on things that don't bring you value, while having the freedom to actually do the things that you do value is the ultimate goal. And as we know, while half of all millionaires operate on a strict, planned-out-in-advance, annual budget, the other half doesn't. Once you establish the correct value for money it becomes natural to save it and to want to see it grow.

A Quick Recap

Specialise so that you can *systemise*. One of the quickest ways to free up your time, and free your mind from worrying about debt, bills and expenses, is to create systems. Freedom First is about developing a healthy view on money, allowing you to spend guilt-free, as well as making it automatic to want to see your savings grow. A little savings is all it takes to start to get free from the short term.

CHAPTER 12

Freedom is having more choices

You are a business already.

> **"Nothing is more difficult, and therefore more precious, than to be able to decide."**
>
> *Napoleon Bonaparte*

'Okay, so I can see why I'd want to be a specialist instead of a generalist; and to be honest, it's a bit of a relief to have permission to focus on my real estate photography instead of offering to do every type of photography. It's a bit scary though, to think that might mean I miss out on some bookings early on.

'If I'm going to focus on doing real estate photography, do I have to come up with a unique angle? I mean, why are people going to book me unless I offer something different?' Melissa asked.

'I know it might seem easy to you,' she continued 'but the thought of starting a business is so alien to me — where do you even start?'

'Well, the easiest answer to both those questions is to realise that you are a business already,' I replied.

Often when faced with starting a business, it's the scary 'unknowns' that stop a lot of people before they've even started: 'How will I deal with tax?', 'Do I need to know a lot of legal stuff?' — practical things that seem daunting at first from the outside. Coming up, I'll give you an insight into how the tax system really works, but the truth is that a lot of these 'procedural' concerns aren't the hurdles most people fear.

You are a business already

If you think back to your education and then to your first job, how much of your education prepared you for the actual practical realities of doing your job? If you were lucky your education taught you a skill you could use; in my case, my physiotherapy degree taught me some of what I needed to actually do physiotherapy on patients, but it taught me nothing about how to work day to day in a hospital, how to navigate the bureaucratic aspects of the job, let alone how to start a private practice. Yet, many of my peers did just that, and started their own businesses straight out of university.

So, in what other ways can working a job be compared to being in business?

In a business, you have a product or service you sell; in a job you sell a service as well (you are like a service-based business)—your 'service' is your job skills, which you were hired for.

In a business, you have customers; in a job, you have a customer who buys your services too: your boss. You 'sell' your customer on your services when you have a job interview. But they're your only customer—lose your one customer, and you are back to square one!

Importantly, as an employee, your business is not unique: plenty of other people have the same skills or received the same education you did, and yet there was still opportunity for you. You didn't have to invent something new that no-one else thought of to get your first customer and start making money (to get hired and start getting paid).

It's the same in any other business: it's not how original, or clever, or new your business idea or product is that often makes the difference. So don't fall into the 'more sophisticated' trap, and think that you have to wait for inspiration to get started in business. If you find that you are coming up with complicated schemes that are a 'sure thing' then you need to take stock—chances are you are trying to avoid failure by coming up with an idea so clever that people will just buy it, and you won't have to risk getting out there and trying to market your product or sell it.

In fact, it's actually more risky to rely on being totally new and innovative. Many businesses with really new ideas often go bust trying to convince or educate the public on why their clever idea is necessary in the first place. It's more important to deliver a quality product than a new one, and it's better to outcompete others by marketing a 'standard' type business better, or running your business better and more efficiently than other people.

Seriously, put in place a system for returning customers' phone calls and you're ahead of far too many businesses already!

Innovation and creativity are incredibly important but innovation should occur after you are already in the marketplace. To truly offer people more value, you have to know what they actually value, and you can't figure that out until you start interacting with them. In his book *The Lean Start-up*, Erick Ries introduced the idea of releasing the 'minimum viable product' to market, with the idea that once your product or service is out there, then you can tweak it to what the market wants. People themselves often don't know what they truly value either, which is why you need to be already charging them money to find out. People pay for what they value. You see what people value by what they do, not what they say.

Which brings me back to the point I made in part II about the lack of feedback trap: without freedom to control both inputs and outputs, you end up less in touch with the market, and therefore less able to respond to changes. Comparing a job to even a small service-based business you'll realise that in a job you:

- can't increase your prices (although you can ask for a pay increase)
- can't decrease your prices (a business may want to offer a discount to stay in business during lean times. Not many people would offer to work a job for less, and even if they did they'd still be at the mercy of a boss who could refuse to raise their salary when business picked up again)
- can be fired at any time — the equivalent of losing 100 per cent of your customers at once
- can't decrease your workload
- can't get rid of bad customers, or choose who you work with
- have no warning that your service is becoming obsolete. (In a business if you start to lose some customers you can always test different things and change what you offer)
- can't change or control your product.

If you view your job as if it were a business, it would be obvious that it doesn't allow you a lot of freedom. You might think I'm belabouring the point, but it's important because there are plenty of people who may have a job that is high paying who think, 'Why would I start a business? I make good money already' or 'If I start a business I'd better start *big*.'

> **I believe you should start a business to have more freedom. Remember: *freedom leads to wealth.***

In fact, if you ask most people why they might want to start a business, they'll tell you 'to get rich' or 'to make more money'.

I believe you should start a business to have more freedom. Remember: *freedom leads to wealth.*

You want to start a business that frees you first, in other words:

- a business that starts making you money straight away. (This applies to people who want to learn an active investing skill too: create investments that make you money now, not later, and you can leverage that equity you create now into the next investment and so on. Even if you work a job, if you want to actively invest, treat it like a business.)

- a business that can be a service-based business or a product-based business, but it needs to be something you can sell *now*.

You don't want to start a business that:

- requires you to go into massive debt, in the hopes of creating the 'next big thing'.

- traps you in dependence at the mercy of one big customer, or one that depends completely on the whims of one platform.

A business that frees you allows you to make *more choices*. Freedom to control more means that you can respond to what the market tells you it wants.

Realising that you are a business already—albeit not a very good one, and that starting a business is similar to getting hired and learning on the job—can make taking those first scary steps a lot easier.

A Quick Recap

It can be scary to try something new, but in a real sense your life is like a business already, just one with limited choices. Without the freedom to control both inputs and outputs, you are less in touch with the market, and less able to respond to changes and to prosper. Freedom is having more choices.

CHAPTER 13

Buy back your time so you can buy back more time

Freedom Escape Velocity.

'Well when you describe a job that way, now I'm really certain I want to quit my job for good,' Melissa laughed.

'I've done what you said, and collected the marketing that other photographers have sent the office and I've got my camera and lenses. But I'm itching to just get started.

'The thing is, I'll only have a couple of shoots a week at first, based on work I'll probably get from this office. I know I should probably try to build my business part-time until I can replace my income, but I'm not sure how I could do that, even if I wanted to. Agents are going to want to book me during the week for starters, not just the weekend.

'While I have my job I can't really start taking bookings—I could try to book agents on a Saturday, but what if they want another day? You said that I've got to think of what the customer wants, not just what would suit me best, and I know agents. Those guys like to leave everything to the last minute and do it in a rush. Besides, weekends are a time they've got a lot else on their plate.'

Melissa was asking me to 'give her permission' to quit her job without any real 'security', so she could be free to really commit to her new business idea, and make it work. I'd spoken with Melissa over the previous few months as the GFC was unfolding. I'd shared my concerns about the downturn and the hard times that would follow the initial fireworks and headlines that were only just reaching our shores.

While it sounds insane to think about starting a business going into a predictable downturn, especially one in real estate, it's not as crazy as you'd first think. In fact, starting a business in a downturn may be the safer thing to do. You can't control your boss's decision to cut staff.

Besides, some of the biggest companies around today all got their start in the Great Depression. While downturns hit the average family pretty hard, they're also a time when big, established companies that are bloated and bureaucratic get hit hard too. After the prolonged, debt-fuelled economic summer we'd been in for decades, there were many companies that were getting away with inefficiencies that would kill them in leaner times. Melissa's previous workplace had its own examples of people hired for dubious reasons and with inflated job titles. In a downturn the employee gets fired, while the small, lean start-up that is free of bureaucracy can respond quickly and grow,

"...some of the biggest companies around today all got their start in the Great Depression." often taking over areas that bigger companies had dominated for years. Even in the real estate industry people will always need to sell houses, and when times get tougher there may be even more call for agents to put effort into marketing properties that could have more or less sold themselves in the past.

I'd decided to mentor Melissa in the beginning because I sensed that she was someone who, like me, put an abnormally strong value on freedom. Whether it was her nature, or all the stuff I was filling her head with, I knew she was right.

After all, it was what I had done, and if I truly believed that you needed to be free first if you wanted to be rich, then it was the only advice I could truthfully give her.

Of course the 'responsible' advice would be to build your business in your spare time until you can make enough to quit your job. But think about what that advice is asking people to do. Someone who works, say, five days a week for a $50000 salary is being asked to create something that earns them at least $50000 a year—in their spare time!

They're being asked to put less effort—two days a week—into something to replace the five days a week they devote to their job. Many people put years into studying for their nine to five jobs, as well as years of experience into the jobs themselves. But for a business—just put in your spare time!

That's not 'safe' advice; it's setting you up to fail.

When you've spent the majority of the hours of the majority of the days in the week working your job, it can be hard to summon up the energy on the only days you have off to invest in a business that, in the beginning stages at least, may not be making much, if anything, compared to your full-time salary. In effect, trying to start a business in your spare time can trap you in the beginning stages indefinitely: endlessly planning, until seeing little result, it becomes easier to give in before you've even started. At least you'll get your weekends back!

I remember watching one of those entrepreneur incubator type shows — you know, the ones with weird names like 'Shark Tank', 'Lion's Den', 'Bear Pit' (I'm not sure about the last one): programs where a panel of successful entrepreneurs listen to proposals by hopeful guests who are looking for funding for their business ideas.

Anyway, there was a pair of hopeful young guys who came on the show, both had pretty good jobs with decent income and they had a business that they hoped the gurus would back. In the background clip they showed the guys and their wives hanging out, socialising together at restaurants. When questioned, one of them admitted that he couldn't devote too much time to the business yet because it wasn't making enough money to 'pay his salary', but once the business could pay him what he 'needed' to maintain his nice lifestyle, then he'd totally commit to it.

Well the gurus gave him an earful: 'Why would we invest our money in your business when you won't even invest your time in it?'

I kind of felt sorry for them. They were only doing what I've seen so many other people do, who have been conditioned by a lifetime living in the Income Trap. And that is fall for the big win temptation. Like buying a lotto ticket (where you put out a small amount of money you can afford to lose, in the hope of winning enough money that you never have to work again), they were hoping that by putting a small amount of time that they could afford to lose (their weekends and so on) into their business idea, they might one day strike it rich. In the meantime they could stay comfortably in the Income Trap, spending as much as they earned, confident that the pay cheque would always be there. But as most people know, buying lotto tickets isn't exactly a sure-fire way to become financially free.

> **..buying lotto tickets isn't exactly a sure-fire way to become financially free.**

The gurus on the show went on to humble-brag about how much they had sacrificed in the beginning, going sometimes years without drawing an income from the business, while living extremely frugally.

But you don't need to start a business with no foreseeable income and be driven to grow it into the next big sensation. Most people who do that don't succeed, and besides, trying to create 'the next big thing' can be a consequence of valuing your ego, of wanting to be a 'big businessman', instead of being driven by a motivation to be free.

Women often find this trap easier to avoid than men, perhaps because men have more ego ...

Having survived the property correction, converted his home into an investment, increased his cashflow and avoided shackling himself to massive debt, Andrew had remained free enough and flexible enough to finally commit to the entrepreneurial path he'd always wanted to pursue.

But that's where his true values began to make themselves felt. Rather than start a business that could free him from his job, he, along with three other friends who worked for the same company, decided to go into business together making themselves directors of their new company: four directors, incorporation, big meetings, paying employees—all while still working their jobs.

Right from the beginning it became clear that it was more important to them to feel big and successful—while sharing the risk of failure with many others—than it was to be free.

Meanwhile, his girlfriend at the time, Julia, had a much simpler motivation. She wasn't driven by ego to create the 'next big thing'. She was simply sick of working for her boss and dreamed of being free.

Being unburdened by ego, it didn't take much for her to quit her job and start up a mobile hairdressing business. She ended up leaving her job well before Andrew, despite him dreaming of doing so for many years before she did. At first she earned a little less than she did in the salon, but it didn't take long before she had replaced, then exceeded, her former income, and now with the freedom of being her own boss too.

Andrew's business, on the other hand, didn't fare so well. The shame was, it was a good idea for a business. It was a service-based business delivering training to doctors, and as their rush of early bookings made clear, it could have replaced the income of any one or even two of them in a short space of time. What's more, the business took advantage of skills that the guys were already using in their jobs, which they were still hanging onto while trying to do their new business on the side.

Unfortunately though, this failure to commit to the business created a conflict of interest which, when it finally came to light, resulted in multiple firings and strife that eventually pulled the company apart.

Had they trusted in the power of growth and focused on freeing themselves first, they could have started out doing some of the training services themselves, instead of rushing to hire employees. Facebook and Google all started with the founders doing the early coding personally. This would have freed them from the need to cling to their jobs, and they could have used that freedom to eventually systemise the business and hire others when the time was right.

In case you are thinking that I'm advising you to choose working in a small business versus striking it rich in a big one, think again. One of the richest men in the city of Brisbane was a man called Stefan Ackerie.

Stefan started out running his own hairdressing business, like Julia, and eventually built an empire of salons and haircare products. He ended up owning million-dollar racing boats, and even built a tower that shone a light around the city. That's how starting a business that frees you first allows you to have the time—and get the feedback from the market—to really grow. Which is better than trying to create a big business in your spare time while your job takes up all your attention (as well as the best hours of the majority of the days of the week).

Part of the reason that people cling to their jobs while trying to make a business work part-time, might be that having lived our lives in the Income Trap, earning money in straight lines, it can be hard to trust in the power of growth, particularly in a concept I call 'Freedom Escape Velocity'.

The power of growth: Freedom Escape Velocity

What I've been describing so far in this chapter is a concept I've come to call 'Freedom Escape Velocity'.

In teaching others, I'd noticed that people who didn't seem to value their freedom as much as I did were always looking for a way to become *totally* financially free at once—or they wouldn't bother to do anything at all. If they couldn't buy back all their time in one big hit, like winning the lotto, they couldn't get motivated to buy back any time at all.

In contrast to this, Freedom First says that you need to buy back *your* time, if you want to buy back *more* time. It's worth buying yourself even a little time back. Why is that?

When you're working a job, you have very little time to call your own, in which to be creative, to invent and to grow. And I'm not just talking about hours in the day, but rather *mental* time too. How often do you come home at the end of a work day and just want to relax and 'veg out'? You may still have a few hours left on the clock, but your mental tank is empty. Working a job, you end up giving the best hours, of the best days, of the best years of your life to someone else.

Thinking about this, I was reading up on ageing research when I came across a researcher who was lecturing on an interesting concept he called 'longevity escape velocity'. He was borrowing a term from aerospace engineering, escape velocity being the speed you need to get to, to escape the pull of Earth's gravity.

Most people, when they hear that actual research into fighting ageing is being conducted, and that some of the biggest names in Silicon Valley are investing heavily into it, are quite surprised. Research to fight diseases seems normal, but ageing has always seemed inevitable. With all the hype out there, nobody is getting visibly younger. And that's what the researcher noticed: most people feel that unless researchers can offer a complete solution, unless someone proposes a way to stop ageing or even reverse it, there is not much point looking into fighting ageing per se at all.

What the researcher noted was that people were failing to understand the power of growth, which we talked about earlier—the power for small changes to add up. Even if research couldn't yet reverse ageing, or halt it in its tracks, if it could at least delay the point at which we start to suffer the effects of ageing, then it could buy us time to find a better solution. Longevity escape velocity, as he called it, was the point at which ageing research gained us more life than we were losing.

So Freedom Escape Velocity can be thought of as the point at which your productive efforts are buying you back more time than they cost you. What this means is that *you don't need to totally replace your income, or create enough wealth to buy back all of your time before you quit your job, retire or start something new.*

With, say, six months' savings, any business you start, or investment you make, doesn't have to replace your income straight away. As long as you start something that brings in some money—in bookings or sales or profits—that early money is adding time onto the end of your freedom window (the amount of time you can survive without a job); instead of having six months of living expenses, you'll have six months plus one day extra the first time you make a sale.

> *Even when David had excitedly gotten off the phone after making that first booking, he still wasn't convinced he'd made the right decision. After only one sale he couldn't see how he could live off it: 'it's only one sale'.*
>
> *But I reassured him that despite the urgency he felt the money wasn't important—even though every fibre of his being was telling him it was—the process was what was important.*

At first, you may spend two or three days or even a week getting that first day of extra freedom, but as soon as you start to buy back some time you've started on an exponential path. If, in that first week, you only make enough money to buy back one day of living expenses, and in the second week you earn enough to cover two days of living expenses and so on, you're on your way to achieving Freedom Escape Velocity. You haven't escaped orbit yet, but each week you are expanding your freedom window. At some point you'll be buying back more than one day's freedom each and every day, and at that point, you've achieved Freedom Escape Velocity.

Because your earnings are coming in in a *non-linear* way, you probably won't even realise when you've passed that point at first. People are terrible at predicting growth, especially if they've been stuck in a trap that reinforces straight line thinking.

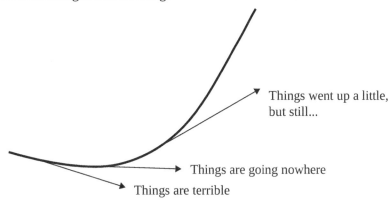

Things went up a little, but still...

Things are going nowhere

Things are terrible

The first month you've made only two weeks of living expenses — bummer, so you send out some marketing. The next month you make five weeks' worth of living expenses; well that could have just been a good month right? The next month you spend four weeks but only make enough to add three and a half weeks of freedom onto your window. The following month it's six weeks of time you've bought back.

As a result of this irregular pattern of income, saving money can actually become easier too. This was something David shared with me early on: by creating wealth, instead of just earning a salary he began to see money as an input, and not just an output. Because he wasn't directly living off his sales (at first he was living off his savings) it was easier to see the money he made from that first sale as a seed he could plant by reinvesting it in his business.

When you earn a salary, you need to budget so you can save a little extra a week for a 'future you' 30 years from now. However, the authors of the book *The Millionaire Next Door* found that almost half of all millionaires don't use a fixed budget and instead operate on a perceived scarcity principle — what I prefer to think of as Perceived Income Level Lag, (or PILL: would you like to take a pill that meant you didn't have to budget?).

Basically, by being free of the Income Trap, those millionaires, naturally and without effort, acted as if their income was lower than it was. How?

Well, when people live pay cheque to pay cheque, they do it largely subconsciously: they don't spend all their money at the beginning of the month, then starve for the rest of the month, nor do they get to the end of the month with money left and just spend it all on the last day. They tend to subconsciously 'estimate' their income and spend right up to it, sometimes running out a few days early or sometimes blowing what's left at the end of the month. It's easy to accommodate to what you 'can' spend when you live in the Income Trap, earning the same money each month, which is how people with vastly different incomes and expenses can all end up equally broke at the end of the month!

> **When you are growing, your perceived income level is on a 'lag'.**

But in the example given above of the first few months in business, you can see that month to month your income was variable, which straight away helps you not to accommodate to it as easily. But on top of that, on average, the income was increasing. That means that each month if you project your earnings forward based on the last month, you'll actually be earning more than you expected. Remember from the diagram above that when things are growing our tendency to think in straight lines means we underestimate them.

So, when you are growing, your perceived income level is on a 'lag'. Most years I have no idea how much money I have made that year until I do my tax. Because of this uncertainty, my brain seems to 'assume' an average income that I find it easy to live within. This is actually the upside to the problem of the human brain being terrible at projecting forward growth. When you are free of the Income Trap you can use that to your advantage, to live within your means without the restriction of a budget!

Finally, Freedom Escape Velocity is so powerful because the freer you get, the easier it is to become more and more free. For one thing, you have more time, but the nature of freedom is that it gives you more choices, so you have more time and more options too.

Provided you choose a business that makes you some money now, or an investment strategy that pays you up front, Freedom Escape Velocity means that you:

- can start with less money than you think
- can start sooner
- don't have to have all the answers at first.

I've met some retirees who only really started investing once they had quit work, because they never had the time to do it before. But after waiting their whole lives to buy back *all* of their time, they're finding that all it took was *enough* time to find the first deal and complete it. They could have retired years earlier.

What a waste of time!

" The secret of happiness is freedom ... and the secret of freedom is courage. "

Thucydides

'Okay, I've done it. I've quit my job.'

'How did it go?' I enquired.

'Pretty good actually. The boss took it better than I expected. He said he was sorry to see me go and was pretty keen to continue to contract the office's photography shoots out to me too. It'll save them a bunch of money. I think you were right about the property correction putting a strain on businesses with bigger payrolls. Not that there has been much of a correction here yet.'

'That's great. So are you ready? The next few weeks are going to be some of the most memorable, scary and exciting weeks of your life.

'You know when you go on a two-week holiday and years later you still remember all the high points of your holiday and none of the stress... long after the other 50 weeks in that particular year have faded in memory? That's what this period of time will be like. Really living, not just going through the motions. Humans are meant to work, and create and grow, and you're certainly going to be growing!'

'That sounds ominous!' Melissa laughed.

'Not at all,' I reassured her.

'You've gotten free—now you've got something to lose. You'll find the motivation takes care of itself.'

'Oh I'm not worried about motivation; I've got so much to do!' she replied.

'Well since I got you into this, I'll give you a hand to get started.'

You can't buy success, but you can look the part

Some people spend a fortune trying to look 'successful' or legitimate when starting a business, hiring staff just for the sake of it, renting expensive office space. That's crazy. You don't need to go to that extent, but if you are starting out there are a few things you can do that don't cost a lot and can make your business look more serious.

I'm not advocating pretending to be bigger than you are; it's smart to start small—Google started in a garage, Facebook in a dorm room. But on the other hand you don't want to look unprofessional either. A website is one thing that can make you look more professional nowadays; a booking number can be another. Being smartly dressed, perhaps with a logo, can be a good, cheap image enhancement. Be smart about it and choose things that add to your image without costing much, or requiring a big commitment of time either. Many a business started a business blog when that was a craze, only to make five posts and give up. That looks worse than not doing it at all. It's the same today with Twitter and Facebook among others. You want a plan for your marketing: if you are spending heaps of time writing tweets or posts but you are not directly measuring conversions into sales you may be wasting your time, especially in the beginning.

So we sat down and made a list of all the things Melissa would need to do to get started.

Some of the things were pretty routine: think of a business name and register it. Open a bank account. Print some business cards.

Other things seemed more daunting: putting up a website and coming up with a plan on how to market, what to offer and how to price her services.

Some of those things could have been done while she was still safe and secure in her job, and I'd discussed this with Melissa, but she'd been adamant that it'd be easier to just start and throw herself into it. Creating a website was something in particular that she felt she'd never get her head around learning to do, if there wasn't some urgency to it.

And she was right. She had a bit of a flair for design, which is not too surprising for a photographer I guess, and had even started a graphic design course online, but never got around to finishing it. Sometimes the best education is the one you have to teach yourself, to achieve a concrete real-life goal that has some urgency to it.

But before she started on the website, we needed to decide what she'd offer and what she'd charge for it. We looked at what other photographers were charging, and it ranged all the way from 'cheap' to 'premium'. Melissa's instinct was to come in towards the low end, which is quite common with new business owners, but I reminded her that she wasn't a commodity business. A commodity business is one where the product you sell is identical to every other product, and therefore the only thing you can compete on is price. Petrol is a commodity, and people seem particularly sensitive to price, often going miles out of their way to save a few cents.

> **Sometimes the best education is the one you have to teach yourself, to achieve a concrete real-life goal that has some urgency to it.**

Looking at other photographers it was clear that not all photography was equal either—the quality ranged as much as the prices did. Melissa's experience in real estate photography combined with the decision to be a specialist, not a generalist, meant that she could realistically price her services higher than she could if real estate photography was just a sideline for her.

Of course, price doesn't always reflect quality, and the most expensive photographers were not automatically producing the highest quality photos. Instead, perhaps they offered a superior service, or positioned themselves more effectively. Which brought us to the question of how exactly Melissa would market herself.

Melissa showed me the marketing she'd collected from other photographers while working at her old job. One immediate thing that jumped out was the average quality—terrible. 'My name is Bob and I take photos.' That's nice Bob, but why should I care?

We learned in part II that you want to be free to get in touch with the market. And the Freedom First Wealth Creation Formula taught us that while you should do what you love, you need to find a way to also do what other people will value.

So many businesses don't think in terms of what their market wants. People hate marketing because they feel they are asking others to give them something. But that's a result of selfish thinking—thinking of the work you want to get, instead of what you can offer. I remember a while back a board game I loved from the 1980s was re-released, but they didn't spend much on marketing and so I didn't hear about it. It quickly sold out and now copies sell for a fortune second hand on eBay. I wish I had been marketed to when the product was first re-released! You've got to stop thinking of what you want and see marketing as a way to give people what they want.

> **So many businesses don't think in terms of what their market wants.**

So the first important question I asked Melissa was, 'Who are your customers?'

Again, you'd be surprised by how many businesses can't answer that. Melissa would be photographing people's homes to help them sell their properties. But in most cases, the homeowner wouldn't be her customer, the real estate agent would.

So the question became: what do agents value?

Most people would say 'getting the sale', but as Melissa explained to me, that's not really true. Most agents care more about getting the listing. They call themselves sales agents and they get paid when properties sell, but many of them are more concerned with selling the homeowner on listing with them in the first place and letting the sales process take care of itself, to an extent, after that. The agent comes to your house personally to get you to list, but often it's their assistant who they then send out to do the open houses on the weekend.

Melissa walked me through the standard listing pitch as it is for an agent. Many agencies don't just want to secure a listing: anyone could convince people to simply list their house for an unrealistically high price to see if someone will bite, when it costs the homeowner nothing to list. Then the agent and agency have to spend time and money marketing a house that the owner may not even really want to sell.

So, agents often want to secure some investment in the sales process from owners as well as the listing, which means not only selling the homeowner on the agent's ability to sell their home, but selling them on the need to invest in some marketing too.

Generally, the tools for doing that are pretty boring. The agent can come armed with facts and figures about how much a certain ad costs and how many extra enquiries that ad might generate.

Boring.

But talking about the process gave me an idea for how Melissa could help the agents.

What if, instead of simply dropping flyers at real estate offices advertising Melissa's business, we created something that the agents might actually value? What if we created a sales pack the agents could use in their listing appointments with potential home owners?

We started brainstorming and came up with a glossy A4 folder with handout leaflets the agents could use to help convince an owner to invest in marketing their property. Instead of boring owners with dry statistics about ads, they could hand owners a colour brochure that showed in images, not numbers, how real estate photography could help sell their house.

Included were examples with before and after photos showing the same property with photos taken by agents/owners, versus photos taken with skill by a photographer with wide-angle lenses, photographed at dusk and professionally edited.

Along with the photos, we included a fact sheet that the agents could use in their presentations, highlighting research done by online property listing sites about the shift towards online marketing and how photos online are now often the first impression many people get of a property. We also included a guide for owners on how to best prepare their house to be photographed professionally. (Apparently, having lived in their homes for many years people collect a lot of 'stuff' that they simply stop seeing, that can be hidden to make a room look better in photos.)

I suggested we should include in each 'kit' a little fact sheet about Melissa and her experience with both marketing and photography in real estate, as well as a call to action.

'Can you write that bit?' Melissa asked. 'I'd feel weird talking about myself.'

Believe it or not, there was a time when not everyone was obsessed with taking selfies and sharing their innermost thoughts with the world on Instagram or Facebook. So, as we put the finishing touches on the kits, I agreed to write up Melissa's bio and she got to work on her website.

The first week of Melissa's freedom was spent immersed in online tutorials and YouTube videos learning to build herself a website. YouTube is an awesome resource for learning practical skills they don't teach at school.

Back then it was a sweet spot (or sour spot?) in time where websites were becoming pretty necessary to have for businesses, but there weren't the many options that there are today for simple DIY 'template' websites, and website designers were still charging a fortune. So Melissa knuckled down and in 10 days built herself a website from scratch, breaking only twice to do shoots for agents at her old office. I was impressed.

Melissa decided that to start with, she'd offer a few different options: a regular shoot, a small unit shoot that would be cheaper and include fewer photos, and a premium dusk shoot. There are only so many dusks available a week. Dusk is the best time of day by far for real estate photography and these shoots often take a lot longer, involve more photos and more time editing in Photoshop afterwards, which justified the price.

...you are never going to know exactly what the market wants until you ask it.

Finally, there were the 'add-ons': floor plans and aerial shoots. Floor plans were easy enough to figure out, and easier to do once Melissa realised you could use a laser distance measurer instead of a tape measure. But aerial shoots were another matter. Some other photography franchises had special vans with extendable rooftop ladders that they used for aerial shots. Other photographers who had a lot of work contracted the shoots out to local light aircraft pilots, often doing several properties in the one flight. We looked into this option, but starting out with a small volume would mean that the cost to contract out these shoots would be sky high (sorry).

And besides, you are never going to know exactly what the market wants until you ask it. So, there was no real way to know how much demand there would be for aerial shoots until Melissa got out there and started booking shoots. Would the ability to do aerial shoots be something that people would see as a 'make or break' service for a real estate photographer? It seemed crazy to invest in a 'truck with ladder' setup, which would cost tens of thousands of dollars, or a drone—drones were pretty new back then and were prohibitively expensive—when Melissa had been so frugal up to that point in starting her business.

So Melissa decided that for now she'd pass on the aerial shoots as an option, at least in the beginning, which turned out to be a good decision.

In the beginning, it can be tempting to throw money at buying the most expensive equipment in an attempt to position yourself as 'the premium brand' in your market, but while you want to be in a branded business, not a commodity business, trying to buy your way to the top at the start rather than earn your way there, is a sure way to go broke. No matter how much you spend to be the 'best' right out of the gate, you can't force people to buy your product and pay you premium prices (especially if you haven't established relationships). Nor can you avoid the need to market yourself—which is why I think a lot of people are tempted to go down this road in the first place. You want to start a business that frees you, and keeps you in touch with the market long enough for it to tell you what it values, and then set about delivering that value to your customers better than anyone else.

As we finished up the kits and the website, Melissa had to decide on how exactly she was going to market her business. We'd created a 'product' in the marketing kits that might be of actual value to agents, certainly compared to a random flier stuck under an office's door. Would we just mail them out to agents and hope that they'd contact Melissa?

Since we had something of value to offer, I encouraged her to ask for something in exchange: perhaps we could cold call the agents and offer them the kits in person?

'Cold call them? No way!'

'I thought you'd say that,' I laughed. 'So what are you comfortable with? When have you promoted yourself before?' I asked.

'Well, when I did job interviews I guess?' Melissa replied, after a pause.

'Absolutely! Like we said before about "being a business already": you've already done sales and marketing! Marketing is like sending out your resume, and a job interview is like face-to-face sales—harder in some ways.

'You told me that you found job interviews easy to do, right? Would you be comfortable meeting with these agents in person to give them the free kits and introduce yourself, maybe over a coffee?'

'Sure I could do that. But how do we get the appointments? I don't want to cold call them,' Melissa asserted.

'You've saved a lot of money making your own website, why don't we outsource the phone calls? I know a top-gun sales guy who could spend a couple of days hitting the phones for you if we put together a list and a script. It's a soft sell — you're actually offering them something in exchange for meeting you.'

'Alright,' Melissa agreed. 'I'd rather pay someone to do that!'

I'm all for people starting a business frugally rather than going into debt, but you don't have to do everything yourself. Do what you are comfortable with, and find a way to get around what you are not.

So, Melissa got to work putting together a list of all the agents in her area and all the surrounding suburbs that she could conceivably do shoots in, and put together a short phone script as well.

The phone calls went well: agents are, by nature, gregarious people and many were happy to meet with Melissa over coffee.

Most were quite impressed that she had gone to the effort of creating something of value for them, instead of just spamming their offices with emails or flyers. When dealing with other businesses, the relationship is as important as the product, and going to the effort to meet with them in person created a good impression.

> **You don't have to do everything yourself.**

In fact the phone calls were going so well that one agent wanted Melissa to come out and do a presentation for the whole office.

I thought that sounded like a great idea: if the boss invited Melissa to speak to all the agents they'd be more likely to book her with his endorsement.

But Melissa disagreed. The thought of presenting to a room full of people terrified her. I'd probably find talking to a room full of people easier than meeting with them all one on one. But I forget that I'm probably weird that way.

So I reassured her that even though the presentation might be a great opportunity, she was in her own business now — which meant she was free to do whatever she was comfortable with, including choose what work she wanted to do, or not do. In a job you only have one customer, your boss, but in a business there will be many more customers.

Of course it can be hard to trust that there will always be more work to be had; even so, it's one thing to turn away a small opportunity, and another to turn down a big opportunity — especially one that promised to quickly fill up her time and replace her income in one fell swoop — which Melissa was soon to find out . . .

But for the moment, having spent her first week and a half setting up her business, half a week on phone calls, then a couple of weeks of one-on-one appointments with principals of real estate agencies, the bookings had started to roll in. It was still only a few shoots a week, in addition to the shoot or two a week that she was still doing for her old agency, but even so it was enough to add to Melissa's freedom window (the amount of time Melissa could live on her savings and income) and gave her confidence that she could really do this.

She could succeed in her own business and be free of a boss for good.

In addition to booking meetings, Melissa had started to email out to her list as well, which included the agents she'd met with and the ones she hadn't, as well as agents further afield than her immediate area. It was in response to one of these emails that Melissa received an interesting proposal. One of the principals of a larger agency had asked to meet Melissa to make her an offer. Curious, Melissa agreed.

A Quick Recap

The freer you get, the easier it is to become more and more free. Each step towards freedom helps you to build the skills you will need for the next step, giving you not only more choices but more time to capitalise on those choices too. The human brain thinks in straight lines. You can use this to your advantage: once free of the Income Trap it becomes easy to live within your means *without* the restriction of a budget.

CHAPTER 14

Get free, so you can get freer

Avoiding the Dependence Trap. The Freedom Quadrant.

> **There is only one cure for the evils which newly acquired freedom produces, and that is MORE freedom.**
>
> *Thomas Macaulay*

'So, come on, I'm dying to know: what was the offer?' I asked her.

'Well, he offered to make me the exclusive photographer for the entire agency!' Melissa replied.

It's important to note at this point that although Melissa had been meeting with many principals, most individual agents at those agencies were still free to choose their own photographer to work with.

Often, after meeting with Melissa, a principal would recommend her to his agents and those who were looking for a new photographer to work with would book her, but until word of mouth spread among the agents themselves, there were always several agents at an agency who had an established relationship with their own photographer, as well as other agents who would do their own photography.

So, from any one agency she contacted, Melissa would only end up working with one or two agents at first, which is what made this offer enticing.

'Okay. That's great!' I enthused.

'He did have one condition though. He wanted to lock in a cheaper price in exchange for about two shoots a day, or 30 to 40 shoots a month. Which, with dusk shoots, editing and floor plans would pretty much fill up the rest of my time.

'He also wants me to do the audiovisual presentations at the monthly group auctions,' she said.

'What does that involve?' I asked.

'Well, each month the agency has a night-time in-house auction, where they promote and sell a bunch of their properties at once. I think the idea is that with a larger group of properties they can attract a larger group of buyers into one place at one time and that drives up the bidding more than if they only had a small group of people at each listing,' Melissa explained.

'So what would you have to do at these nights?'

'That's the thing: if I take this on I'd be expected to do a short video of each property in addition to the photos. Then, on the night of the auction, they want me to run the audiovisual presentation, so I guess that would mean that I'd have to put together a slide show, and set up the equipment. I'm not really sure. But it's taking me away from being a "specialist" into "generalist" territory. I'd have to figure out video production, get my head around AV equipment... it sounds like a hassle,' Melissa concluded.

'You could outsource that part of the job if it makes sense financially. I've got a great guy I used to work with who's a bit of a whiz at the AV stuff. We could get a quote from him,' I suggested.

'Yeah, I guess,' Melissa replied. 'The thing is, he does want me to do the photo shoots at a lower rate, so I'm not sure how much room I'll have to outsource the monthly auction AV.'

'These shoots per month he's estimated you'd have — he's given you a bit of a range there — has he guaranteed a minimum amount you can work with? Like, if they have less than 30 shoots per month, then they lose the discount rate that month?' I asked.

'To be honest he was pretty vague on that. He certainly didn't offer to sign a contract, no,' Melissa replied.

'They have a photographer who currently does most of the shoots and also does the videoing and monthly auction night AV. She's apparently leaving, which is why they offered this job to me,' she continued.

'Wait, you said she does most of the shoots? I thought the principal was offering you an exclusive setup with all his agents,' I asked, surprised.

'Well, it's a large agency and this photographer is doing the shoots for the majority of the agents, but one of the agents uses their own photographer. I think they offer this agent a bit of leeway because she's a top performer.'

'That's interesting. Tell me, what would you say is most tempting about this offer?' I asked.

'I guess it's the chance to pick up a lot of work quickly. I mean I've only just started and this could see me fully booked already. Are you talking about what values this meets? I see where this is going ...' Melissa groaned, a smile on her face.

Over the months since our first meeting I'd been talking to her about my thoughts on freedom, valuing freedom and the traps that come from not being free. This was a real chance for her to examine her values in light of a real-world opportunity.

'Now that I think about it I guess that there is the temptation to work for less in exchange for a bit of security. And filling up my days with work is comfortable, like a job, so the temptation of the Income Trap might be a factor?'

'Right,' I agreed. 'The fact you are even looking this gift horse in the mouth at all is a good sign though. You wouldn't believe how many people would be tempted to become a generalist, and even take a pay cut for the security of a big contract.

'The other trap I'd say is relevant here is the Dependence Trap. If you take on this work, what will you have to give up?' I asked her.

'I hadn't really thought of that. If he came through with as much work as he promised, which I'm starting to doubt, it'd mean I'd have less time for the agents I've already established a relationship with. Although there's only a handful so far, they're great to work with. I'm really enjoying being able to choose who I can work with. That's a benefit of freedom I hadn't thought about much beforehand.'

'That's a biggie,' I agreed. 'There is one thing you can get out of this though. And that's the tale of two photographers. One photographer at this agency does the majority of the shoots for a low price and has to juggle a bunch of other tasks as well, such as videoing, putting together presentations and running the AV for the company each month. She's basically an employee with all the work she does, but one without the benefits of employment.

'The other photographer works with the top salesperson only—for a premium price—and while they probably don't make as much money from this one agency, they definitely make more per agent. And they're free to find other agents just like this one at other agencies, finding the cream of the crop, if you like.'

'Well when you put it that way...' Melissa smiled.

So Melissa chose to pass on the illusion of security, for the freedom to continue to build her own list of agents, which seemed like an easy decision to make—at first.

That was until her faith in the process was really tested.

Up until that point Melissa had picked up several new clients, but was still doing work for a couple of agents from her old workplace. Shortly after passing on the exclusive offer, however, something strange began to happen.

Out of the blue her old office started to drag out paying her. She contacted the accounts department, but was given the run around. The delay seemed to be coming from higher up. It was strange: her old boss had seemed happy for her, and they had parted on good terms, but now that Melissa was running her own business and no longer his employee, he seemed more reluctant to pay her.

She got on well with the agents she was working with there, and was reluctant to stop working with them, but they had no control over when she got paid, and it was causing stress and taking more and more effort each month to get payment from the office.

It was one thing to 'pass up' a new opportunity. But it was another altogether to have to face letting go of agents that had been good clients in the past, and face a cut to her existing income.

'Look on the bright side, not many people get to quit their job and fire their boss too!'

'Some bright side—I'm losing nearly 25 per cent of my work if I let them go,' Melissa complained when we discussed the problem.

'Most people, if their boss stopped paying them, would lose 100 per cent of their income,' I replied. 'But I hear you. It sucks that you've had to jump through hoops just to get paid.'

Unless you are living week to week you should never be afraid to let your bad customers go, even if, like in Melissa's case, you are not fully booked yet. I get that it's hard to trust in the nature of growth at first when you only have a few clients and work might seem scarce. But if you've been growing steadily and continue to market your business, you will eventually get very busy.

Perhaps more than you'd like, too. And it's pretty hard when you are busy to start looking for higher quality customers — customers that give you more work with less hassle — when you are run off your feet chasing after bad ones.

If you've gone to the trouble to buy back your time, you don't want to give it away too cheaply.

Getting busier and busier will make you more money — up to a point. But like we've learned all along, getting freer will always make you richer.

Getting busier and busier will make you more money linearly. You may make more total money the longer you work, up until the point you're fully booked. But you want to make more money *per hour* you work. That's exponential, and that's tapping into the power of growth.

You may have bought back your time, but now that you've got control of your time, it's time to figure out how to use it more productively, so ultimately you have *more* free time too.

You want to use your free time to do Freedom Quadrant activities.

Freedom Quadrant activities

In 1954, former US President Dwight D Eisenhower (who was quoting Dr J Roscoe Miller) said, 'I have two kinds of problems: the urgent and the important. The urgent are not important, and the important are never urgent.' This became known as the 'Eisenhower Principle'. Later authors such as Stephen Covey used Eisenhower's principle as the basis for a four-quadrant diagram illustrating that tasks or activities could be either:

1   *urgent and important* — tasks that require immediate attention, that are important.

2   *important but not urgent* — tasks that are important but aren't currently urgent.

3   *urgent but not important*—tasks that require immediate attention but don't advance your goals

4   *not urgent, not important*—tasks that don't need to be done now and aren't important.

Task	Urgent	Not urgent
Important	Quadrant 1	Quadrant 2
Not Important	Quadrant 3	Quadrant 4

Covey and others agree that after dealing with the things that are important *and* urgent, your focus should be on devoting time to the second group of activities (Quadrant 2 in Covey's parlance)—things that are important, but not urgent.

You've probably already figured out the 'flaw' in this advice though: 'How can I tell if something that is urgent isn't really important, and what things that aren't immediate priorities on my to-do list are important that I should be doing?'

Covey's answer was that you need to refer to your goals. If an activity advances your goals, it's important. If it's urgent, but not moving you towards your goals, then it's not important. I agree.

But, while it's all very well to say we should try to do things that move us towards our goals and not waste time doing things that don't, as we learned earlier, our actions tend to flow from our values, and not really from our stated goals.

That's the reason why people often end up confused when they say they want to achieve something only to constantly sabotage themselves with unproductive behaviour. The student knows that if they do some work towards their end-of-semester assignment now, instead of playing computer games, they will be better off.

So we need to examine our values.

What I want to do, is take Eisenhower's one-line observation and Covey's two-dimensional quadrants, and add a third dimension.

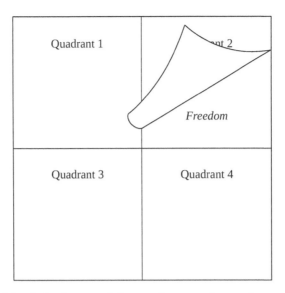

I want to peel back the layers of the quadrants and see what motivation lies under them. If someone is spending all their time in one quadrant, or on one type of task, what could be motivating them?

Quadrant 4: not urgent, not important

This is the one our student finds themselves in. They could be working on their assignment early, but instead, they are procrastinating. This is the quadrant of someone who is valuing comfort.

Quadrant 3: urgent but not important

This is a quadrant somebody who values the status of being a big businessperson might find themselves in: running around, constantly busy for the sake of looking busy.

Quadrant 1: urgent and important

At first glance this quadrant doesn't suggest any value. We all have to do things that are important when they are also urgent. But, if you're finding yourself spending all your time in this quadrant, it suggests that you may be valuing being important, and being in control. This is the quadrant of people who have trouble delegating work.

Quadrant 2: important but not urgent

If you want to spend more time in this quadrant, doing things that are important to you, you need to focus on adopting the value that supports this quadrant: Freedom.

Quadrant 2 is the Freedom Quadrant

"For every minute spent organising, an hour is earned."

Benjamin Franklin

For the workaholic who can't delegate tasks, starting to value their time and their freedom can help them to think of ways, and put in place systems, that shift some of their work to others. For the student who faces the pain of a dreaded task and flees into escapism, valuing their freedom more can help them to realise that *there is a difference between escaping and getting free,* and that they can free themselves of the pain of a difficult task best by facing it.

So how do you get freer in a small business? Look at how you are spending your time each week. How much time are you spending doing things that aren't important? Or are you booking yourself up completely, spending all week doing things that are urgent and important? Could you find some time each week to spend in the Freedom Quadrant where you can look at your business and ask yourself 'What is something I could do that could make me freer? Is there a part of my business that I could work on to increase my returns, or decrease my work?'

After all, there are really only two ways to get freer in a small business:

- *Do the same amount of work for more money:* get more money per hour; do higher value work/have higher end services; create branded products — turn your service into product.

- *Make the same amount of money for less work:* 'work' less per sale; create systems — leverage the work you do.

> **❝Confront the difficult, while it is still easy;
> accomplish the great task, by a series of
> small acts.❞**
>
> *Tao Te Ching*

*'Well now that I've fired my old boss and lost the work I was
getting from that office, I certainly have more time to invest in
the business. So what are some Freedom Quadrant activities?
Obviously marketing comes to mind.'*

*'Absolutely. It wouldn't hurt to look at how you will be marketing
going forward now that you're established. It would be even better
if we can come up with a plan to systemise it too, to free you from
having to always come up with something new,' I replied. 'But why
just stop at marketing?'*

'What do you mean?'

*'Freedom is about having more choices. It's time you learned to
pull the levers.'*

'Levers?'

*'I guess I'd better introduce you to the levers you didn't even know
you had!'*

A Quick Recap

Once you have bought back some time, don't give it away too
easily: it's time to figure out how to use it more productively, so that
ultimately you will have more free time too. Having freedom as a
Dominant Value means you are alert to opportunities to do 'Freedom
Quadrant' activities.

CHAPTER 15
Pulling the levers

The more choices you have, the more 'levers' you can control.

> **Liberty is the right to choose. Freedom is the result of the right choice.**
>
> *Jules Renard*

The freer you are, the more control you have. Freedom is quite literally the ability to choose.

For most people working a job, it's not always apparent how little control they have, and that's partly why when you ask them why they would like to start a business, they answer 'to make more money'. Before, I insisted that you should want to start a business that frees you, a business that gives you more control. *Why is the freedom to make choices more important than money?* In part II we looked at this question in the section on cycles, and the 'lack of feedback' trap. One day you are working a highly skilled job earning a good salary; the next, and due to forces outside of your control, the market changes and suddenly you are being asked to train your replacement. But the more choices you have, the more 'levers' you can control. When the market changes, you can respond.

When you are in control of a ship it's because you have your hands on the wheel: you get to pull the levers and decide where to go. Otherwise you are just a passenger.

So, now that you've taken control of your ship, what can you do that you couldn't before? The list is almost unlimited!

Since Melissa had brought up marketing, I decided to go through the marketing process with her and see how many things we could influence, and what effect just tweaking all the different 'levers' could have on her bottom line.

'Say you own a shop; you might run a promotion that gets people in the door. That's your response rate. Then it's up to you or your salespeople to convert those leads into sales. That's your conversion rate.

'Once you've measured those numbers you can adjust some levers. What that means is you can try different marketing or different offers, and measure how that affects your leads or response rate. Then, you could try adjusting what the salespeople say to potential customers to see how that changes your conversion rate of those leads.

'When you first got the telemarketer to ring agents and book them into a meeting with you, that was getting leads. When you sat down with the principals and sold them on your business, that resulted in conversions,' I explained.

'Since then, you've put together a list of email "leads"—people who may be interested in your product—so for now we can start at the conversion step: how many bookings do you get from each email you send? We'll call them your first round customers.

'Now there's a lot we can tweak with marketing. We can send out two different offers—one to half your list, another to the other half of your list—and measure the difference to see which offer was more effective. That's called A/B testing. But we'll come back to marketing soon, after we look at all the other levers you can adjust.

'Once you've got a customer, what can you do to get more sales from that customer?

'You've put in all this effort to meet with principals and you've picked up an agent or two from several different agencies. But there are more agents at each agency! Some have a photographer they use already; others are still taking the photos themselves.

'Is there anything you could do that might encourage the agents you are working with to "spread the word" to the other agents they know? That would be working on adjusting the "referral rate lever".

'Once you've got some referrals, we can then look at your total customers (first round plus referrals). What can you do to influence how much they spend?' I asked.

'I guess I could encourage them to try a dusk shoot, which I charge more for?' Melissa replied.

'Sure, that's a great idea. I'd call that your "average $ spent" lever. How much do your customers spend on average per transaction?

'There's more to this lever though: you can also see what you can do to encourage your clients to buy more "extras" each time they make a booking: in your case floor plans, and any other extras you can think of. You could do an offer that makes it tempting to "order the whole package".

'We've looked at the average amount spent per transaction, but what about the average number of transactions a customer makes?

'If you market a special offer and pick up a new customer, what can you do to make sure you get more than one shoot out of them: what could you do to encourage an ongoing relationship?

'You don't want to fall into the trap of offering a discount shoot, only to have people book you for that one shoot and no more,' I explained.

'I do really go out of my way to make sure I give a good service so I haven't had too many examples of that to be honest.'

'Well that's okay. What about the agents you do work with? Do they use you for all their listings or only some? What could you do to increase the number of shoots they book you for? Do they just book you for their "premium" shoots? Could you get them to use you for their small unit shoots as well? That would be tweaking the "average number of transactions" lever.

'Now there are a couple more levers I'll mention: "margins", which are how much money you have left after you take into account your expenses; and "taxes": how much you have left after the tax man takes a chunk. Then I want to run through a hypothetical to see how much you can achieve even if you only tweak each lever a little bit.

'It's important to see how, by putting aside a small amount of time for Freedom Quadrant activities each week or month to make even small changes, you can make a huge difference to your bottom line.'

Take a hypothetical business that over the last year had the following figures, and then increase the leads, conversion rates and so on by only 10 per cent.

Levers	1st year	Increase 10%
Number of marketing leads (you can break these down into cost–benefit per channel)	2000	2200
× Conversions (%)	25%	27.5%
= First round customers	500	605
× Referral rate	5%	5.5%
= Referrals	25	33
Referrals + First round customers		
= Total customers	525	638
× Average no. transactions	5	5.5
× Average $ spent	$100	$110
= Turnover	$262 500	$385 990
*Margins (turnover – total costs)/turnover	30%	33%
= Profit	$78 750	$127 376.70
× After tax take	70 per cent	77 per cent
= Net profit after tax	$55 125	$98 080.05

From $55 125 to $98 080.05!

By only 'tweaking' each lever 10 per cent, you've increased your net profit by 78 per cent!

If you worked on each lever until you increased it by 50 per cent, how much would your net profit increase?

You'd have a turnover of $1.814 million dollars, or $816 328 profit before tax.

Even leaving aside tax, that's still a 937 per cent increase on profits before tax.

Little changes that you make to several different levers can make a huge difference.

'Okay, so you haven't been in business a year yet, but already you can start to make some adjustments and measure the results. Now,

at this stage of your business it's early days so tax isn't going to be such an issue, because you haven't earned much yet.'

'Thanks,' Melissa replied sarcastically.

'Unlike the example I gave you, you have fewer customers who do more transactions with you each year. So, trying to increase the number of transactions of your existing customers might not be as important as getting one new customer and establishing a relationship with them. That will give you an idea of where to start focusing, and which lever you should adjust first.

'Also, your margins are pretty high already because you are doing everything yourself. If you eventually grow and need to take on employees, then looking at the margin lever will become more important too.

'Of course you can look at margin as it relates to a lot of things, for example your time. What's the most profitable thing you do at the moment?'

'I guess it's my dusk shoots?'

'That's the highest value thing you do, in terms of what you get paid for it, but how much work do you do for that money?'

'Well, when you put it that way, dusk shoots do take a lot of time to shoot, and even more time to edit... it only takes me about an hour to draw up a floor plan. So I guess floor plans would actually be my highest "margin" thing?'

'That's a really good insight. We had no idea when you started that floor plans would be your most profitable service. That's why it's important to get in touch with the market so it can tell you what it values most.

'It's good to think about this now, before you get fully booked. If you'd tried to increase your Average $ Spent per transaction by encouraging all your agents to do more dusk shoots, you might have made more per agent, but you would have ended up with less free time per week.

'Now that you know your highest margin service, it might be worth putting the focus on encouraging your agents to do more floor plans instead, leaving you more time each week to maybe even take on an extra agent.'

'Considering dusk shoots are limited by how many I can do anyway, it's kind of good to know floor plans are more profitable. Okay, so how do I get agents to do more floor plans?'

'You could try what McDonald's does and just ask! Make it a habit to say, "Do you want floor plans with that?"'

Melissa groaned. 'Well at least if I make it a habit to ask them when they book a shoot, if they do want floor plans I'll be able to draw them up while I'm onsite. Occasionally an agent will ask for them later after buyers have started to look at the property and then I have to go out all over again to measure them up. If I do them at the same time as the photos I'm working on my margins too!'

'That's right! It's a good idea to make it a habit too — that's what I meant by "specialise so you can systemise". Asking "Do you want floor plans with that?" every time is creating a system. And it's something you can systemise because you are specialising in one type of photography.

'You'll really appreciate having thought things through now, and having put little systems like this in place, if you ever decide to take on employees.'

Having adjusted one lever already, we decided that since Melissa had passed on the security of the exclusive agency deal, and had let her old agency go too, the next lever to focus on was increasing leads.

'I could email out an offer for 10 per cent off my regular prices this month?' Melissa suggested.

'You could. The thing about offering discounts is twofold: firstly it does kind of put out there the idea that your product is overpriced. And you can only do it so often before people come to see that as your "real" price, and then wait until the next discount to book you.

'While you've got this time on your hands it'd be nice to put together more of a "system" for marketing instead of just a one-off.

'Secondly, there's the economics of it. Let's say your margins are 20 per cent, if you offer a 10 per cent discount you are effectively giving away half your profits, but you are only offering the consumer 10 per cent off. If you are giving away half your profits, you might as well give them all away (best done on things that have "soft costs" for you, like your time) and offer the customer something much more enticing: instead of 10 per cent off they could get 100 per cent off! "Free" is much more powerful than "discount", and it doesn't diminish the perceived value of your service like discounting does either.'

'If this is another example of how freedom leads to wealth I'd like to see it. How does working for free make me more money again?' Melissa asked.

'Well, obviously you're not doing all your shoots for free, but you could offer to do the first shoot free for new agents. Or maybe we could focus on the referral lever and offer a free shoot for any of your existing agents who refer another agent to you?'

'That's a good idea, actually,' Melissa agreed.

'I like that you're thinking of doing marketing; that is, a direct call to action. In fact, I'm a big fan of "call to action" or "offer-based" marketing. The reason is because you can measure it. As we were talking about with the levers, if you can measure your performance you can improve it, and even small improvements add up.'

Too many people buy into the 'Mad Men' 60s era ad agency style marketing: that marketing is all about raising brand awareness or other things you can't measure. If you can't measure, how do you know any adjustments you've made to your marketing lever have been successful?

Since the advent of what the kids call 'social', the tendency to favour this type of marketing has only increased. Instead of throwing money at 1960s ad guys in suits, we are now throwing money at social media gurus in skinny jeans! Just because it's on a new platform or has a new name, it doesn't mean that marketing fundamentals have somehow changed.

Some people might find the recipes and jokes that some businesses share on their social media of value, but what you really want to be doing is offering value in your area of expertise. Trust me, your clients can get their 'hot political takes' elsewhere!

Your customers may want to have a relationship with you, so not every email has to be asking for a sale. But any marketing you do that's not directly asking for a sale should still be offering some value.

In Melissa's case that meant the idea was to offer value that those on her list could only get from a professional photographer. This is why the 'listicle' style of internet article became so popular: people love learning new facts, especially new facts from someone they respect as an expert, that can satisfy their curiosity, teach them something about the world, and that they can then share with their social circle and sound like an expert themselves!

'Remember the agency that offered you the exclusive deal, how there were two photographers? Which type of photographer do you want to be? The one who does a high volume of work for a low price, or the photographer who does a lower volume for a "premium" price?

'We can send out offers and you will get more leads. And getting busier and busier will make you more money—linearly. But you bought back your time so you could buy back more time. Instead of trying to just get more work, it's time to get more money for the work you do.'

'Okay, sounds good. So how do we do that?'

'When you started out you offered the agents who agreed to meet with you something for free that got you a lot of bookings, helped you build an email list and also enabled you to position yourself as more of a premium photographer right from the beginning.'

'The marketing kits,' Melissa replied. 'They worked well because it gave me something to offer them, instead of just asking the agents for business.'

'Exactly. It also displayed your skills as a photographer and as someone who understood the needs of agents. So what if we did something like that again, only online this time?

'I'm thinking of something you could turn into a series of emails, so you can plan them out now and still have something to go on with when you get busy again.'

Too many small businesses treat marketing as first aid: a quick fix in an emergency. When work quietens down, quickly churn out some marketing. When work picks up, slack off on the marketing. And the cycle repeats.

'Ah, systemise the marketing,' Melissa exclaimed. 'I like it. I hate trying to think of things to email out, especially when I'm busy.'

'Alright, well, it'd have to offer a lot of value if there is no physical thing to give away this time, if you want a similar response,' I suggested. 'How would you feel about this: what if you put together a five-week photography course for agents, teaching them how to take better photos?'

'Wait. Why would I do that? That's what I charge people to do! Why would I want to teach them to do it themselves?' Melissa asked in shock. Up until now she'd been pretty open to the ideas I'd floated.

'On the surface it seems mad, I agree. And it's really stretching the whole "offer it for free" principle. But let's think about it for a minute. Even over a five-week course, could you teach them everything you know about photography? And even if you could, could they ever approach your level of experience doing the occasional shoot when you do them full-time?'

'Well no, I guess not.'

'So you are unlikely to lose the agents who already use you. They've already shown they are prepared to pay to have someone do a quality job. Besides, a lot of them hire you because they know their time is more productively spent doing what they do best, getting listings and selling. So which agents would this appeal to most?'

'The agents who do their own shoots already?' Melissa guessed.

'Right. Those are the agents on your list who were probably never going to book you anyway. They're happy to get by with their own photos. So you're not losing anything there either. If you view these emails as "relationship building" marketing then you are offering a lot of value, at no real cost to yourself.

'Some of those agents will no doubt take what you teach them and use it to improve the photography they do. But others might realise for the first time what a gulf there is between what they've been doing and professional photography. Good taste is learned! You may be in effect creating a new market for yourself of newly informed consumers!'

'Okay,' Melissa said, warming to the idea. 'I can see that. In fact I could do the referral offer we were talking about in the middle of this course. Offer my existing customers a free shoot if they sign up one of the other agents in their office who may have been doing their own photography up until now.

'Oh, and I could do a quiz at the end of the course and the first new agent to respond with the right answers could win a free professional shoot too!'

'That's great; combine your call to action emails, offers and relationship marketing all into one! Now you're rolling.'

There was one added benefit of creating the course that didn't become obvious until later, and that was how it also helped to raise Melissa's perceived expertise and value in the eyes of agents who were already booking her.

Counterintuitively, putting together a course to teach agents how to do better photography not only didn't stop them using Melissa as a photographer, but instead positioned her as the person who taught people how to do photography. One of her agents reported that he'd been approached by another agent in the office who'd been following along online doing the course, and they wanted to know if Melissa was really his photographer!

'Help! I've got a problem!'

It had been a few months since Melissa had lost the work from her old agency and we had invested some of her newly freed-up time into coming up with a marketing plan. I'd been following along with her email course and had seen that Melissa had not only understood the idea of blending relationship marketing with calls to action well, but had found a way to further systemise her marketing by sending out the occasional link to a blog that highlighted 'dodgy real estate photos', which was not only quite funny to read, but was also a clever way to take a lot of the work out of her marketing. So I was surprised when Melissa told me she needed help.

'What's the problem?' I asked, genuinely surprised. 'The marketing not going well?'

'No, actually the complete opposite—I'm run off my feet. I've picked up a couple of new agents who are great, but I'm getting more enquiries than I can handle. There are only so many hours in the day!'

'That's not a problem, that's great,' I laughed.

'No, it is a problem. I hate having to turn away work. What do I do?'

'Other than just turn away the work?' I asked.

'I'd really hate having to do that, but I'm not too keen to take on an employee either. What if the work drops off and then I have to find work for another person too? I've been enjoying my independence so much. I'm not sure I'm ready to commit to that yet.'

'That's fair enough. I'm glad you are still thinking in terms of valuing your freedom. Employees can both free you further, or potentially cost you your freedom. It's good not to rush into taking

people on just because you are busy, or out of some sort of scarcity mentality or fear of turning away work. Too many businesses feel obligated to grow quickly for growth's sake,' I replied.

I was reminded of a story about a Japanese manufacturing firm that, let's say for the sake of the story, made widgets. They produced 50,000 widgets a year at a price of $5 per unit. One day a big American company came to Japan and approached the firm with an offer: 'How much can you make us widgets for if we order 1 000 000 of them?' the Americans asked, sure that the small firm would be impressed with such a large order. The owner of the Japanese firm thought about it for a minute and said: '$10 per widget.'

'What?!' the Americans replied. 'You don't understand; we offered you a very big contract. You should offer us less per item, not more.'

'No, you don't understand,' the Japanese owner explained. 'We are set up to produce 50 000 units a year in volume. If we took on your order we'd have to invest in a new factory, new machines and take on many new workers just to meet your order. It would cost us more per unit to produce 1 000 000 widgets than it would to produce just 50 000. We would have to change our entire business, for just your order.'

Don't be afraid to turn away work if it could end up costing you more than it's worth, in money, or time.

'Since you are still valuing your freedom,' I said to Melissa, 'I've got one more technique you can try before you decide how you want to grow from here. It's a great technique because it can increase your freedom and increase your wealth at the same time.'

'Okay, sounds great!' Melissa replied enthusiastically.

'Not so fast,' I cautioned. 'If you don't like turning away work, you might struggle with this.'

'Stop teasing and spit it out,' she laughed.

'Okay, here it is: you've got to raise your prices.'

'Alright, you were right. I'd feel bad about raising my prices, especially for my existing agents.'

'Why's that?' I asked.

'Well, I guess I feel obligated to my clients. They have given me a lot of work, which I appreciate. And I guess I'm also worried that if I increase my prices I might lose some of them.'

'Okay, well let's look at both parts of that. As far as losing clients, let's say you make 10 per cent profit per client. Now I know you make more than that, which is one of the reasons you chose this business, but many businesses operate on lower margins than that. So for every $100 a client spends you make $10. If you raised your prices by 10 per cent you've doubled your profits. In this example you could lose half your clients and still come out even, right?'

'Sure, I guess.'

'But wait, if you lost half your customers you wouldn't come out even, you'd come out ahead.'

'How's that?'

'Well, you're not taking into account the unseen. If your profit stays the same, but you now have half the amount of work to do, you just gained a lot of freedom! Besides, in reality, it's highly likely you won't lose any clients at all.

'But there is another aspect to think about too. You said you appreciated your existing clients. But now that you are run off your feet with bookings, you're not as available for them as you were in the beginning. If you raise your prices and that does nothing more than deter the odd bargain shopper looking for cheap shoots, you've actually done your existing clients a favour by making yourself more available for them and allowing them more choices when they book you, and the ability to book you with shorter notice too, which is something I'm sure your regulars would value.'

'I guess you're right,' Melissa conceded.

'You may eventually want to take on staff,' I said, 'but you should want to do that when you can see a way that it can free you, which means you have systemised your business and can delegate or outsource parts of your workload. It then becomes an active choice. But, what a lot of people who suddenly find themselves booked out do, is try to avoid turning down work by quickly taking someone on as an employee—someone who may take up way more of your time than they save you, if you haven't first systemised your business. And then on top of that, they end up raising their prices anyway to cover the cost of the employee. By raising your prices first you not only give yourself

some breathing room, but you give yourself greater margins to work with, if and when you decide to expand.'

'I still feel nervous about asking for more,' Melissa admitted, 'but if it's a choice between turning away work, taking on employees, or this, I'll give it a go.'

A Quick Recap

Now that you've given yourself more choices, use them! Identify 'levers' in your life or in your business. Try tweaking some levers and see what a big impact a series of small changes can make, and why being freer to choose, even in just a small way, can make you rich.

CHAPTER 16
Free from tax

The real tax secrets of the rich. Thinking in four dimensions.

Tax. To most people it's a four-letter word.

Once you start making even a modest amount of money, tax quickly becomes one of your biggest expenses. I remember reading that a serf in the Middle Ages could perform his feudal duties to his lord in fewer months of the year than it takes the average employee today to earn enough money to cover their tax bill. Not only that but they had more public holidays back then too!

When it comes to wealth building, personal finance or even dinner table discussions, there is hardly a topic that is debated with more passion. Why do we hate tax so much? After all, given the choice, most of us would rather live in a country with well-developed laws, freedoms and personal security, than one without. And if push comes to shove most people will acknowledge that tax is the way we have to pay for all that.

I think the reason tax is so universally hated is because of the way most people first experience tax. For most, tax is something we don't get a say in: it's taken out of our salaries before we even get paid.

> **The trick is to stop thinking of it as 'your' money.**
> *IRS auditor, anonymous*

When the pay slip comes, there it is, in insultingly clear figures: 'This is your gross salary (what you could have earned); this is your net salary (what the tax department is letting you keep); and finally this is the tax that we have already

213

taken out of your pay cheque. And if you think we got it wrong you can spend hours sifting through your receipts and figure it out yourself, and maybe, at the end of the year we'll let you have a little of it back, minus of course the interest we earned hanging onto your money all year (if you're good).'

And it gets worse from there. If we manage to get ahead under the current system and see our pay cheques go up with each pay rise, we eventually see that the more we make, the greater the percentage or proportion of our money that gets taken in tax.

In every other area of life, if you want to save money you simply spend less, buy less stuff or use fewer services. But when it comes to tax as the 'fee' we all pay to live in a secure country, we often are entitled to fewer services the more we earn and the more we pay in 'fees'.

This system of rewards/punishments can often lead people to do crazy stuff when it comes to tax and benefits. The incentive of access to government benefits can see some people try to earn less money to stay entitled to those benefits. On the other hand the disincentive of paying higher taxes the more you earn can see others commit fraud to avoid paying them!

In fact, every time there is a tax increase there is a rise in tax evasion. This may be one reason that you see celebrities caught in tax scandals: it must be hard to go from being a low income earning, out of work actor, entitled to arts grants and other social benefits, to a high income earning, high tax paying individual in one leap.

So it's easy to see why people get emotional about the topic of tax.

Due to his illness, David had faced these perverse incentives and rewards/punishments when he first started his business. To get out of the Dependence Trap he had to risk going backwards despite earning more money. In a job, a small pay raise would have been enough to tip him over the edge, and he would have needed several raises in a row to earn enough to get back to even. But thankfully after a year of hard work and the advantages of growth that come when you're free of the Income Trap, he was facing a different kind of money problem altogether.

In his first year of business he'd managed to clear $70 000, but as he told me, that was because he was able to claim a lot of deductions, which kept his taxable income figure low. However, in his second year he was projecting he'd make at least $100 000 and he wouldn't be so lucky as to have a lot of deductions to offset that income as he did in his first year.

Tax secrets of the rich

So what is the 'secret' to paying less tax? Is it that the rich have company structures that pay lower rates of tax? Or is it that the rich can hire expensive accountants who can find them special deductions that the poor and middle class can't?

I've seen plenty of people run out and set up all sorts of company structures for businesses they don't even end up starting. It's tempting because you can feel that for a few grand you can be 'doing what the rich do'. But it's an expensive waste of time if you don't end up starting anything.

I've also seen plenty of people pay an arm and a leg to accountants who promise them clever tax deductions that end up being complicated investments that lose them money. (Never make an investment for the 'deductions' it will give you, or you could end up deducting a good portion of your equity too.)

> **The real secret of tax is that the tax system rewards the financially free, not just the rich.**

No. The real tax secret of the rich isn't special deductions.

It's not complicated legal structures.

The real secret of tax is that the tax system rewards the financially free, not just the rich.

Of course, the rich do tend to be freer on average. But not always. A high income earning professional working a job may not have a lot of actual freedom in terms of the choices they can make regarding their income and so they end up paying the highest rate and amount of tax, despite technically being rich.

Being free is more important than being rich.

Tax: thinking in two dimensions

If, like David, your first thoughts about tax are 'How do I find more deductions?' you can be forgiven. Most people work jobs, most people earn a set amount each week, and most people don't have much money left over at the end of the year.

Because of that, most people have already earned all the money they are going to earn that year by tax time. Their income is fixed. So, all that's left for the average employee to do is find some deductions to offset against that income.

Besides that, most popular books on tax tend to reinforce this 'deduction' focus, because most popular books aim to reach the largest number of people—which means targeting people working for a salary.

We talked before about how one of the costs of the Income Trap is that it causes people to think in straight lines. Nowhere is that more obvious than with tax. Trying to increase your expenses, or even trying to decrease your income by working fewer hours, is very two-dimensional thinking: expenses up or income down.

As legitimate deductions cost you a dollar to save you 30 cents, and reducing your income to pay less tax is like cutting off your nose to spite your face, it's no surprise that many people aren't very excited about learning about tax either.

> **Increase your freedom so that come tax time you can make some real choices.**

Worse yet, having so little control, some people even fall into the trap of doing things that, while quite common, are still illegal—such as deducting stuff that isn't business related to increase their expenses, or worse, hiding cash they are paid to decrease their income. It's not worth risking your freedom by breaking the law just to shave a little tax off the edges.

It's much better to increase your freedom so that come tax time you can make some real choices, and legally cut a big chunk off your tax bill instead.

Once you are free of 'dependence on income', and are less attached to actually receiving the money you create in small weekly parcels, you can expand your thinking and start to think in three or more dimensions.

Tax: thinking in three dimensions

Like I explained to David, one of the advantages of a small business over a job—even if you make no more money—is that you have the freedom to choose, the freedom to 'control more levers'.

So when it comes to tax, instead of thinking linearly—earning more or less money *this year*—what if you could earn more or less money *in* this year?

This is adding a third dimension of time to your thinking.

Instead of just thinking 'up and down', now you can think 'backwards and forwards' too.

If your business is growing and there are predictable expenses that you will incur next year, can you bring those expenses forward to this year and increase your deductions that way? I'm not talking about seeking out *extra* deductions, instead I'm talking about *moving* the deductions you will already make backwards and forwards in time.

If you negotiate in bulk you may even be able to save money by buying in advance too. It's another way that having even just a little savings can free you to do things that can make you richer.

Income works the same way as expenses. You may choose to book a major contract or job for July instead of June, meaning that you earn that income in the next tax year instead of this one. Or, if you suspect that as your business is growing quickly you will earn a lot more in your second year than in your first you might even do the opposite: bring forward your income to this year.

Now this is really stretching the way most people are conditioned to think about tax. It's a complete one-eighty in thinking to save tax by *increasing* your income! But by pulling forward income into your first year of business, you can actually save money because income tax rates are always less at lower levels of income.

In David's case some of the money that was going to be taxed at the $100 000 dollar level in his second year, could have attracted less tax if he'd earned it in his first year at the $70 000 level.

Planning ahead to profit

One way to bring forward your income is to offer a promotion: attract new customers, and encourage customers that would have booked in July to book you earlier instead. This is one exception to the 'don't discount' rule I shared with Melissa. A discount for your clients could pay for itself if it saves you 100 per cent in tax (why 100 per cent? Well the lowest tax brackets often have zero income tax rates—zero tax is pretty hard to beat!). There's no point wasting those lower income tax brackets this year if you haven't filled them up—it may be the last year you have the chance to earn income at those low rates!

Now that I've got you thinking in three dimensions, what about your expenses?

Think it's too hard to bring forward income? What about shifting back your expenses instead? Is there a major expense you are contemplating that you could push back; could you run down inventory in June and buy in bulk in July?

These are the reasons you see big companies offer end of financial year deals.

Even if you don't have your own business, you can of course still do this if you are an investor. Choosing when to sell your investments, and therefore what tax year to take your profits in, can have a huge impact.

When George Lucas sold the Star Wars franchise he not only made US$4.05 billion—half in cash, half in stock—but he saved 5 per cent tax on the lot (so roughly $202 500 000) by doing it when he did, instead of waiting until the new tax changes kicked in (which would see the long term capital gains tax rate increase from 15 per cent to 20 per cent). But I'm sure saving $202.5 million in tax played no part in his decision to sell his rights to Star Wars when he did ...

And if three-dimensional thinking is too basic for you, what about thinking in four dimensions?

Rather than timing when we earn income, what if we could get rid of it entirely—transform it into something else—and pay no tax at all?

Income versus growth

If someone asked me to simplify the vast topic of tax as much as possible, I would point out that there are generally two main types of tax: tax on income, and tax on growth.

Or to put it another way, *you're taxed on the wealth you earn, and not on the wealth you create*.

Let's say you want to retire young and live on $50 000 a year. For argument's sake, let's imagine two hypothetical investments: one that returns 5 per cent *income* per year (let's call this investment 1) and one that grows by 5 per cent a year (we'll call it investment 2). How much money would you need to have in each case to have $50 000 in income? One million dollars, right?

...you're taxed on the wealth you earn, and not on the wealth you create.

Hang on. Even though $50000 is 5 per cent of $1 million, what about tax?

If investment 1 is paying you 5 per cent income or $50000 a year, you have to pay tax on the whole $50000 because it's income. At a tax rate of, let's say, 30 per cent, you'd be left with only $35000 after tax (when you factor in tax-free thresholds and lower tax brackets, the effective rate of tax you pay is always going to be less than whatever the marginal tax rate is for a given amount of income, but this is just an example).

With investment 2, which grows by 5 per cent per year—or in other words increases in value by $50000—you could sell off $50000 worth of it (if it was something like shares) and if you'd held it for 12 months or more you'd only pay tax on half that amount because it's a capital gain and therefore the capital gains 50 per cent deduction applies. So you'd end up with $42500 after tax.

In other words, in the pure income example, if you wanted $50000 a year to live on after tax you'd need $1428571.42 in savings.

In the pure growth example, you'd only need $1176470.

Which is $252101 less you'd need to have in savings.

We can make the difference even more obvious when we consider that if you were retiring young (or at any age really nowadays) you need to account for inflation eating away at the value of your savings. One million dollars of capital and $50000 a year might seem like a lot now, but what about in 30 years' time?

The usual figure that is given to set aside is 2 per cent. So if we factor in that you want to live off $50000 after tax and after setting aside 2 per cent to cover inflation what do we come up with?

This is where the fact that you only pay tax on any growth you consume becomes apparent. For investment 1 you'd have to earn enough from the income-only investment to be able to put some money aside, after it had been taxed, to add to your savings to ensure they grow enough to match inflation. Imagine investment one is a bank account that earns 5 per cent interest.

But for investment 2, the one that grows by 5 per cent, you simply leave your 2 per cent in the investment, where it isn't taxed at all because you don't take it out. Imagine investment two is shares that don't pay any income.

How much difference would that make?

- *Investment 1:* 'all income' — $50 000 income, taxed at 30 per cent leaves you $35 000. Put $20 000 back into savings (so you have $1 020 000 in savings) to cover inflation, leaving you with $15 000 to live on.

- *Investment 2:* 'all growth' — grows by $50 000. Leave $20 000 in the investment to cover inflation (so you now have $1 020 000 in savings), sell $30 000 worth of 'shares', pay tax on half, taxed at 30 per cent leaves you $25 500 to live on.

Or, put another way, how much money would you need in each example to live on $50 000 after tax and inflation?

The answer is $1 666 666 in investment 1 versus $3 333 333 in investment 2 example.

In other words you'd need twice the amount of savings.

Now that example might be interesting if you have a nice pile of savings and are looking to retire early, or like my mother at the beginning of the Income Trap chapter you're wondering where your 'income' in retirement will come from. If you are a retiree who wants the security of an income stream and are tempted to sell all your assets to purchase an annuity, the costs of living for a long time off an income-only investment should be of interest to you.

In real life though, *most assets will give a mixture of income and growth.*

If you receive rent from a property, you are receiving income, so you pay income taxes on it. If you receive a lump sum from the sale of the same property, you are receiving a capital gain and the capital gains rate applies. So the same 'asset' can give you income, or growth, and the tax advantage comes not because of where the money came from but how the money came to you. Did it come as income, or as a capital gain? And there is even a third way to receive money from the same asset that isn't taxed at all and that is to draw out your equity, or growth, by borrowing money against the asset instead of selling it.

> **Income is to the rich what payday loans are to the poor and middle class — an expensive way to fund your lifestyle!**
>
> *Matthew Klan*

It's not where it comes from, it's how you receive it.

Or whether you receive it at all.

Turning income into growth

It turns out that the real tax secret of the rich and the reason they sometimes pay comparatively low rates of tax is that they receive most of their 'income' each year from capital sources:

- According to the IRS, those who earn over $1 million a year receive 67 per cent of their money, on average, from 'capital' or assets, and only 33 per cent from salary or wage income.

- The 'super rich', who, according to the IRS earn over $10 million a year, receive an even larger portion of their money from capital: 81 per cent compared to only 19 per cent from salary or wage income.

Now part of that is just a fact of getting richer. The more assets you have, the more of your total income each year comes from those assets, compared to wages. Someone with no savings at all sees 100 per cent of the wealth they earn each year come from their wage, and they get taxed at the highest rates too.

But part of that is also that the rich know that you're taxed on the wealth you earn, and not on the wealth you create.

To illustrate this there is a club known as the Zero Income Founders club. Zero Income Founders are those CEOs or company founders who pay themselves a symbolic salary of zero, or sometimes $1 per annum. By doing so they hope to signal to investors and employees that they are committed to seeing the company succeed and grow, and not just running the company to pull down a nice salary. They often own a majority of shares and they only make money themselves if the company's shares grow.

But you don't have to be a company founder, or already rich, to benefit from the advantages of growth over income.

Turning income into growth as an employee?

Even if you are simply an employee there are ways you can immediately turn income into growth: salary sacrificing is a strategy that allows you to directly turn some income each year into retirement savings or assets. Or, more actively, you could turn 'income into growth' by taking some time off each year—perhaps unpaid leave—and use that time to work on a project, such as renovating a house. If it was a principle place of residence you could sell it after 12 months completely tax free, allowing you for part of the year at least, to do what the rich (and more importantly the financially free) do and work for growth, not for income.

After all, having the freedom to not only 'work for growth' but to *actually grow* your skills and *yourself* is one of the most powerful reasons to get free first.

A Quick Recap

The real tax secret of the rich is that the tax system rewards the financially *free*, not just the rich. When it comes to tax, stop thinking two dimensionally in terms of income and deductions, and instead start to think in three or even four dimensions. Think about how you could *create* instead of earn, and work for *growth* instead of income.

CHAPTER 17
Free to grow

Free from the Income Trap — working for growth.

So I'd given David a lot to think about with tax, and had taken him from straight-line 'deduction thinking' to thinking three-dimensionally: realising the power that being in control of more levers afforded him to make more choice, such as moving income up and down, backwards and forwards, or 'transforming' it entirely.

The last bit — working for growth — David found particularly interesting.

In one conversation he admitted that when he started his business he'd only been thinking in terms of how much income he could make doing it.

But now he had another goal: a goal that made facing higher tax rates in his second year more bearable.

Instead of just making enough to get by, he could be building up a nest egg for his future — *without ever having to set aside money to 'save' for retirement.*

The business he was building had a value. His business was an asset. And assets are taxed differently.

- In Australia if you are nearing retirement and you've been in business for over 15 years you can sell your business for up to $6 million dollars *tax free*.

- If you sell when you are younger, even if you have been in business for less than 15 years, you can still get a 50 per cent discount on capital gains for the sale of 'active assets' like a business.

- Up to $500 000 of capital gains can be put straight into a retirement account at any age without paying tax on it at all.

- Or you can defer the 'capital gains' from the sale of a business entirely if you roll them into a replacement asset.

This gave David a lot more choices, and a lot more incentive to work on not just generating income but building his business too, which could provide for his retirement, give him something he could pass on to his children, or even just be something he could sell and roll the proceeds into a new business, perhaps starting that special effects business he'd always dreamed of.

> **There is no more fatal blunderer than he who consumes the greater part of his life getting his living.**
> *Henry David Thoreau*

So many people work their entire lives, and every hour they spend doing so gets turned into income. After a lifetime of work they've built up no value. At the end of your working life no matter how much extra training you did for your job it's still not something you can sell like you could an asset; 100 per cent of the value you created over your entire working life was taxed, while your work has helped create an asset for someone else.

If you create a business that you could sell for $1 million, that's $1 million dollars you've created tax free that could be a retirement nest egg: you could sell it and pay no tax, or at worst only pay tax on half.

You could roll the proceeds into another business tax free.

You could continue to grow it while drawing out the money as a loan, again tax free, to buy other investments.

Turning income into growth in a business is as simple as freeing up the time to work on Freedom Quadrant activities: perhaps turning away a couple of hours of work a week in exchange for working on systemising your business, which in turn should free you up further, as well as increase the value of your business.

For those who want to practise Freedom First to become financially free, but don't want to start a business, the same principle still applies: free yourself from the Income Trap—or at least from dependence on it. You can start to be less dependent on your job and its income by having some savings.

You can turn 'income into growth' in a job with salary sacrificing.

But you can do it more directly too. If you are faced with the choice to work 40+ hours a week to maximise your income—as opposed to working a little less and investing the time into growing yourself, and your skills—that's the smarter choice.

> ❝ **If a man empties his purse into his head, no man can take it from him. An investment in knowledge pays the best interest.** ❞
>
> *Benjamin Franklin*

One skill you develop in your spare time during your working life could mean the difference between retiring from your job with no residual value (you can't sell your job, you can just stop doing it), to being able to retire with skills you could use to invest, or even earn some money part-time, in a way that's fun and is no pressure.

Any skill you learn that could earn you a little income in retirement has a value.

And the value goes beyond the financial. We look at our jobs as purely economic activities. But people have a need for so much more than money. People need to create.

They need to create value, and to be valued. There is nothing worse than working your whole life for income, only to retire and feel that you have nothing of value left to contribute.

❝...**people have a need for so much more than money. People need to create.**❞

Working on growth: building assets within assets

But while David was focused on the big picture now, I wasn't finished with him yet.

While his business was something that had a value—that he could one day sell as an asset—there were other ways he could focus on building an asset *within* his business that could make him money *now*.

One of the advantages we looked at earlier that came from getting free was being able to be in touch with the market. The market is the network of minds that connects consumers and producers and is where wealth creation happens. By getting in touch with the market directly when he first quit his job, David was able to directly see what it was that consumers valued. And the market had told him what to specialise in to make the most money. But now that he'd been in business for a while he'd done more than just 'get in touch with the market', he'd created a network of his own.

And that network itself could be an asset.

A good example is the company 23andme. The human genome was first sequenced in 2000 for a cost of approximately $2.7 billion for the publicly funded effort. By 2006, the cost had fallen to approximately $20 million, a decade later in 2016 it was under $1500 and since then the cost of sequencing DNA has come down to the point where it is feasible for consumers to have their own DNA sequenced.

23andMe, started by Linda Avey, Paul Cusenza and Anne Wojcicki (the former wife of Google co-founder Sergey Brin) is a business that offers a service: order one of their DNA sampling kits, take a sample and send it to them and they'll sequence your DNA for a pretty low price, and even give you some insight into what all the information contained in it might mean. A sufficient number of people were curious enough to order a kit and make this a viable business.

But 23andMe, from its beginning, was more than simply a 'service'-based business.

While it might make 'income' from selling its kits, it was simultaneously working on the 'growth' of its assets. In the case of 23andMe that asset was the collected DNA of all its customers. Having such a large database of DNA, the company was able to rent out this database to researchers and drug companies around the world who could use this information for everything from testing new drugs to uncovering new genes by looking at sample sizes far larger than most researchers had access to.

Aside from being a little creepy, what 23andMe did from the start was create a service-based business that would pay them to build an asset as well.

Now you may recognise the second part of this business model from other tech companies. In fact, many of our biggest tech companies started at the 'build the asset' stage and completely ignored the 'earn income' phase.

Facebook, for example, provides a service, but not one that anyone was prepared to pay for. But by building such a large user base, Facebook has been able to 'monetise' its list or database by selling it to advertisers ... and others.

However, this is not a good model to follow if you value being financially free.

For a start, it involves losing money every year as you give away a service, on the gamble that enough people will adopt your service to make it profitable to sell those people as a list to others. And secondly, these businesses often end up going into debt or dependence, on venture capitalists and others, to keep them afloat while waiting for the gamble to pay off. If you look carefully you'll notice many big companies today don't make a profit, but they

> **"Start a business that frees you: start a business that has a service or product that you can make money from selling straight away."**

provide a value to someone who keeps them afloat regardless. You can't rely on that happening to you, and you shouldn't want to end up dependent on the whims of a big moneyed backer with an agenda either.

23andMe, on the other hand, is a much better model to follow. Like I said earlier, start a business that frees you: start a business that has a service or product that you can make money from selling straight away. Then use your newly freed-up time and expanded range of choices to 'turn income into growth' by focusing on growing the parts of your business that are not immediately visible.

The visible part of David's business was the service he provided: repairing phones. It was a great business to start because it very quickly set him free, and provided him with immediate sales. But in the process David had been building an asset that wasn't immediately visible: his list.

When he first started his business, I told him: get the contact details/emails of all your customers. He'd been pretty passive about it at first, leaving it up to customers to add him on Facebook. At first glance there wouldn't seem much point in building a database—after all he'd specialised in repairing phones, and it's not like people break their phones regularly. How do you market to former customers: 'If you break your phone again this week I've got a special offer on'?

But even though he'd started out as a generalist, and shifted to becoming a specialist, what David didn't realise was that he could provide extra value to his customers without having to go back to being a generalist and offering a bunch of different services to increase his revenue.

The people who'd come to David to have their phones repaired left not only happy with the job he'd done, but with an appreciation for David as a 'tech expert'. David had been building up his value in the eyes of his customers by being a specialist, and the best guy in town at what he did.

David could take advantage of the network he was building by creating a dialogue with his list and discovering what other needs they had.

This is the hidden power of being a 'specialist small business' and having a list. Your list will respect your expertise and follow your recommendations. So David could now build relationships with other businesses in a similar field and refer his customers to them, perhaps in exchange for a referral fee. Other businesses might pay to 'rent' his list for an email blast. His list had value.

This is not hard selling. In fact, it's not selling at all. David is constantly telling me about the latest gadget he's bought and he doesn't make a cent from that, and I often don't buy whatever the latest thing is; but I still like hearing about it. There is so much great stuff and innovation and information out there but our time is too limited to follow all of it. It's good to have a friend who is into something you like more than you are, so they can save you time by highlighting all the cool bits for you.

The act of contacting your list will itself get you new work independent of the content of the email. Whenever Melissa bought a new piece of equipment for her business she would write a review and share it with her list. New business is generated just by reminding people you are there. And if you can remind them in a way that adds value for them, so much the better.

Plugging into your list, adding value for them, recommending things that you use/like, can also have benefits beyond the extra bookings or extra revenue from referrals.

David had been tending his list on Facebook for a while when out of the blue he was contacted with an opportunity from someone who had never used his service before, but was nevertheless able to appreciate his expertise by seeing how others on Facebook spoke highly of him. He hooked David up with his son who had just landed a contract to handle hundreds of surplus government phones a month, providing a whole new stream of work for him.

By focusing on growth and tuning into your network on more channels, you'll find more opportunities than you could imagine. You enter an exponential growth curve that you simply don't have access to in a job.

The more freedom you have, the more opportunities come your way, and the freer you are to seize them!

'It didn't work.'

'What didn't work?' I asked, surprised.

'You said if I raised my prices I could not only end up richer, but freer too if I lost some agents because of the price rise ... but I didn't lose any!' Melissa replied with a grin.

'I decided if I wanted to get freer I'd have to do something about it,' she continued more seriously. 'It's hard when you are run off your feet. But you talking about the quadrants definitely helped.

'I was busy during the day doing shoots, but still had to come home at night and spend time on the computer. And that's what gave me an idea. I don't need to take on an employee yet if I just outsource part of my job.

'What if I could contract someone to do some of the back end stuff? Like floor plans and photo editing?

'I think it was because I do that stuff at home at night that I got the idea. So even though I was run off my feet I placed a small ad with a "work from home" opportunity, for people with Photoshop or Visio skills,' Melissa explained.

'I've seen plenty of those work from home ads before, but they always look like scams,' I laughed.

'I know, but this was an honest to goodness opportunity for someone to work from home—for real!' Melissa exclaimed. 'I was worried that people would think it wasn't legit either. But I got over 300 responses! Many of them mums. I couldn't believe it. It was actually pretty overwhelming and humbling too.'

Until you have kids you have no idea how demanding of your attention they will be. There are plenty of 'packaged solutions' that promise to allow you to work from home, (and make a lot of money!) but what you really need is not just a way to work from home, but one that doesn't require you to go door to door, or drop everything to take a call; an opportunity that allows you to work any hours: around baby's naps, outside of normal working hours or late at night if that is the only time you can find. Learning a skill, and looking for a 'business to business' niche, like Melissa created, might require a little more work initially, but may actually allow you to achieve the work–life balance that is so lacking in our modern 'mass employment' economy.

'Humbling?'

'Just that so many people were looking to me for work. I've never been an employer before: I still have to pinch myself that I'm my own boss sometimes, let alone anyone else's. And I know how much it means to me not to have to work for anyone else ever again. I mean I'm not rich or anything yet, but now that I've done this I can't ever see myself going back to a job. It was really important for me just to have someone who could tell me that I could do it, that it wasn't as hard as it looked from the outside. I really have to thank you for that.'

'Oh that's okay,' I replied. 'It sounds like now you've got the opportunity to pay it forward at least.'

'Yeah that's true, I guess. Most of the people who responded to the ad weren't looking to make a full-time business out of it — even though they could have, especially if they got themselves several photographers to work for.

'Most were just looking to make their part-time jobs survivable, with some work they could do at night. It really opened my eyes to how much people are struggling in this economy, with jobs that tie them up all week only to give them a few hours' work. There's no job security any more.

'And it amazed me how many people have taught themselves a valuable skill: Photoshop is not that easy to learn! Nearly all of them were self-taught: one guy linked me to his YouTube channel in his resume. He'd taught himself the Adobe Suite programs so he could make better infographics for the videos on his YouTube channel!'

I've got a saying: 'Watch YouTube to learn, publish to YouTube to earn.' YouTube is a fantastic place to learn new skills.

'You remember David? When he started his business he taught himself how to repair phones largely from YouTube. He'd done some repairs before at his old job, but with new phones coming out every day YouTube was a real help. And it's free. Free education!' I said to Melissa.

'That reminds me,' she replied excitedly, 'you know how you said one of the ways to get freer in a small business was to do higher value work? Well one of my agents was asking me about HDR photography. He'd heard that another agent's photographer was doing it, so I looked into it, watched some tutorials on YouTube and it's not that hard to do. Of course some people overdo it and their photos start to look really fake but done well it can look quite good.'

'So what's it involve?'

'HDR stands for High Dynamic Range photography. Basically, you capture several exposures of a scene, and then use software to combine them to give a more realistic photo, which is similar to what the human eye and brain does when you look at a high contrast scene.'

'Oh, I would have guessed it had something to do with high def,' I replied.

'I'm pretty sure some agents think that too, now that I've started offering it as an option!' Melissa laughed.

'Hey that's great. Let the market tell you what it wants!' I said. 'So what about the outsourcing. What happened with that?'

'Oh, that went well; at least as far as the floor plans were concerned. I sketch them up onsite then email a scan to my contractors at night. I've found a couple of guys who are great, and turn them around really quickly. It didn't take long to train them either.

'The photo editing is another matter. I'm really picky about quality, and while I had plenty of people who were keen on the work, teaching them to do it to my standards was not so easy. I'm still working with a couple of girls, but it's taking a lot of back and forth. I'm not prepared to deliver to my agents anything that represents my business that's not 100 per cent right in my eyes. I'm sure some of them wouldn't mind, but I do. So I'm still working on that. But it has been great to be able to outsource one part of my business so far.'

'Well I guess with the floor plans it's pretty objective: the rooms are either drawn to the right measurements or not.'

'Exactly.'

'But with the photo editing you're having to do a lot more training huh? Can I give you one tip? Take the time now to record your *training. With computer work like photo editing, that can be really easy: there are programs that allow you to record whatever is on your screen.*

'Make sure that if you are spending a lot of time training someone you take a little extra time to do some Freedom Quadrant work and record it, that way if you have to end up hiring new editors you won't have to start the training process all over again.

'Not only do you make things easier by systemising and formalising the training, but you are "working for growth" in that having training systems in place increases your business's potential sale value to a buyer too.

'Besides, you never know when you can turn a skill or service you provide into a product. By placing that ad, you've gotten in touch with the market and uncovered a niche demand I wouldn't have imagined existed: people who, for whatever reason, have taught themselves some Photoshop and are interested in using that skill productively.'

'Okay, I'll keep that in mind!'

August 2011

Melissa called me up with an interesting proposal. She was keen to catch up and share with me how her business was going, but she wondered if I could meet her at one of the shoots she was doing in the suburb of Milton. She had discovered something she was sure I'd be interested in.

It had been nearly a year since Melissa had first started to get free of her business, but it had been over 40 years since the city of Brisbane had suffered a huge flood. When she rang, the waters had just started to recede after the biggest flood in most people's memories, so my curiosity was piqued.

Australia, like South America, experiences what are known as La Nina weather cycles: multi-year-long cycles that deliver greater than average rainfall (in Australia) in the wet season each year, followed by multi-year-long El Nino cycles that deliver lower than average rainfall and drought.

Humans are bad at predicting cycles at the best of times, but when these 'larger' cycles last for years and sit on top of more regular cycles like the yearly seasons, they can be even harder to comprehend.

At the height of the last El Niño cycle in Australia, several high profile people convinced state governments that the drought would never end. The effects of the El Niño cycle were attributed to broader climate change and once again the subtleties of cycles were lost in a desire to see straight lines and permanent trends.

Governments around Australia invested billions of dollars in desalination plants to turn sea water into drinking water and failed to build proposed dams, in the belief that the rains would never come again. But eventually the cycles ended and the rains came with the new La Nina cycle. 2010 and 2011 were the third wettest and second wettest calendar years on record for Australia. But as dams hadn't been built, rivers flooded, houses and lives were lost, and billion dollar desalination plants sat in mothballs.

Together, the two years were the wettest 24-month period in Australian history. The previous record had been in 1973–1974. People in Brisbane often talked about the 'floods of '74' where large parts of the city that were normally well above flood levels went underwater; they were a part of the local lexicon, and figured significantly in the collective memory of the people of Brisbane.

But 1974 was nearly 40 years in the past. Markets are capable of pricing in a lot of things, but they don't do well at pricing in events that come around only every couple of generations. Was it possible that now that the last two years had set rainfall records, for a while at least, people would see this level of flooding as the 'new normal'?

As Melissa met me outside the house that she was photographing and floor planning, I began to have an inkling as to why she'd invited me there. To be honest I was surprised I hadn't thought of it myself, but that's the advantage Melissa had of 'being in the market'.

Before we could go in and look at the place, Melissa had some updates for me. The first was that she'd taken on a full-time employee! She introduced me to Larissa, who was at the shoot with her, and as Larissa excused herself to continue taking the photos Melissa caught me up on her progress.

I wisely decided against making a crack about 'Melissa and Larissa, the photography sisters', and instead asked her to fill me in on the changes she'd made since we last spoke.

It was clear that she had continued to 'tap into the network' and find out from her consumers what it was they valued, as she'd added another premium service to her line-up: interactive floorplans and panoramic 3D photos. As Melissa explained it, this allowed people perusing an online listing to click on a floorplan to see the picture of each particular room on the plan. The 3D photo option allowed an agent to give a buyer the chance to 'step into' a particular feature room in the property and look around—all before seeing the house in real life.

But what I was most interested in was how she'd come to take on an employee. Unlike some people who rush to employ people so they can have a 'big' business, or because they are busy and don't want to turn away work, I knew Melissa wasn't about to take on an employee unless she could see how it could free her, and not just create more work.

'I was outsourcing the floor plans and the editing, but as you know I was pretty fussy about the quality of the editing. Recording everything like you suggested helped, but eventually I decided to take on Larissa because of what else she could do as well.

'So many people responded to the ad, and most of them just wanted a little bit more money, but Larissa really seemed like someone who was keen to take on more responsibility and even run her own business one day,' Melissa explained.

'It's funny you say that because I remember David telling me how as soon as he went on commission and started showing some real drive and bringing in new business, his old boss started feeling threatened,' I reminded her. 'Whereas you went out of your way to hire someone like that?'

'Yeah, I don't understand David's boss. As I've learned there's a lot more to running a business than just doing the service part of it. I'm not worried about Larissa starting her own business, in fact part of the reason I hired her is that I think she could be someone great to hand over to one day.

'Plus, not only has hiring her allowed me to control the editing better, and lessen the time I spend on site, but it's forced me to systemise parts of the business I never would have before—things that just I was doing.'

This is another reason I suggest starting a business that frees you, first.

Starting small, you initially may do more of the tasks yourself, but the upside of that is when it comes time to outsource or to employ others, you've had a chance to figure out the best way to do things. Even some of the biggest, flashiest tech companies today started out with their founders doing the coding. Employees are never as motivated as founders are to find the most efficient way to get things done.

'I've got a checklist for Larissa to follow for what to do onsite now, and what's more, I did what you said about recording the photo editing training I was doing for the contractors. That came in really handy when I hired Larissa because I'd already put together a lot of her training, so it got her up to speed in no time.

'But now that I've got a little more time on my hands I was thinking about what you said about an untapped market of people with Photoshop skills, and remembering how well my photography course went over when I emailed it out.

'Since I already have hours of recordings teaching people how to properly edit real estate photos, why don't I polish it up and sell it as a course?'

'That's a great idea!' I said. 'You've taken the first step towards turning your service into a product—a virtual one at that!'

Virtualising your skill

There are guys working very 'manual' type businesses thinking, 'How will I ever get free of working in my business when it's so hands on?' (Which reminds me of my days as a physiotherapist: literally a hands-on business!) Little do these skilled workers realise that they've got skills that other people may want to learn—a very easy way to 'productise' their service is to teach others! There are YouTube channels about carpentry with millions of views from hobbyists looking to do small projects in their spare time.

I congratulated Melissa on her progress; it was clear that she wasn't just focusing on generating more income, but on building a real asset too. Not only had she freed herself from a job, but she was well on her way to freeing herself within her business, and freeing up her time as well.

'On that note, that reminds me why I invited you to meet me here. Come and check out the house,' Melissa said.

As she led me around the house I was surprised to find that the flood damage was much less than I'd expected.

Watching the flood coverage on the news I'd seen images of people wading through mud, damaged furniture piled up outside their houses. But once the mud had been cleared away, the interior wasn't as damaged as I'd imagined.

In fact, it looked like after the wet plasterboard had been cut away at a height of about a metre off the floor, the rest of the walls were left intact while the underlying frame was exposed and allowed to dry.

'So is this a good example of a Salvo?' she asked.

'Salvo' refers to part of a property strategy I call 'Salvo-Reno-Primo', which I was teaching about towards the end of the boom. When every TV channel was showing property renovation shows, and the demand for 'fixer-uppers' was at its peak, it was becoming more and more difficult to buy a 'Reno' at a reasonable price in the hopes of doing it up and selling it as a premium or 'Primo' property. If people are paying above 'fair value' for a Reno, what do you do? Instead of being a buyer of the overpriced Renos like everyone else, become a seller of Renos instead! How do you do that? By finding what I call Salvos, or salvage properties—properties with major problems, that might be beyond the average home renovator—and fixing the major problem, then selling them as simpler Renos to a market that's going crazy for easy fixer-uppers. Like that Leo Tolstoy quote from Anna Karenina, 'All happy families are alike; each unhappy family is unhappy in its own way,' the beauty of the Salvo-Reno-Primo strategy is that while there are only a few things that make a premium property 'premium', there are many different things that might make a property a Salvo, and the savvy active investor can specialise (and therefore systemise) in fixing a particular subset of those problems, such as zoning issues, or asbestos contamination.

'Well it does require a little work, but much less than I expected,' I told her.

'I'd call this something between a "Salvo" and a "Bargain Purchase" instead.

'A Bargain Purchase is a great way to get your equity up front which is the essence of Freedom First active property investing. There are plenty of reasons something may be a bargain purchase, but in this case you've found something that may be "undervalued" due to cycles.'

A different way to think of what was happening to the houses in this usually premium suburb is a market 'mispricing'. People were used to seeing this suburb as a premium inner city suburb and not as a 'flood prone' suburb.

But while the memories of the recent floods were fresh in people's minds, that perception had changed. However, this suburb was not a flood-prone suburb—except in the exceptional case of a 'once every 40 years' flood.

That's almost two generation cycles. A property could change hands several times before it ever saw flooding again.

How long before people stopped 'mispricing' this suburb as a flood prone one, and went back to pricing it as a desirable inner city one? My guess is it would be less than a year, but worst case scenario after a 'normal' rainy season or two passed without further incident, I was sure perceptions would change.

After a little research, I saw that this house had previously sold in 2007 for $650 000. The Aussie housing market had pulled back a little since then — nothing compared to the United States; it had mostly just paused.

The share market on the other hand had corrected sharply during the GFC, and unlike the US, by 2011 the Australian stock market had not recovered to its pre-GFC highs — but it had recovered. And by passively investing the profits from her business in the stock market over the past couple of years Melissa's savings had grown passively with it.

Of course it was tempting for me to want to coach Melissa to actively invest in the stock market, but she had an active investment strategy already — her business — and if you are not 'in touch' with a market, it's best to just invest passively in it. Besides, the return on her initial active investment in her business far outstripped anything she could have hoped to do in the stock market in the same space of time.

But one market Melissa was in touch with through her business was the housing market. Had Melissa identified an opportunity to turn some of her passive savings into an active growth play?

Well, one month later the property Melissa showed me sold for just $480 000, well below what it was worth only months before, confirming that she had found a real opportunity.

We got to work. There were dozens of houses in similar situations across several suburbs.

It took less than a year before the affected properties would bounce back and be valued higher once again.

And a few short years after that, not only would property sales in the suburb go on to surpass their 2007 peak, but Melissa would go on to sell her business, retiring for the first time in her mid twenties.

A Quick Recap

Turning income into growth in a business can be as simple as freeing up the time to work on 'Freedom Quadrant' activities—increasing the value of your business—or as sophisticated as identifying assets within your asset and developing those.

In a job you can turn income into growth directly with things such as salary sacrificing, or by investing some time and money in your education or learning an investment skill. You can also indirectly turn income into growth by focusing on taking jobs or projects that give you more skills and allow you to grow, rather than those that just pay the highest income.

You are your best asset. The more you grow and the more freedom you have, the more opportunities will come your way, and the freer you are to seize them.

CHAPTER 18

The path of Freedom First

A compass not a ladder.

For many people, being free of a job is possibly the biggest freedom they could desire. However, it's also true that for many people stuck in a job the thought of starting a business is terrifying. Fortunately, this is not 'Quit Your Job and Start a Business First'.

It's Freedom First.

But for those who do find the idea of starting a business attractive but scary, if they are honest and they do a thorough Values Audit, they may find that what's really difficult for them to give up is the status of their current job, or perhaps the security of it.

Many people in this position who don't realise that it is their values that are holding them back, often say 'But I don't have any skills, there's nothing I do that I could start a business with.' But we've seen that you can start a business with the most basic skills—even based around a hobby you have, and not any 'formal' qualification.

It's important to understand and accept what it is that you truly value.

Freedom First is a guiding *principle*.

If you want to become financially free, you must get free *first*. It's about learning to value your freedom *more*, not abandoning your other values.

> ❝ **Many are stubborn in pursuit of the path they have chosen. Few in pursuit of the goal.** ❞
>
> *Friedrich Nietzsche*

It's important to realise that Freedom First is like a compass, and not a ladder.

It gives you a guiding principle to apply, rather than a set of predefined steps.

A compass, not a ladder

Of course we've seen that there are certain signposts along the way—certain bearings you can check to ensure you're moving in the right direction:

- Are you aiming for security, or heading for dependency, when you really want freedom?
- Are you moving from dependence towards independence and interdependence?
- Are you moving away from pain, and towards pleasure?
- Are you receiving income, or working for lump-sums?
- Are you *earning* money, or *creating* wealth?
- Are you living week to week (in the Income Trap) or are you progressing towards living month to month, and eventually year to year?
- Are you working just to pay the bills, or taking on projects and working for the skills?
- Are you following orders, or taking control of the levers?
- Are you spending more time in the Freedom Quadrant?
- Are you depending on assets always rising, or are you in control of your growth?
- Are you getting more in touch with the market and network of minds?
- Is your mind constantly tasked with the short term, or are you freeing your mind to think, to create, and to grow?

Freedom First is a principle: you can apply it to whatever area of your life you want — the more the better.

And because it's a compass and not a ladder it's okay that people may be starting at different levels.

It's not how much money you have, it's what you do with it.

Some people work hard for many years until they've 'saved up enough' to be investors. But having a million dollars doesn't mean you can be a big shot investor, it just means you have a lot of capital to invest, or to lose. And if you've worked and saved your whole life for that capital, that's not a strategy you can repeat. On the other hand, if you've created your wealth, you can create it again. It's better to start investing early with a small amount of money and build up your skills and experience than wait years building up your savings and developing no skills.

> **❝ I've met some retirees who only really started investing once they had quit work, because they never had the time to do it before. But after waiting their whole lives to buy back all of their time, they're finding that all it would have taken was enough time to find the first deal and complete it. They could have retired years earlier. What a waste of time! ❞**
>
> *Matthew Klan*

And it's not just about money.

Hannah Arendt's book *The Human Condition*, makes an interesting point that the ancients used to have two words for what we now just call work. There was 'work', and there was 'labour'. Labour was considered almost lowly. It was the activity that you did to make ends meet — you laboured to put food on the table. The effort put into labour was consumed, whereas 'work' was often something larger, and lasting, that you could put yourself into: think of 'great works' or 'public works'.

Now we call everything we do work, although nearly everything we do is labour — what we create is consumed, either immediately or in the future. Although we are richer than ever before, the ancients would consider us impoverished. Hardly any of us get to step back from 'labouring' to look at the big picture and truly work towards something bigger than ourselves. If you could free yourself from the short term—free yourself from 'labouring' to make ends meet—what great work could you be capable of?

I'm reminded of the story of the Parable of the Talents (Matthew 25:14–30) where a rich master leaves his servants to watch over his money, or 'talents', while he's away. In the story, the servant who does the most with the money he is left in charge of, is rewarded the most, while the servant who chooses to take no risks but instead keeps the money he was left safe, is punished. 'So take the bag of gold from him and give it to the one who has ten bags. For whoever has, will be given more, and they will have an abundance. Whoever does not have, even what they have will be taken from them. And throw that worthless servant outside, into the darkness, where there will be weeping and gnashing of teeth.' Harsh.

The story talks about 'talents': 'he gave five talents to the first servant' etc. A talent in this instance is usually interpreted as a measurement—so a talent could be one measure of silver, or one measure of gold.

But I like to think that this story can be about more than just money: we are all born with unique talents that are ours to use or waste. What is your story? What are your unique talents? In what ways could you be freer right now, and what could being freer allow you to do, to be, to create?

The greatest asset we all have in common with each other—that we can invest or waste—is time.

There's no better time to buy back your time, than now.

CHAPTER 19
Free minds create

" I know but one freedom and that is the freedom of the mind. "

Antoine de Saint-Exupéry

Postscript

I spoke again with Melissa a couple of years after she sold her business.

She had trained her replacement, and eventually sold the business to her in several instalments, with a period of overlap where Melissa continued to do the marketing for her, providing Melissa with not only a lump sum, but a small income stream during the transition.

Having 'retired' so young I was curious to see what Melissa was up to.

Was financial freedom sitting on the beach every day, while everyone else was at work?

Well, that was definitely part of it, she informed me happily. But something else had happened when Melissa had finally gotten free of the Income Trap entirely.

Like a lot of people discover (sometimes almost too late in life once they retire the more traditional way), freedom from the nine to five, freedom to choose what to do during the best hours of each day, and every day, freedom to think and to create is incredibly liberating.

It looked like Melissa's freedom, rather than cause her to waste away in idle pursuits, had instead only begun to unleash her creative juices.

In her first job Melissa had been dependent; after starting to save and value her freedom her new job offered her more independence, but it wasn't until she'd started her own business that she'd become truly independent. But like we saw in chapter 7, there are levels higher than just independence, and freedom doesn't mean being alone.

Having escaped the Dependence Trap and achieved independence, she was now free to seek out opportunities at the highest levels: interdependence.

'I sold my list of agents with the business, but I didn't sell my list of people who contacted me to learn how to edit real estate photos or people who bought my course,' Melissa informed me, with a light in her eyes.

'There's a young guy down the coast who's looking to create an app that allows agents to upload their photos to a website and have professional photo editors process them for them — it's a great idea! I wish I'd thought of it,' she continued.

'But I can tell you exactly why I didn't: I found it really hard to outsource editing because it was a high-skill task, maybe even more so than taking the photos. My experience was that contractors weren't consistently producing to my standard, but that was my standard.

'Perhaps what I want, and what others are prepared to pay for are two different things. That's for the customer to place a value on— not me. It was really hard to see that, while I was busy working "in" the business,' Melissa confided.

'But I can understand how seeing things from my perspective stopped me thinking of this idea myself. While the agents who hired me had pretty high standards too, agents who take their own photos to save money might really value a service like this. And if it's set up with an editor rating system, or a sliding pay scale, who knows? It could actually create competition and drive the quality of the editing up too,' Melissa concluded, the idea clearly forming as she spoke.

'Regardless, the idea of a real estate photography editing app is definitely an example of virtualising or "productising" a service — and it takes advantage of a resource I'd already built: a list of contractors who can edit real estate photos.

'I'm even convinced it wouldn't eat into the business of actual real estate photographers either: I've seen the photos agents take by themselves!

'Like you taught me, you can do something that seems like it might cut into your business, but if it reaches people who were never going

to pay for your service in the first place, and introduces others to your service for the first time, then even giving away stuff for free can end up growing your business.

'The more that there is an expectation that the standard of photography has to increase in the industry, the more people will end up using professional photographers too: even if some end up trying to make do with taking the photos themselves.

'So I might contact the guy developing the app and see if there is a way we can do a joint venture. As soon as he starts hiring contractors with Photoshop skills, he's going to realise there is a difference between "doing Photoshop" and using Photoshop to professionally edit real estate photos. The training that I recorded for my Photoshop editors and turned into a course could be of real value,' Melissa enthused.

'Also, since selling the business, drone photography has become a real thing. I used to love playing with remote controlled cars as a girl, so that sounds like a fun skill I could learn in my "retirement". I could hire myself out to several photography businesses at once. Who knows? After the flood-affected houses, my confidence in property investing has increased and now that I've bought back several years' worth of my time with the sale of the business I'm definitely free enough of the Income Trap to be able to work for growth instead.

'While I'm enjoying my freedom for now, whatever I end up doing next, I know one thing: I won't be doing it because I need money for the bills that week. And I won't be looking for someone to be my boss either.

'I'll be doing something that I'm interested in, something that I can get passionate about that can help other people too. And I've got the confidence and experience now to know I can do that for myself.'

I was so glad to hear that, and I knew exactly what Melissa meant. It was how I chose to live my life: following my interests and satisfying my curiosities. Over the years my interests had changed, but if you can become passionate about something, and you have the time to pursue it, sometimes you'll find that your expertise and passion can lead you to see a solution that has been overlooked by everyone else. Having been a lifter for most of my life, and trained as a physiotherapist it always surprised me when I'd visit commercial gyms and their bench press stations would have no safety equipment to stop users from dropping the bar on themselves. Once upon a time there was no such thing as safeties for the bench press exercise, but over the years first elite level football gyms, then even well-kitted-out home gym users began doing the bench press exercise inside of what is known as safety racks. But commercial gyms around the world hadn't caught on. It was like every car on the street had seatbelts, except for taxis. It was bizarre. But I hadn't given it much thought for years until I read an article about a young man in Queensland, not far from where I used to live, who died in a tragic bench press accident. I set to work combining my knowledge of lifting and my experience with building equipment for my own home gym, to come up with a solution that was affordable for commercial gyms to implement, without having to replace all their existing benches.

I shared my idea with Melissa and we talked about how it could not only save lives, but countless serious injuries each year.

> *'Well if you are going to patent that, do you need someone who can draw up 3D designs?' Melissa asked. 'And you're probably going to want a website too, right?' she added.*

I smiled.

It looks like Melissa's retirement may not last that long after all.

Index

Ready to take the next step on your Freedom First journey?

As a thank you for buying this book we would like to invite you to attend a Freedom First LIVE event, absolutely free. At this life-changing event you will learn directly from Matthew how to:

*   Escape the Income Trap
*   Elicit your values, and start valuing Freedom First
*   Get in touch with the network of minds, unleash your motivation and tap into the power of growth to accelerate toward your goals

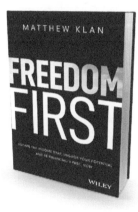

You will:

*   Discover how to get financially freer *right now*, not in 20 years, and why retiring early may not only be easier than you imagined but e*ssential* if you want to prosper
*   Learn about the bigger cycles and trends that are affecting us all, and how to profit from them
*   Learn advanced strategies for taking back control of your investments. Learn the tax secrets of the rich and how to start a business that frees you.

Don't be a slave to a job, debt or the markets. Break the cycle and join others who are discovering a new answer.

Freedom First is a movement. Being free doesn't mean being alone.

Seating is limited so don't miss out. To book your free seat go to matthewklan.com/events

Printed and bound by CPI Group (UK) Ltd, Croydon, CR0 4YY

17/02/2022

03112681-0001